Lesbian and Gay
Foster Care and Adoption

D0165490

of related interest

Adopting
Real Life Stories
Ann Morris
Foreword by Hugh Thornbery CBE
ISBN 978 1 84905 660 1
eISBN 978 1 78450 155 6

Life Story Books for Adopted and Fostered Children, Second Edition
A Family Friendly Approach
Joy Rees
Foreword by Alan Burnell
ISBN 978 1 78592 167 4
eISBN 978 1 78450 436 6

Welcome to Fostering
A Guide to Becoming and Being a Foster Carer
Andy Elvin and Martin Barrow
Foreword by Lorraine Pascale
ISBN 978 1 78592 204 6
eISBN 978 1 78450 480 9

Preparing for Adoption
Everything Adopting Parents Need to Know About
Preparations, Introductions and the First Few Weeks
Julia Davis
ISBN 978 1 84905 456 0
eISBN 978 0 85700 831 2

No Matter What
An Adoptive Family's Story of Hope, Love and Healing
Sally Donovan
ISBN 978 1 84905 431 7
eISBN 978 0 85700 781 0

The Unofficial Guide to Adoptive Parenting
The Small Stuff, The Big Stuff and The Stuff in Between
Sally Donovan
ISBN 978 1 84905 536 9
eISBN 978 0 85700 959 3

LESBIAN and GAY FOSTER CARE and ADOPTION

Second Edition

STEPHEN HICKS and JANET McDERMOTT

Jessica Kingsley *Publishers*
London and Philadelphia

First published in 1999
This edition published in 2018
by Jessica Kingsley Publishers
73 Collier Street
London N1 9BE, UK
and
400 Market Street, Suite 400
Philadelphia, PA 19106, USA

www.jkp.com

Copyright © Stephen Hicks and Janet McDermott 1999, 2018

All rights reserved. No part of this publication may be reproduced in any
material form (including photocopying, storing in any medium by electronic
means or transmitting) without the written permission of the copyright owner
except in accordance with the provisions of the law or under terms of a licence
issued in the UK by the Copyright Licensing Agency Ltd. www.cla.co.uk or in
overseas territories by the relevant reproduction rights organisation, for details
see www.ifrro.org. Applications for the copyright owner's written permission to
reproduce any part of this publication should be addressed to the publisher.

Warning: The doing of an unauthorised act in relation to a copyright work
may result in both a civil claim for damages and criminal prosecution.

Library of Congress Cataloging in Publication Data
A CIP catalog record for this book is available from the Library of Congress

British Library Cataloguing in Publication Data
A CIP catalogue record for this book is available from the British Library

ISBN 978 1 84905 519 2
eISBN 978 0 85700 939 5

Printed and bound in the United States

Contents

ORIGINAL (1999) STORIES WITH 2017–18 UPDATES

Nita and Clare are a lesbian couple who adopted three Asian girls in separate adoptions. They reflect on the barriers they faced to building their family and how the family has changed and evolved.

Paul and Richard, a gay couple, talk about some of the struggles facing gay adopters in earlier times. They tell the story of fostering and then adopting their son, Patrick.

Lee, a trans man, tells the story of how he fostered over 50 children over the years, and adopted five. His story reflects upon his time as a lesbian foster carer and adopter, before gender transition.

Elizabeth and Mary, a lesbian couple, talk about offering respite care to a disabled boy, Peter, and how they went on to foster another child, Daniel, on a long-term basis. They reflect upon the plans for them to adopt Daniel and why this never happened.

Kath talks about the separate adoptions of her three daughters, their life as a family and her current relationships with her daughters and grandchildren.

NEW STORIES

INTRODUCTION

Thirty years ago, a handful of lesbian and gay foster and adoptive parents in London were interviewed about their experiences of being assessed and, in a few cases, of having children placed with them. The resulting report, *Fostering and Adoption by Lesbians and Gay Men* (Skeates and Jabri 1988), was the first British publication to address this area of family life and social work practice. Ten years later, the network set up by those first carers in London, the Lesbian and Gay Foster and Adoptive Parents Network (LAGFAPN), had expanded to include around 50 lesbian and gay foster and adoptive parents across the country and included a second network base in the North of England, the Northern Support Group. In 1997, the London and Northern networks embarked on a joint project to publish their members' stories in a book for prospective lesbian and gay applicants and fostering and adoption professionals. We published that book in 1999 under the title *Lesbian and Gay Fostering and Adoption: Extraordinary Yet Ordinary* (Hicks and McDermott 1999). It documented the journeys of 17 households, comprising 27 adults bringing up 40 children. In our Introduction to the book we optimistically compared the picture our stories painted to the 1988 study by Skeates and Jabri, noting that, 'Ten years on, the lesbian and gay community has far more experience of people who have actually been approved to foster and adopt children, and are doing so...' (Hicks and McDermott 1999, p.11). Those families represented progress unimaginable to the original 13 contributors in the 1988 study, some of whom never had children placed with them even after being approved by a local authority. But the numbers in 1999 still represented a tiny percentage of adoption and fostering placements in the UK (New Family Social 2015).

In contrast to the above picture, figures released by the Department for Education (DfE) in September 2016 showed that in the year 2015–16 there had been 450 adoptions by same-sex couples in England, accounting for almost one in ten (9.6%) of the total number. This included 20 adoptions by same-sex couples in Wales, with the figures for Scotland, though not released at the time, expected to be similar (New Family Social 2015). This figure did not include the dozens more adoptions by single lesbian, gay, bisexual and transgender (LGBT) adopters. It is clear that, in the two decades since we compiled our first book, there has been a sea change in social attitudes and professional practice towards assessing lesbian and gay applicants, placing children with them, and perceiving the LGBT community as a source of prospective carers for looked-after children. In addition, since both earlier publications there have been major changes in legislation relating to child protection, fostering, adoption and the human rights of LGBT people. New spaces are emerging in which those who refuse identification with binary categories of male and female are able to express themselves and assert a range of non-binary, gender non-conforming and genderqueer identities (Green and Peterson 2003), but this increasing openness to different sexualities and fluid definitions of gender is unfortunately still being matched by homophobic responses, particularly in relation to having children and parenting (Weeks, Heaphy and Donovan 2001).

The Skeates and Jabri (1988) publication and the first edition of our book were written in a climate of isolation and adversity, in the face of institutionally sanctioned homophobia. In the same year as the Skeates and Jabri study was published, Section 28 of the Local Government Act 1988 was enacted in England, Wales and Scotland, stating that local authorities should 'not intentionally promote homosexuality or publish material with the intention of promoting homosexuality' or 'promote the teaching in any maintained school of the acceptability of homosexuality as a pretended family relationship.' Although no prosecutions were ever brought under this legislation, its suggestion of 'pretended' *versus* 'real' family relationships chimed with established norms around gender, family and the sanctity of marriage, then only legal between a man and a woman. Inequality in the age of sexual consent for gay men was still enshrined in law, while lesbian and gay relationships had limited recognition in society. By 1999, there was legislation in place on sex discrimination, equal pay, race relations and disability discrimination, and public bodies were being encouraged to embrace equal opportunities policies. However, the presence of Section 28 on the statute books inhibited many from extending their equalities practice to protecting lesbians and gay men from discrimination. Nevertheless, there was active and concerted opposition to Section 28 from lesbian and gay activists and their supporters and some opposition within statutory bodies. Some fostering and adoption agencies actively pursued inclusive recruitment policies indicating their openness to black, working-class, single and lesbian and gay applicants. The majority, however, operated risk-averse professional cultures, and some subscribed to the belief that only married couples or, in circumstances of extreme necessity, single heterosexual carers, could meet the needs of children.

In such an environment it was inevitable that, behind those early pioneers in 1988 who dared to make themselves visible, there were a significant number of others who were fostering, and in some cases adopting, as 'single' carers. They were ushered through approval processes by social workers who, knowingly or not, colluded to avoid inquiry into the sexuality of applicants presenting as single. Responses in lesbian and gay communities at the time ranged from the conviction that no one who seriously wanted to foster or adopt would jeopardise their chances by outing themselves to an explicitly homophobic system to the belief that nothing would change unless we were prepared to come out.

Thus, our 1999 book emerged out of campaigning and support groups set up by activists trying to voice the experiences of those who remained hidden in the application process and those who dared to apply as 'out' lesbians and gay men. Members of these groups were tired of being misrepresented in the media and frustrated by the lack of opportunity to get the complexity and subtlety of their perspectives across in such debates. Most media representation at the time was sensationalist and dealt in caricatures of lesbian and gay experience; for example, the 1990 *Sunday Express* article, 'Stop this outrage!', which argued against all gay adoption in vociferous terms (30 September 1990, p.1). Nevertheless, creative challenges to such negative public and media attitudes came from the lesbian and gay activist group Outrage!, established in 1990, and Pratibha Parmar's pioneering film for the Channel 4 *Out on Tuesday* series (Parmar 1989), which revealed that, although lesbian and gay foster care and adoption had been going on for some time, the issue of sexuality was often hidden or denied, a position of 'tacit acceptance'.

Based in London, the Lesbian and Gay Foster and Adoptive Parents Network (LAGFAPN) was established in 1988/89 and offered a point of contact for the whole country, working with the National Foster Care Association to provide information to any lesbian or gay enquirers. Positive Parenting, a campaigning group set up in Manchester following attempts by the Conservative Government to ban 'gay rights' within fostering services under the Children Act 1989 *Consultation Paper No. 16* (DH 1990), also engaged Manchester City Council in very early dialogue on this issue, designing information leaflets and holding public information events. In 1994, LAGFAPN and Positive Parenting held a national conference for lesbian and gay foster and adoptive parents and prospective applicants in Manchester and, out of that conference, the Northern Support Group was born. This group supported applicants and carers in the North of England until it merged with New Family Social in 2011.

We wrote the first edition of this book on behalf of LAGFAPN, the Northern Support Group and the Positive Parenting campaign. At that time, still five years before Section 28 was finally taken off the statute books in 2003 (2000 in Scotland), the book project felt like an important tool in 'proving' ourselves to a sceptical, or downright hostile, public, but also in offering informative and complex accounts that we hoped would support both lesbians and gay men interested in foster care or adoption and also social workers attempting to engage with practice based on anti-oppressive principles. Our aim was to challenge the suggestion that lesbians and gay men were unsuitable carers for children, and to enable fairer and more balanced assessments of lesbians and gay applicants by documenting good practice. The book's subtitle, *Extraordinary Yet Ordinary*, attempted to communicate both the extraordinary journeys network members had been on to arrive at the reality of building their families, and the utterly unremarkable preoccupations of their daily lives as ordinary parents. In this sense, the stories in the book demonstrated lived experiences of families forming, bonding and problem-solving within structures that were considered radical and controversial by mainstream opinion at the time.

When significant legislation achieves an improvement in human rights and is accompanied by a positive shift in public attitudes, there is a temptation to heave a collective sigh of relief. However, gains are fragile and, although entrenched prejudices may recede, they do not go away. There are always new challenges as oppressive forces regroup and push back. As Cath, in Teresa and Cath's story in this volume, says:

> …the term 'lesbian' is rarely used these days. I think it's an attempt to lower negativity. Society is a long way off attributing anything positive to being lesbian. Homophobia is just too rife, too deep in people's souls.

In contrast, many recent applicants emphasise experiences of being treated equally. For instance, Jamie, in Jamie and Simon's story, says:

> Even when we go to fostering support groups, being gay is seen as part of the norm. Everyone expects there will be a variety of carers. There doesn't seem to be as much of a stigma attached to being gay these days.

However, it is worth noting here that most of the lesbian carers in our newer cohort of contributors are black, and so we suspect that they may have more experiences of intersecting forms of discrimination and oppression than some of the white, gay men.

In writing this revised edition of the book we wanted to document both the gains over the last 20 to 30 years and also the enduring challenges and continuing gaps in understanding and practice in this area. We examine what has changed and what remains as valid today as 30 years ago, and we review the impacts on agency practice of legal and policy changes, research, shifts in social attitudes and constructions of sexuality, gender, family, race and identity. In the following pages we return to eight of the foster and adoptive parents, three couples and two single people, whose stories originally appeared in the 1999 edition, to glimpse something of their family lives during the past two decades and hear how they view their experiences now. We have also interviewed two single carers and six couples, who have been approved and had children placed in more recent years, to contrast their experiences with those of the lesbians and gay men who paved their way.

How we wrote the book(s)

Collecting the stories has been both a similar and different enterprise this time around. In 1997/98 the two of us were founder and active members of the Northern Support Group and we volunteered to assemble the stories and write the accompanying thematic essay on behalf of the national support and campaigning networks. The project was directed by a small committee of LAGFAPN, Northern Support Group and Positive Parenting members, and was experienced as a collective effort. None of these groups is active now, so, in gathering the stories for this second book, we worked with New Family Social to contact recent adopters and foster carers and interviewed a number of carers in our own networks in Yorkshire and the North West, where we are based. Of the 13 households included in this new edition, six are based in Yorkshire, three in the North West, two in London and two in the East of England.

We circulated invitations for contributors through the national online network provided by New Family Social, to those Northern Support Group members we were still in touch with and through our own networks. These included a number of the original participants and, out of these, two single carers and three couples agreed to contribute updates on their family lives over the 20 years since the first edition. This has certainly been one of the most interesting aspects of researching and writing this revised edition for us as, not only were we able to follow up on LGBT carers who, in some cases, now describe themselves as grandparents, but we were also able to ask them about their lives 20 years on and also what they thought of their younger selves in print. As Kath noted, 'I found it strange reading my previous contribution after so long. I didn't recognise the voice somehow. So much has happened and I've learnt so much.' We also located and interviewed eight new contributors whose stories span the last two decades as we wanted to assess how far things had changed, if at all, in terms of LGBT carers' experiences of social work assessment and placement practices in those intervening years.

Unlike the first book with its guiding committee, this edition has been produced by the two of us alone, with very welcome assistance in writing up the stories from Ann Morris. We have drawn on our own experiences as founder members and activists in the Northern Support Group, and as a lesbian and a gay man who have fostered or adopted children ourselves. With a teenager and young adult still at home for one of us, and recent family experience of respite care for disabled children, we combine 25 years of first-hand experience, academic inquiry and active involvement in the education and training of social work professionals and fostering and adoption panels. In some respects, the lessons learned in that time point to a continuing need to represent the voices of lesbian and gay foster carers and adopters as both 'different' and 'equal', since our argument would be that, even though in some respects there has been a move towards greater equality in relation to questions of sexuality and gender, being an LGBT parent still raises many questions about how the world is experienced differently from those positions and how LGBT people are regarded by others. This ongoing task of making visible LGBT foster carers and adopters' unique experiences and their shared understandings of difference is vital, since, when being compared with heterosexual or normative family notions, neither 'sameness' nor 'difference' adequately sums things up. This is because these are:

> ...subject positions that [reflect] only a rigid and limited understanding of [lesbian and gay parents'] narrated experiences... [their] subjectivities are not *completely* constituted by normalizing discourses, nor are they radical examples of resistance. (Hequembourg 2007, pp.5, 51)

A changing landscape

It is important to note that since publication of our first edition there have been considerable legal changes in relation to both LGBT lives and also parenting. In the UK, for example, at the time that we published our first edition, adoption by gay, lesbian or same-sex couples was not legally possible. Only married or single people were officially able to adopt and so, in relation to lesbian or gay couples, only one partner was able to be the named adopter, with many seeking a residence order under the Children Act 1989 to secure wider parenting rights, a situation repeated in various US states (Mallon 2018).

The UK Adoption and Children Act 2002 allowed, for the first time, adoption by unmarried couples, including those of the same sex. The Civil Partnership Act 2004 and Marriage (Same Sex Couples) Act 2013 also allow couples to secure some kinship rights. Teresa, in Teresa and Cath's story, says:

> Initially one of us was actually going to be the adopter and one of us was going to get a residence order, but the rules changed while we were going through the process and so eventually both of us adopted the children, as a couple. We must have been one of the first lesbian couples that adopted as a couple.

The UK Equality Act 2006 and its associated Sexual Orientation Regulations (2007) effectively banned discrimination against any LGBT person by those providing goods and services, including social services such as foster care and adoption. Although the UK Government allowed a 'grace period' in order for those agencies opposed to all homosexual adoption or foster care to reconsider their policies, the Equality Act 2010 in theory ought to prevent discrimination against LGBT people approaching any social welfare agency. The Human Fertilisation and Embryology Act 2008 recognises lesbian and gay parents in law, and changes to adoption and foster care minimum standards also emphasise equality. This is not to say that these changes have not been without their problems. Marriage or civil partnership legislation, for example, has effectively forced some couples to secure rights that ought to be open to all parents, regardless of relationship type, through these means. In addition, the tightening of social work assessment timescales under statutory guidance (DfE 2013) has arguably added greater pressure, and less time for contemplation, to the process of consideration of and by prospective carers.

Recent research studies

Rivers' historical study of lesbian and gay parents and their children (Rivers 2013) reminds us that most activism and research regarding lesbian and gay foster care and adoption is fairly recent, but also that the arguments concerning LGBT parenting – both within the LGBT community as well as more widely – have changed markedly in their focus over the years. The research has grown considerably since we published the first edition of this book, so much so that it would be impossible for us to do it full justice here, and so our readers are signposted to comprehensive overviews (see, for example, Brown, Sebba and Luke 2015; Goldberg and Allen 2013; Pyne 2012; Short *et al.* 2007). However, we did want to review some of the key studies, since they offer an important complementary narrative to the stories collected in this book.

Intersectionality and diversity in LGBT parenting

Although people often talk about 'LGBT parenting', it is important to note that much of the existing research and writing actually deals with lesbian and gay (or sometimes, 'same-sex') parenting, with few studies turning their attention to transgender and, even more rarely, bisexual parents. Contemporary research on trans parents argues that, although there is no evidence that relationships with children suffer, there is discrimination in child custody (or residence), visitation (or contact) and child welfare (Downing 2013; Hines 2007; Pyne 2012). Stotzer *et al.*'s review argues that between a quarter and a half of all trans people are parents and, although some reported no contact with their children after gender transition, most had good relationships. However, most would not approach adoption agencies because of anticipated rejection or the lack of policy addressing transgender people (Stotzer, Herman and Hasenbush 2014).

Although the participants in Pyne's study did not have direct experience of adoption, many reported a perception that they would not be successful if they approached adoption agencies and so they did not pursue this (Pyne 2012). Riggs *et al.*'s Australian survey of 160 trans or gender diverse people found that 24.4 per cent were parents, but only one had fostered and none had adopted (Riggs, Power and von Doussa 2016). A further 18.4 per cent said they would consider having children in the future, with eight of these saying they would like to foster or adopt. A correlation here between age and a perceived possibility of fostering or adopting may indicate that younger trans people see this as more of a possibility.

Bisexual parents are less frequently the subject of research but do feature in a number of studies (Delvoye and Tasker 2016; Eady *et al.* 2009; Mamo 2007; Tasker and Delvoye 2015). Ross and Dobinson's study of 43 LGBT adoption applicants in Ontario, Canada, suggests 'stereotypes and beliefs about bisexual parents may create significant, though not insurmountable, barriers for them in their attempts to prove their worth as parents or potential parents' (Ross and Dobinson 2013, p.98), with fears that adoption workers would perceive bisexual people as unable to commit to stable relationships featuring in the experiences and perceptions of the five bisexual participants.

Moore and Brainer's discussion of race and ethnicity in the lives of LGBT parents argues that 'researchers need to be cognizant of how methods and sampling have shaped what we know, and do not know, about sexual minority parents and their children' (Moore and Brainer 2013, p.145), with the result that limited sampling or restrictive definitions of who counts have promoted studies dominated by white, middle-class, urban respondents. When the interests of gay and lesbian parents are seen as separate to those of black, Asian and other minority ethnic groups, it is black lesbian, gay and other sexual minority families' experiences that are often overlooked. Further, Moore and Brainer remind us that in some ethnic communities, gay and lesbian parenting might emerge through processes other than those in which the adult comes out, forms a gay identity and then moves on to become a parent. Children from former heterosexual relationships or those within extended family and social networks, including 'Black children who might otherwise languish in the foster care system' (Moore and Brainer 2013, p.140), and those cared for by other family members due to immigration issues, all feature in studies that consider more racially diverse samples.

Hicks' longitudinal, qualitative study of 15 lesbian or gay parents includes a focus on the reported experiences of four black and mixed race lesbian mothers. He argues that the social work assessment of prospective adopters often avoids overt discussion of questions of race, yet black lesbians argued for a more rigorous and open discussion of how race is relevant to adoption – that is, that it is a social issue to do with how race is constructed and viewed rather than being merely an individual and psychological one to do with an identity. Louise, a mixed race lesbian mother, for example, reminds us that in certain social contexts she notices that some white people are uncomfortable with her and that she is made to feel out of place – 'barriers I think that my kids will have to face' (quoted in Hicks 2011, p.149).

On questions of social class, Gabb's research, based on diaries, interviews and observations of 14 lesbian parents and their 10 children in the North of England, and Taylor's interviews with 60 gay and lesbian parents in the UK, also suggest that the notion that all LGBT parenting involves egalitarian or shared divisions of labour within the home is a largely middle-class one, derived from research that does not ask questions about class or that is based solely on middle-class samples (Gabb 2008; Taylor 2009). Gabb and Taylor both argue that poverty or lack of opportunity may mean, for example, that a lesbian couple appearing to occupy traditionally gendered homemaker/breadwinner roles may derive some sense of ordinariness or respectability from this arrangement, an important dynamic in a social context that is otherwise stigmatising. They may also lack the choice or opportunity to adopt what is considered to be a more egalitarian model of family life, since this model is sometimes derived from research with couples in which both partners work part time or can afford to pay for day/childcare (Dunne 2000; Sullivan 2004; Weeks *et al.* 2001).

There was very little research into gay male adoption at the time of our first book, partly because not that many gay men had adopted at that stage. Some reported prejudicial attitudes based on gendered notions that men did not make good carers of children or on homophobic associations between homosexuality and child abuse (Hicks 2006). Many also suggested that adoption and foster care agencies were much less likely to consider gay men as potential carers of children than they were lesbians and, where gay men were positively considered, they were much more likely to be seen as appropriate for the fostering of teenagers rather than the adoption of younger children (Hicks and McDermott 1999; Skeates and Jabri 1988). However, in the subsequent years, gay men were able to shift some of these attitudes. Some agencies also progressed their values concerning male and gay carers, so that gay male adoption, including the care of babies and young children, became a reality, something reflected in more recent research.

Mallon's study of 20 gay foster or adoptive fathers in New York and Los Angeles, for example, reports that, although successful in their applications to be considered, these men said that they had to contend with the views of others, and even sometimes their own, which suggested that men are not the 'natural' carers of children and, in some cases, that they ought not to be (Mallon 2004). Mallon found that some men did not come out as gay to social work agencies or that some of those agencies adopted an implicit 'don't ask, don't tell' approach (Mallon 2007, 2011, 2012), but also adds that many of the gay men saw adoption as their 'first choice' (Mallon 2008, p.289) for parenting rather than a second best, something that he suggests is rarely acknowledged by social welfare agencies, many of whom are more used to adopters who approach them after failing to have biological children.

Lewin's study, which looked at 95 gay fathers in Chicago, the San Francisco Bay Area, Los Angeles and Iowa City, found that 14 of the couples had opted for the public domestic adoption route, seven international adoption, six the private domestic adoption option and one couple a combination of domestic and international adoption. Of the single adopters in Lewin's sample, five had opted for domestic and one for international adoption (Lewin 2009). Nevertheless, it is worth noting that at the time of the study two states had gay adoption bans in place. A minority of the men also reported some hostility from other gay people to the idea of gay parenting: 'Paul and Keith exchanged a knowing look and then Paul said, "Oh, we're not gay anymore. We pick our friends by what time their kids' nap time is"' (quoted in Lewin 2009, p.152).

Queering assumptions?

Queer theory has provoked some interesting questions about why much of the early research into lesbian or gay families appeared mainly concerned with reassuring audiences that such families were 'just like' or 'the same as' heterosexual ones, with the children exhibiting similar outcomes along the lines of peer relationships, gender and psycho-sexual development. Of course in some ways this is understandable – much of the early research was used to challenge virulently homophobic ideas about gay or lesbian parents that resulted, quite frequently, in those parents losing legal custody (or residence) of and contact with their children (Golombok, Spencer and Rutter 1983; Golombok and Tasker 1994, 1996; Green 1978; Hitchens and Price 1978; Hoeffer 1981; Hunter and Polikoff 1976; Kirkpatrick, Smith and Roy 1981; Tasker and Golombok 1995, 1997). Indeed, Patterson has added that 'not a single study has found children of gay or lesbian parents to be disadvantaged in any significant respect relative to children of heterosexual parents' (Patterson 1992, p.1036).

From a queer perspective, however, because 'anti-gay scholars seek evidence of harm, sympathetic researchers defensively stress its absence' (Stacey and Biblarz 2001, p.160), with gay and lesbian parents 'apologetically normalized, their sameness maximized, and their differences...minimized' (Clarke, Kitzinger and Potter 2004, p.546). Studies influenced by queer theories have suggested that LGBT parenting research based solely on white, middle-class, urban samples is in danger of reproducing normativities, that LGBT parents ought not to be merely compared with a heterosexual standard, and also that the experiences of such families are neither inherently transgressive nor assimilationist; rather, that the 'different/not different' trope is rather limiting as it tends to uphold often implicit, heterosexual norms and overlooks the complexity of LGBT parents' lives. Thus, while LGBT families may have very different experiences to heterosexual ones, this ought not to suggest, for example, that they are automatically challenging of traditional gender roles (Hequembourg 2007; Hicks 2011, 2013; Mamo 2007). Or, as Goldberg's study of gay adoption has it, gay fathers 'may *alternately* or *simultaneously* draw from or derive meaning from normative conceptualizations of family, fatherhood, and parenthood, even as they create their own "nontraditional" families' (Goldberg 2012, p.12).

Anti-gay parenting studies and their resurgence

After publication of the first edition of this book, a number of pieces opposed to all LGBT parenting emerged (Almond 2006;

Holloway 2002; Morgan 2002; Phillips 1999). These variously describe non-heterosexual relationships as dysfunctional, unstable and fleeting, inadequate in relation to the 'gold standard' of the heterosexual, married couple (Morgan 2002, p.44), and as the cause of gender 'confusion' in children (Morgan 2002, p.78). Of course, it is vital to remember here that these perspectives are published by conservative and, in some cases, Christian organisations opposed to homosexuality, such as The Christian Institute or the Social Market Foundation. Morgan, for example, wrote off the first edition of our book as mere 'self-congratulatory testimonials' (Morgan 2002, p.49), and suggested that our work was masquerading as research evidence that proved nothing. It was, however, hardly generous to suggest that we were making strong research claims in a book that was a collection of personal accounts, not a research study as such, and in which we merely noted a 'number of important themes which recur throughout the book' (Hicks and McDermott 1999, p.14).

Further, Morgan's (2002) assertion that research provides evidence of gender confusion amongst the children of lesbians and gay men is based on misinterpretation. A study by Hoeffer (1981), which used social learning theory to suggest that children acquire a 'sex-role', considered children's toy preferences, toys that were pre-determined as gender-typed and, based on this, suggested a sex-role type for each child. Putting aside qualms about such sex-role determination and its methods for a moment, Hoeffer actually reported that there were no significant differences in toy preferences between the children of heterosexual and lesbian mothers, and that most of them chose traditionally gender-typed toys (Hoeffer 1981, p.542). However, she also argued that some lesbian mothers were less likely to insist their children play with traditionally gender-typed toys. In Morgan's account, this becomes 'evidence' that children with gay or lesbian parents suffer terrible gender confusion.

Such concerns have also risen again recently with the resurgence of anti-LGBT parenting studies (Regnerus 2012a, b; Sullins 2015, 2016). Regnerus' New Family Structures Study, for example, based on a survey of 2988 young adults, including 175 who said that their mother had, at some point, had a same-sex romantic relationship and 73 who said the same of their father, suggests that the children of lesbian mothers and gay fathers are more open to, though not more likely to be in, a same-sex relationship. However, it also suggests that such children are more prone to sexual victimisation and poor health and psycho-social outcomes (Regnerus 2012a). Regnerus claims this is because 'the small or nonprobability samples so often relied upon in nearly all previous studies…have very likely underestimated the number and magnitude of real differences between the children of lesbian mothers (and to a lesser extent, gay fathers) and those raised in other types of households' (Regnerus 2012a, p.765).

However, this study has been subject to rigorous criticism (Cheng and Powell 2015; Gates *et al.* 2012; Perrin, Cohen and Caren 2013), since it suffers from various limitations, such as the conflation of once having 'a romantic relationship with someone of the same-sex' (Regnerus 2012a, p.756) with being a lesbian or gay parent and 'questionable use of the terms "lesbian," "lesbian mothers," "gay," and "gay fathers" given the coding of parents within the…study' (Barrett 2012, p.1354). The possible conflation of relationship change or instability (via divorce, remarriage and single parenthood) with having a lesbian or gay parent and the inability to 'isolate the effect of having a parent who had a same-sex relationship from the effect of experiencing multiple family forms' (Osborne 2012, p.779) are also serious concerns with the study. Finally, basic errors in some of the stated data analysis and the lack of any clear link, much less any causal relationship, between having a lesbian or gay parent and poor psycho-sexual outcomes in children are also major limitations.

The question of gender

One of the concerns of those opposed to LGBT parenting, and also a concern that frequently comes up even where LGBT parenting is supported, is to do with the supposed gender effects of growing up with same-sex, gender non-conforming, trans, gay or lesbian parents. The concern is usually that the LGBT people do not always conform to expected gender roles and therefore their children will grow up either with distorted views of gender or with an abnormal gender identity (Hicks 2008, 2013). This was something that the contributors to our first edition commented on, with some identifying what they saw as inappropriate gender roles attributed to them by others and also debates amongst some social workers about whether it was appropriate for lesbians or gay men to care for girls or boys. As Berkowitz and Ryan comment:

> …lesbian and gay parents are subject to increased moral judgment than that of their heterosexual counterparts and are thus more aware of their accountability to others in their interaction work… This is because the gender expressions and identities of children raised by sexual minority parents are assessed by a range of actors, included but not limited to: their extended families, friends, acquaintances, their children's friends, the parents of these friends, their children's teachers, curious strangers, invested academics and politicians, and finally, other sexual minority parents. (Berkowitz and Ryan 2011, p.333)

Pyne's research with transgender parents, for example, suggests that they do create 'change by acting in small everyday ways, quietly chipping away at stereotypes and prompting others to re-think gender' (Pyne 2012, p.31), and other studies also suggest that LGBT parents positively question standard gender roles (Sullivan 2004). Gay fathers report 'gender role strain' caused by the felt need to conform to expected masculinity (Benson, Silverstein and Auerbach 2005, p.3), and Epstein's interviews with lesbian mothers who identify as 'butch' reveal assumptions that mothers are expected to be typically 'feminine' or unremarkably gendered (Epstein 2002). However, studies also demonstrate that many LGBT parents express a mixture of gendered positions, often dependent on social context (Doucet 2006; Stacey 2011).

On the question of supposed gender 'effects' on children, researchers have argued that these children do not exhibit any gender confusion, and that their parents or families offer adequate role models. However, there is also evidence that those parents are careful not to impose rigid gender roles or expectations on their children (Biblarz and Stacey, 2010; Fulcher, Sutfin and Patterson 2008; MacCallum and Golombok 2004). But at the same time, they may also be acutely conscious of the judgements of others concerning their children's gender development or expression and, for these reasons, may also seek to reassure some of these concerns. In Berkowitz and Ryan's study, for example:

> ...many gay fathers in [the] sample (n = 16) mentioned something about including a woman or women in their child's life. Profoundly aware of reigning cultural discourses that construct female femininity and male masculinity as opposite, complementary, and duly required for children's development, gay fathers frequently mentioned the importance of ensuring the presence of female role models in their children's lives. (Berkowitz and Ryan 2011, p.343)

In the fields of foster care and adoption, lesbian and gay applicants frequently report that they have to reassure social workers or child placement panels/decision-makers about adequate and standard gender role models in the home or in their daily lives (Cocker 2011; Hicks 2011; Riggs 2007, 2010, 2011; Ross *et al.* 2009; Wood 2016, 2017), with some expressing frustration at assumptions about stereotypical gender roles. Gay male adopters have reported the strain of fitting neither into parenting cultures often geared towards women nor the work-dominated worlds of men (Mallon 2004), but Goldberg notes that, while gay and lesbian families may deconstruct and reconstruct 'gender, sex, and family in complex ways' (Goldberg 2010, p.10), such families are neither essentially 'assimilationist or radical' (Goldberg 2010, p.11). Wood adds that gay or lesbian adoption or foster care applicants are often asked about gender role models by social workers, with those applicants adding that their responses to such questions were an 'exaggerated performance' of gendered expectations (Wood 2016, p.1717).

Research studies on lesbian and gay foster care and adoption

There is now a broader range of research on gay and lesbian foster care and adoption than when we published the first edition of this book, including the first ever UK-based comparative study of gay, lesbian and heterosexual adoptive families (Golombok *et al.* 2014; Jennings *et al.* 2014; Mellish *et al.* 2013). Mallon's study reminds us that most find the experience of adopting a child transformative or, as one gay adopter put it, 'Five years ago I adopted Peter, and I have never been the same since' (quoted in Mallon 2004, p.xi). Still, he adds that gay men and lesbians remain 'an underused resource' by adoption and fostering agencies (Mallon 2006, p.1). As with the Mallon study, Goldberg also notes that many gay adopters do not see biological parenting links as a priority, but also report some prejudice from adoption agencies and, as with other studies (Goldberg and Gianino 2012; Mallon 2004), quite a number had been asked to adopt transracially (Goldberg 2012). In an earlier Goldberg study, although nearly 83 per cent of participants were white, around 50 per cent had adopted transracially, in part because they were more likely to consider this as an option (Goldberg 2010).

The UK comparative study found no statistically significant differences between gay, lesbian or heterosexual adoptive families in terms of parent or child wellbeing or development. The gay dads were slightly more positive in their interactions with their children and the heterosexual dads slightly more disciplinarily aggressive (Mellish *et al.* 2013, p.10), but there were no significant differences in terms of contact with birth parents. However, some 54 per cent of the gay and 75 per cent of the lesbian adopters reported some negativity towards them during the adoption process compared with only 30 per cent of the heterosexual families (Mellish *et al.* 2013, p.33). Although the gay male adopters were more likely to have older boys placed with them than others, they were more warm and interactive or expressive with their children than the heterosexual families, which may be because 'the screening process is especially stringent for gay couples who wish to adopt, resulting in even higher levels of psychological wellbeing and commitment to parenting among adoptive gay fathers than adoptive lesbian or heterosexual parents' (Golombok *et al.* 2014, p.464).

Other UK-based research has argued that gay or lesbian applicants do not feel they should conceal their sexuality from social workers, and are now far less likely to report being rejected by agencies on the basis of their sexuality. In addition, they are now more likely to take placements of children from a range of ages, including babies, with diverse needs (Wood 2016, 2017). Nevertheless the 'complicated displays' of self (Wood 2016, p.1714) identified by applicants are about the 'front' that they feel they may be expected to put on for social work agencies in order to demonstrate their potential as parents. Although many of the adopters in Wood's study saw this as a first choice of parenting route, several were asked by social workers to reflect on grief as a result of infertility which, as reported in other studies (Hicks 2000), was not always relevant.

Two national US surveys of adoption agencies have demonstrated varying attitudes and practices concerning lesbian or gay adoption. In Brodzinsky *et al.*'s 2002 survey, just 26 per cent of agencies responded – some choosing not to do so for moral or religious opposition to homosexuality – and although 63 per cent of those who did respond said they would work with such applicants, they found that:

> …public agencies were significantly more likely to place a child with lesbians or gay men, followed by private, nonreligious agencies, Jewish affiliated agencies and mainstream Protestant affiliated agencies. Only agencies affiliated with the Catholic church and more fundamentalist Christian beliefs made no placements with individuals known to be lesbian or gay. (Brodzinsky, Patterson and Vaziri 2002, pp.14–15)

In a follow-up study, 34.1 per cent did not respond as they refused to work with gay or lesbian clients, mainly for religious reasons. Sixty-five per cent of those who did respond had a policy of working with lesbians and gay men and 60 per cent had accepted such applicants as adopters, although this was more likely to be the case with 'special needs' agencies. In some cases, a gay or lesbian sexuality went against agency policy (23.3%), or was seen as a lifestyle (20.3%) or sexuality (14.5%) incompatible with adoption (Brodzinsky 2012; Brodzinsky and Staff of the Evan B. Donaldson Adoption Institute 2003). Brodzinsky *et al.* (2012) also argue that, although in the US there is now greater acceptance of gay and lesbian adoption, 'caseworkers' discomfort in discussing issues related to sexual orientation and sexuality, as well as their homophobic beliefs and attitudes, creates an atmosphere of tension, confrontation, and conflict' (Brodzinsky, Green and Katuzny 2012, p.236).

This is echoed in other studies that demonstrate a growing trend towards acceptance of lesbian and gay adoption (Pertman and Howard 2012) and a lessening one of placing children with 'special needs', or those most 'hard to place', with such families (Brooks and Goldberg 2001; Brooks, Kim and Wind 2012). Indeed, the comparative survey of Florida-based heterosexual and gay/lesbian adopters by Averett *et al.* demonstrated no propensity to place certain 'types' of children with lesbian or gay adopters and no significant outcome differences based on sexuality, with issues such as household income or pre-adoptive history of the children having a much greater impact on children's behaviour (Averett, Nalavany and Ryan 2009).

The role of social work

Moving on finally to research that considers the role of social work assessment and support for LGBT foster carers and adopters, Brown *et al.*'s literature review notes that 'assessments [of such prospective carers] need to be enabling, rigorous, and analytic, covering all subjects considered with all foster carers; but in addition social work assessors, with the LGBT applicants, should think through areas pertinent to a person's gender and sexuality relevant to them becoming foster carers' (Brown *et al.* 2015, p.14). This is so that issues of sexuality are neither ignored nor over-emphasised. In part, this requires that 'social workers have the confidence, skills, attitudes and knowledge to work effectively with all foster carers irrespective of their sexuality or gender' (Brown *et al.* 2015, p.20) since, in the recent past, in their 'encounters with adoptive and social services, lesbians and gay men experienced new manifestations of [the] social acrimony against non-heterosexual parenting' (Rivers 2013, p.173).

Many LGBT foster carers and adopters report, as did the contributors to our first edition, that they 'shopped around' for positive and/or equality-focused agencies to approach when they were thinking about applying. In Gianino's study, for example, in most cases interviewees reported that they were 'highly selective' in their choice of agencies, based on reputation and on the interviewees' stated desires to be out or known as gay adopters (Gianino 2008, p.214). Shelley-Sireci and Ciano-Boyce's comparative survey of the experiences of 18 lesbian and 44 heterosexual adopters in Massachusetts found no differences in their overall ratings of the adoption experience. However, lesbians were significantly more likely to perceive and experience discrimination than the heterosexual adopters, and while 81 per cent of the lesbians felt they had to omit some information from their home study social work assessment, only 24 per cent of heterosexual parents reported this (Shelley-Sireci and Ciano-Boyce 2002).

Cocker's interviews with 11 lesbians assessed as potential adopters report broadly positive experiences of social workers. Indeed, those lesbians valued the opportunities that social work assessment offered them to think through and face some important questions about their future adoption of children (Cocker 2011). Most of the 96 lesbian adopters included in Ryan and Whitlock's survey across the US reported positive experiences of adoption agencies but, in all cases, some negative bias regarding their sexuality was reported, with 5.2 per cent and 10.4 per cent reporting discrimination from social workers or adoption agency staff respectively (Ryan and Whitlock 2008, 2009). Similarly, Riggs' Australian survey of 60 lesbian or gay foster carers (and follow-up interviews with 30) notes that most relied heavily on the commitment of a few social workers and that all reported anxieties about possible or experienced homophobia within the welfare system. Indeed, Riggs argues such foster carers are 'forced to engage with a system that most often does not provide clear endorsement for their role as carers and which thus requires carers to be reliant upon the goodwill of individual workers' (Riggs 2011, p.221).

Positive experiences of social work agencies and their employees are also reported in various other studies (Berkowitz 2011; Brown 2011; Dalton and Bielby 2000; Dugmore and Cocker 2008; Logan and Sellick 2007; Lott-Whitehead and Tully 1999) and evidenced in examples of social work practice guidance aimed at improving work with LGBT carers, a quite considerable and positive change since publication of the first edition of our book (Brodzinsky and Goldberg 2016; Brown and Cocker 2011; Cocker and Brown 2010; Hicks and Greaves 2007; de Jong and Donnelly 2015; Mallon and Betts 2005; National Resource Center for Permanency and Family Connections 2012a, b; Sudol 2010). Mallon has noted that, in the US, many 'child welfare agencies across the country have broken through their own organizational bias against LGBT people and are already placing children with LGBT parents', but adds that, 'by and large, there are few child welfare agencies that seem to be openly discussing this process' (Mallon 2018, p.182). He adds that it is essential for social work practitioners to 'read the research and to analyze, interpret, and discuss the research findings and practice implications for effective practice with [LGBT parents]' (Mallon 2018, p.193).

Differences and similarities over two decades

Comparing the profiles of participants in both the 1999 and 2018 editions reveals some similarities and also significant differences in terms of (successful) applications, assessment and the placement of children. The 1999 book documented the stories of ten couples and seven single foster or adoptive parents. The balance of single carers and couples is similar in the current edition, with nine couples and four single carers telling their stories. However, the balance between genders has shifted significantly. In 1999, there were twice as many women interviewed as men (18 women and 9 men) and all the adopters were lesbians, reflecting the considerable barriers facing gay men seeking to adopt at that time. This balance is reversed in the current study, in which 13 men and 9 women participated. What has also changed significantly is the recognition and acceptance of people changing their gender or resisting a fixed attribution of gender. Two of the 13 men in this edition are transgender; one applied to his agency as a transgender man and the other recently began his transition after his adopted and fostered children had matured.

The changing landscape described earlier has had a big impact on the experiences of LGBT applicants approaching agencies to foster and adopt. Whereas applicants in earlier decades were more fearful and hesitant, expecting rejection, recent applicants describe feeling confident and assertive about putting themselves forward:

> We never thought that we couldn't be parents; that never crossed our minds... When we initially contacted the agency, we were worried that they might say no because we were gay, so we decided to be up front and came out straight away. It was fine, they were keen to take on a diverse set of carers and we were up for the challenge. (Jamie, in Jamie and Simon's story)

Although Jamie and Simon's confidence is tempered by their worries about an agency possibly rejecting them because they are gay, their response is illustrative of the greater likelihood of our recent contributors being out or open about sexuality. As Darrell also notes, in Darrell and David's story:

> [We] were a bit worried when we first approached our local authority. Although we used to live in the city, we now live out in the sticks and living in a village we wondered what our neighbours would think, but they have been very supportive. We were also worried about how we would be perceived by the local authority as a gay couple, but actually they told us, 'You're not the first.'

For single adopters, sexuality or sexual orientation may not be immediately apparent to agencies in the way it usually is for couples. Nevertheless, single contributors who have applied in recent years all describe being out in their assessment and had no doubts about being so, even where they were initially anxious about how they would be responded to. This marks a significant change from the first edition, in which several single contributors reported not having been out as lesbian or gay, or social workers deliberately not asking about their sexuality with the presumed intention of wanting the assessment to go through without any difficulties:

> In a way I wish I had come out at the beginning, when I first started fostering. But I suppose in another way I don't think it would've been quite as acceptable at that time. I think most people were accepting, but if it had been in their face I think we would probably not have been allowed to foster in all honesty. (Lee, in Lee's story)

James, in Dilip and James' story, also highlight ways in which fostering or adoption impact on coming out to wider family and networks:

> As we were planning to adopt, we had to come out to extended members of our family. The majority of my uncles and aunts knew I was gay, but I'd never had a direct conversation with them about it. I think my parents had probably talked to them about it. As the adoption got closer, I realised we were just going to be outed all over the place once the kids were with us. We had to get on and tell people about the adoption and about being gay because the kids would just tell everybody. One of the sticking points, the reason why I hadn't been more open about being gay, was that I'd never come out to one aunt, who I am particularly close to, but who doesn't live in the UK. I'd never had the conversation with other uncles and aunts, because it felt like it would be a deception not telling her first. So, I emailed her and we had various email exchanges and tearful phone conversations. I'd left it far too long and wished I'd done it a long time ago.

James also notes that being 'outed' in public settings may have positive consequences:

> There was one really nice incident in Morrisons supermarket. We went there one evening and we were all tired and we hadn't had any tea, so we thought we'd just go to Morrisons' café and get a quick meal for the kids. I was in the queue and you went and did some shopping and Anthony and Jake stayed with me to get the food and the woman behind the till said, 'Oh you've got the easy job tonight, while mummy goes and does the shopping', or something like that and the kids were calling me, 'Papa.' And she said, 'What do they call mummy?' and I said, 'Oh no, it's daddy.' She said, 'Oh they've got two dads! That's lovely.' It was kind of completely unexpected, but it was kind of nice.

Most of the contributors to both editions came to fostering and adoption as their first choice for bringing children into their lives, rather than pursuing other options such as reproductive technologies, alternative conception or surrogacy. As Andrew, in Mike and Andrew's story, notes, '[We] had a lot less to talk about than other adopters [on our preparation course], who had to address the loss of not being able to conceive naturally. Adoption was our first choice and it made the whole process very exciting for us.' Of the 17 foster and adoptive families in 1999, 12 (70%) had fostered or adopted as a first choice. Two single lesbians and one partner in a lesbian couple had birth children before fostering or adopting, and two lesbian couples had tried and abandoned alternative insemination at an earlier point in their lives. Five of these households continue their story in this edition. Of the eight new households in this edition, six (75%) fostered or adopted as a first choice. One partner in a lesbian couple had birth children before fostering or adopting, and one single gay man had explored being a known sperm donor to a lesbian couple with the intention of being involved in the child's life, but the arrangement had fallen through. Dylan, a transgender male adopter, echoes the sentiments of many contributors for whom fostering or adoption was a first choice:

I always knew I would adopt, even as a child – it seems a waste to produce more children when there are already children needing loving, safe families. (Dylan, in Dylan's story)

Darrell, in Darrell and David's story, described this response from a rural county authority, which appreciated and valued the fact that they had come to adoption as a first choice:

They had approved several same-sex couples already and their policy was to support diversity. And they are not alone in actively recruiting same-sex couples; their attitude was that we come to the adoption process 100 per cent invested in it having only considered this route, whereas heterosexual couples may have suffered many setbacks and heartaches before deciding to adopt.

Some of the earlier contributors described being influenced to apply by seeing local authority advertising that welcomed a diverse range of applicants. Others were motivated by campaigning messages from lesbian and gay rights activists. Elizabeth and Mary saw the *Out on Tuesday* (Channel 4) programme mentioned earlier, showing lesbians and gay men providing local authority care (Parmar 1989), and were spurred on to contact their local fostering agency. Paul and Richard said being involved in raising awareness and challenging policy through the gay rights movement in the 1970s and 1980s gave them the confidence to pursue fostering and, eventually, adoption. In contrast, the accounts of recent foster and adoptive parents place more emphasis on support networks and less on activism. On the whole, their experiences are of greater acceptance by others, confidence in approaching agencies and being far less likely to see fostering or adoption as impossible. This is partly because many agencies have now developed positive practice and have more experience of working with LGBT carers, but perhaps also reflects what Weeks *et al.* identify as 'stories of impossibility' moving towards 'stories of choice' regarding LGBT parenting (Weeks *et al.* 2001, pp.161–8).

Contributors in this edition appear to feel less judged or 'on trial' than those of 20 years ago. For instance, Elizabeth and Mary say:

There was a time that if you talked more openly as a couple about a problem, people would be thinking, 'Oh it's because he's been placed with a lesbian couple.' Whereas we hope that's a bit easier now. It was our fear that people would judge us as lesbians; that's inhibiting, it stops you discussing things openly.

All the contributors talk about how much more open society is now to accepting the idea of LGBT people fostering and adopting, or accepting LGBT relationships and families in general. This difference is expressed most passionately by the returning contributors from the first edition. For instance, Paul, in Paul and Richard's story, says:

Things have changed enormously for the LBGT community in the past 20 years. I mean we were around when being gay was illegal! We were the first on the register in our local authority when we became civil partners – we got council champagne in plastic glasses! We also married as soon as this became lawful. In the 1990s, we didn't even imagine that these things would be possible. Things have changed so much.

However, there are also reported experiences of homophobia and heteronormative assumptions in this book, as well as those of racism and stereotypically gendered ideas. For example, Barbara and Shazia, a black lesbian couple contributing to this edition, experienced prejudice in their journey towards being approved, while others still carry recollections of past discrimination with them today. The single foster carers and adopters in both editions also highlight particular resistance to them as lone parents. Kath describes a 'pecking order' described to her by one agency, with Kath on the bottom rung:

In one conversation I had with a manager a few years ago, she inferred that I may experience less homophobia as a single lesbian adopter; however, in the same conversation she told me that at the national register of adopters, lesbian and gay couples were second in popularity to heterosexual couples for children needing placements, leaving single adopters, and presumably lesbian and gay single adopters, last in popularity?

Rob describes the challenges of introducing a new partner as a single carer:

> Although I am a single carer, I am currently in a relationship, but at this point my partner hasn't moved in and he doesn't take any role with the kids at all, except as a friend when he's around… Asking him to get police-checked really freaked me out, but he was brilliant about it. His relationship with the kids is still quite distant; they know him but it's very much me that's the foster carer.

Kath describes a very conscious choice to prioritise adopting her daughters, knowing this would probably involve a commitment also to remaining single:

> I entered adoption as a single parent and I am still a single parent. For the most part I have chosen this and I consider it would be very hard to find someone who could have committed to my family in the same way. I have also been so stretched for much of my parenting life and have not had the resources to consider someone else's needs.

Interestingly, very few couples in this edition refer to civil partnerships as having any bearing on their application to foster or adopt, even though Paul and Richard suggest that gay marriage or civil partnership would have made things a lot easier for them. Dilip and James only mention this to highlight that having a civil partnership was not seen as relevant by their agency. As James says:

> The social worker said that she really wanted to document the nature of our relationship rather than putting any emphasis on the length of time we had lived together.

Dilip goes on to say:

> And that was nice, it cleared the way. We're not in a civil partnership or married and I don't think they asked about that – that's never been a stumbling block, and it wasn't an issue at panel.

A noticeable change in this edition of the book is the percentage of men who have adopted. While no gay men in our 1999 edition had adopted, three of the five adoptive couples in the current edition are gay, and both transgender contributors – one of whom is gay – are also adopters. This reflects a wider acceptance of gay men, and men in general, as potential carers for children, although there is still evidence of prejudice against some trans and gay male parents. It also reflects the greater overall proportion of carers adopting, rather than fostering, in this 2018 edition. In the 1999 edition, nine households were fostering, seven were adopting, one lesbian carer was offering respite care and another had both fostered and adopted children. In the current edition, the greatest number of carers has adopted, with seven households adopting, five fostering, one contributor having both fostered and adopted, and three households having also provided respite care. This reflects a greater propensity for agencies to place children for adoption, an increased (and not always welcome) state emphasis on adoption and, though not statistically significant, raises the question of whether the improved ease of navigating the adoption process for lesbians and gay men may reduce the availability of this group of carers for fostering. The increase in LGBT applicants being approved to both foster and adopt means there has also been a significant increase in LGBT foster carers becoming available for children, but the acceleration in LGBT adopters being approved has been more rapid than the trend for both.

In 1999, 5 out of the 27 carers interviewed were from black or minority ethnic backgrounds (18%). The number of black contributors has not changed in this edition, but represents a greater percentage, 23 per cent of the total of 22, reflecting a small increase in the proportion of lesbian and gay foster carers and adopters coming forward from black and minority ethnic backgrounds. In 1999, two of the five black carers were single carers and three were in couples with white partners. In this edition, there is one black lesbian couple and the other three black carers, one man and two women, are in couples with white partners. The increasing numbers of black lesbians and gay men choosing to apply to adopt or foster is linked to a greater confidence and prevalence of lesbians and gay men coming out in black and minority ethnic families and communities. However, what remains constant is that most of the black and mixed race contributors in both editions describe experiences of racism in assessment and placement, whether from agencies, other carers or birth families. Some of the most extreme experiences are the experiences of the black lesbian couple in the 2018 edition, labelled as 'aggressive' by their assessing social worker. As Barbara says:

> She agreed to start the assessment and then, even before she actually started, she told us she was going to close the case. I asked why and she said, 'Well, I feel like you're really aggressive.' I said, 'I wonder why you'd use that word, because there are many words you could use for me but I don't think aggressive is one of them, I don't think it describes me anywhere near accurately.' (Barbara and Shazia's story)

Barbara and Shazia also encountered overt racist abuse on an equality and diversity training course, which was not challenged by the trainer, and were not supported concerning racist abuse from children placed with them:

> We had one boy who was 15 and I don't think it was appropriate for him to be here, mainly because of his history. But we were told, 'It's for one night, possibly two nights.' He was here for five months… He was very, very abusive about our sexuality and he was always calling us 'Nigger' or 'Paki'…a whole range of things. It wasn't the right place for him to be. We could take that abuse, but I don't think you should be in a situation where that's what was happening. It wasn't healthy for him or for us. (Barbara, in Barbara and Shazia's story)

Changing trends are evident in the placement of children with black and mixed race households. Although all the black and mixed race carers and/or couples in both editions of the book have had black or mixed race children placed with them, Nita, Clare, Dilip, James, Barbara and Shazia all highlight potentially inappropriate racial 'matches' in their cases, and Barbara and Shazia have had more white than black children placed with them. Their longest placement, for nearly five years, was of a severely disabled white boy. Discomfort with their race, gender and sexuality was apparent in their initial failed assessment by the local authority, which led to them approaching and being approved by an independent agency. Yet, since their approval by another agency, the local authority has relied on them consistently as expert carers, but has not maximised their potential as carers for black children, and has avoided identifying race as a relevant factor in placing children with them. This may also highlight state policies, such as in the DfE (2013) *Statutory Guidance on Adoption*, downplaying the relevance of race in matching considerations:

> We're both black, we want black children. We know that there's this disproportionate number of black children in care. But the agency advised us not to say that we would just take black children. And we'd hear other foster carers talking about the children they were looking after. One said, 'Oh we've got three Asian kids, we just get them a takeaway for food.' And I asked him what language they speak and he says, 'Oh, Muslim.' And I said, 'That'll be their religion, not their language.' I mean, I can't imagine how it was for these children. (Barbara, in Barbara and Shazia's story)

Barbara and Shazia's story shows that barriers linked to race and sexuality experienced by black contributors in 1999 are still present in agency thinking and practice. The focus in 1999 was on policies of 'same race placement', which led to many successful placements of black children, but racist and homophobic assumptions around language, religion and nationality also resulted in barriers to matching and placement, based on stereotypes of certain ethnic and religious communities. Nita and Clare's 1999 story recounts how they were refused a match with a sibling group of Asian girls by a local authority panel, which suggested that, 'as lesbianism is not an accepted lifestyle in the Hindu faith, it could be argued under the Children Act that [Nita and Clare's] "chosen way of life" meant that they could not provide a suitable environment for the upbringing of these children.' These and some other sibling groups Nita and Clare enquired about were ultimately never placed as sibling groups, even though Nita and Clare were offering them a secure and loving home.

By 2014, when Barbara and Shazia were first interviewed, social work practice was moving away from 'same race placement' towards a more individualistic approach led by policies concerning the need for increased adoption numbers, something that remains controversial. This approach, which often problematically ignores questions of 'race' altogether (Hicks 2011), is summed up by Dilip with some irony:

> In adoption today, there's more of a 'what do you want?' than a 'let's match you', which was, I suppose, the situation ten years ago. (Dilip and James' story)

Yet, as Cath points out, questions of race are always pertinent to the placement of children and require carers able to address such concerns:

> They have their own confusion about identity because they are mixed race. I mean they've been 'racist'. June was very muddled up. I remember her coming home and thinking she was a white girl for ages... I can remember Joseph saying to me, 'I'm so glad I'm not black.' And it was very, very painful. He's got better. He has got a struggle anyway because of his appearance. Appearance-wise, people think he's white a lot of the time. I don't think he really knows what to do about that. He did say he'd rather be black or white but not this, neither one nor the other. You can see that because he's so much lighter than June is. (Teresa and Cath's story)

The assessment process

Most of the participants in the 1999 edition experienced some prejudice from agencies either in the assessment process or in pursuing placements, and some had repeated experiences of rejection and homophobic attitudes. Others described very positive experiences, but these were more unusual. In this edition the picture is more universally positive, with most noting accepting responses from agencies:

> We've never felt that, as a same-sex couple, we have been treated differently by the agency – it's just been, 'You're a carer and this is your job.' They do tell the kids and their families that they are going to a same-sex couple. Nowadays, it's not about same-sex couples – it's more about social care and changing the attitudes of parents who have to understand that carers come in all shapes and sizes... I think an advantage for our agency is the fact that we don't have any kids, we've got two spare bedrooms, we're young, and we can take on almost any placement that comes through. (Jamie, in Jamie and Simon's story)

Kath reflects on the changes since she first adopted in 1995:

> I think it is far easier for lesbians and gay men to adopt now. I sit on an adoption panel and many lesbians and a number of gay men have come through this agency very positively. I think some of the younger prospective adopters have no idea about the struggles that have gone before them. Having said that, I am sure there are other agencies continuing to struggle with this issue, and I continue to question and challenge assumptions and examples of homophobia within this agency.

Dylan, who was out as a transgender man at the point of applying to adopt, reports a positive experience, which included being supported by the social work team when he encountered transphobia in a panel member:

> The social workers handled my gender identity really well. I felt well looked after by them. The only difficult person was the medical adviser...who [refused] to approve me based on psychological integrity... She clearly had no experience of trans issues. It was upsetting, but my social worker stood up for me and [they] offered to pay £700 for an assessment from an independent

psychiatrist… The social work team also did some trans awareness training with the panel before my panel date.

The experience of the black lesbians and the couples with one black partner in this edition is more mixed and is linked to the intersections of racism, sexism and homophobia. Lee notes the continuing prevalence of racism in some agency responses:

> I come across prejudice in my role in the independent fostering agency when assessing carers, as I hear some terrible views expressed about people from a different culture; I feel sad that these levels of prejudice still exist. Why is that still happening?

For many participants in earlier decades, initial adoption or foster care preparation groups were stressful experiences as they were usually the only participants who were not heterosexual and were not confident of support from the facilitators. Kath describes the preparation group in her first adoption as follows:

> The first preparation group I attended included 22 heterosexual couples and me…a not out single lesbian. There were a number of social workers involved and this was an exceptionally big group, to deal with a backlog across the county. From the outset I felt isolated and found many of the small group discussions uncomfortable.

The 2018 cohort describes more positive experiences of these groups. Indeed, Darrell, in Darrell and David's story, describes how a whole support network has developed out of their preparation group:

> We're also still in contact with several adopters from our preparation course so that's a great network – we really bonded as a group on the course and they're local, whereas other friends are all over the country.

Barbara, in Barbara and Shazia's story, found the experience less helpful:

> We were probably the only lesbians in the group – probably the only lesbian, gay and black people in the group, actually. That wasn't acknowledged in the preparation groups for social services

41

or for the private company. They say anybody can foster and adopt, but you get the feeling that the other couples don't expect there to be gay and lesbian people amidst them. It's like something they read about but that doesn't exist.

The extent to which contributors were asked directly about their sexuality varied in both cohorts, but the overwhelming consensus was that social workers, then and now, avoided direct questions about their sexuality:

It felt as though generalisations were being made during the assessment. The social worker almost skated over questions of sexuality, in a funny way. It didn't sound like she had registered the implications in her mind and we didn't really talk about our sexuality. We talked about a support group where there are a lot of men and she said that, in her experience, there are a lot more gay men than lesbians wanting to adopt, and she wondered why. I said that it was possibly more complicated for gay men to create a family biologically, but she'd not thought that through even though she had worked with both gay men and lesbians. (James, in Dilip and James' story)

However, Dilip also highlighted the positive responses of social work agencies:

Both panels were lovely – the approval panel and the matching panel, very positive. The woman who chaired the second panel started off by saying, 'This is a match with some complexities, but, on the whole, we're optimistic.' The complexities weren't about being gay – these brothers had a very difficult start to life. They asked a lot of questions... The only time they talked about us being same sex was when they talked about schools and recommended a school that they felt was positive towards LGBT families. They probably just wanted to make it clear that they didn't have a problem with our sexuality. Their major concern was the approval of our families and whether the children would be embraced into the wider family unit.

Almost all contributors were asked about how they were going to provide role models of the opposite gender in their assessment. Many acknowledged the importance of the issue, but questioned the stereotypical assumptions implied in the way it was raised with them:

> She also asked about gender role models. It's an important question and it was important for me to think that through. I remember thinking at first that the children might have more men than women in their life with me, but it hasn't worked out like that at all. Most of the foster carers I know are female, and I ended up linking with them as well as with friends amongst the staff at the school where I work, who are also mostly female. (Rob)

Lee also added:

> There used to be an emphasis – which is not necessarily correct – about ensuring female carers have male role models for the children in their care and *vice versa*, a belief that they needed these role models to become well-balanced people. But even when I had a partner, when we were going through the adoption process for Paul and Rebecca, I felt it wasn't about the roles that we had as a partnership or the roles taken within the house. The boys were taught to cook as well as Rebecca, the boys were also expected to help with the cleaning and they also did 'boy' things in the garden, like climbing trees, but then so did Rebecca. So, I think there was a realisation that there were no defined roles, and that they were still well-balanced people.

However, Dilip also notes of their social work assessment, 'They didn't do the "gender role model" thing or ask if the children would come into contact with people of the opposite sex.'

Placement

Many of the carers in the 1999 edition experienced long delays after approval before a child was placed with them. Nita and Clare waited two years from being approved to having their first child placed.

Most of the participants in the second edition had children placed very quickly, some as soon as they were approved. Only one couple approved to adopt had to wait a year, which was considered unusual by social workers and was linked to a particular regulatory change in 2014 that slowed the number of children being placed for adoption.

In both the 1999 and 2018 cohorts, around two-thirds of the interviewees were working in the caring professions and had extensive prior experience of supporting vulnerable children; 18 out of 27 in 1999, and 15 out of 22 in 2018. They are not all middle class, but some talk about how 'knowing the system' has helped them have confidence with agencies:

> I think the fact that we both worked within social work meant we had a sense of reality about what adoption meant and how it could work. (Dilip, in Dilip and James' story)

Or to advocate for their children's needs:

> It's all fire-fighting. We make a lot of noise, but we're not unpleasant. We've had to be firm about advocating for our child and asking for what we need. (Mike, in Mike and Andrew's story)

Lee identifies how experiences as a professional carer and mature student may have distanced him from his working-class background:

> I suppose I am middle class now. I'm almost ashamed of it to an extent, but I know where I have come from. I'm middle class from a working-class background. A lot of the kids – and the carers – are from working-class backgrounds.

Of the 17 households included in the first book, around 65 per cent (11 families) were caring for disabled children. The proportion is slightly less in 2018, with 7 families out of 13 (54%) including children with disabilities. The first edition showed evidence of lesbian and gay carers being seen as a 'last resort' for children who were hard to place elsewhere. For example, Lee said of his adopted son, Marcus, in 1999:

He came to me five years ago as a 'hard to place' child. The plans were for him to be adopted but no carers could be found despite advertising. Marcus was seen as having very great needs and the prognosis for him was very poor… When I said I'd adopt him, the social workers made it very clear to me that I was very lucky to do so because they wouldn't normally allow single people to adopt! They had no other options for Marcus, needless to say.

The proportion of very young children placed with contributors has increased significantly since 1999, with only 4 out of 17 households (less than a quarter) having children under five placed with them in 1999. In 2018, just under half of the households, 6 out of 13, had children under five placed with them and five out of the six children placed were aged under two at the point of placement. Most significantly, one of the gay male couples, Darrell and David, was approved for children aged two to six and the child placed with them was actually under two (22 months old), reflecting a confidence in placing very young children with gay men not seen in our previous study. Nita and Clare's third adoption also demonstrates a willingness of agencies and birth parents to choose lesbian and gay adopters and foster carers for babies and very young children, on this occasion, in preference to heterosexual carers:

> [Meena's birth mother] was presented with our family profile and a profile of a heterosexual couple and she chose us as an adoptive family because we offered two older sisters for Meena and parents who were both teachers and also a writer and an artist. The fact that we were also a lesbian couple didn't seem to concern her at all. (Clare, in Nita and Clare's story)

The vast majority of men in our book, both single carers and couples, had boys placed with them. In the 1999 cohort, all the men had only cared for boys. In the 2018 cohort, some gay male single carers and couples had been approved for either boys or girls, but all had boys placed with them at the time they were interviewed, as did Dylan, the transgender man. The picture was more mixed with lesbian carers. In 1999, three of the four single lesbians and two of the three lesbian couples had girls placed with them for adoption. The third couple had a baby boy placed with them for adoption after adopting two girls. One single lesbian carer had fostered both boys and girls and had adopted three of the boys she had cared for. The other single lesbian adopter in the 1999 cohort adopted a total of three girls, as did one of the lesbian couples appearing in both editions. The other lesbian adoptive couple appearing in this edition has taken a sibling group of a boy and a girl. The other lesbian foster carers in this edition, in addition to the transgender carer who both fostered and adopted, have both had a majority of boys placed with them.

The preponderance of boys placed across all categories of carer reflects, in part, the greater number of boys being looked after in local authority care across the country and also needing adoption placements. The placement of only girls with some lesbian carers and only boys with some gay men has been to do with the stated views and preferences of the carers themselves about which gender they feel most suited to care for. There also seems to be a tendency on the part of agencies to match the gender of the carers with the gender of the child, but more markedly so when placing boys with gay men. This suggests a persistence in assumptions around the suitability of women as carers for all children and a concomitant hesitancy around the suitability of men as carers for girls, although this may also be changing as there are examples of gay men adopting girls elsewhere (Goldberg 2012; Lewin 2009; Mallon 2004), with the Northern Support Group at one time including a gay couple who adopted a brother and sister.

Several participants in both cohorts spoke about the stereotypical perception of gay men as not being 'natural' carers or as posing a sexual abuse risk. This is picked up in Jamie and Simon's story:

We have been trained to cope with false allegations. They didn't talk specifically about same-sex couples, more about allegations being made against anyone and everyone. The training looked at safer caring, protecting the child, protecting yourself. We were given simple guidelines, like never go into their bedrooms, knock and say you want to see them, things like that. It's guidance for safe caring. There were two classes on safe caring and for each child there is a safe care policy – as well as all the risk assessment and tons of other policies on smoking, on everything you can think of. (Jamie, in Jamie and Simon's story)

This points to the fact that there is a need to balance safe care, including the protection of both children and carers, with what might be seen as heteronormative assumptions about male carers in families, as Rob's story notes:

The one thing that haunted me as a single gay carer was my fear of having allegations made about me and stuff… I do remember on the week-long course there were several occasions when people were talking about how unsafe it was to leave your husband or your male partner with a child, or let them bathe the children or be with them by themselves. I'm like, 'Hang on, first, I am a man and I'm single and second, if I do have a partner they're going to be a man as well. It's like, what are you saying?' I challenged that and it made them stop and think, but there were a couple of people that still spoke a little bit to that agenda saying that the statistics were very damning, but that's not what you want to hear as a single male carer who is a little bit freaked out about possible allegations.

Many of the foster carers and adopters in the first edition had experienced homophobia from social workers, foster carers, birth families, schools or other parents, and prejudice from their own families. Lee described some difficult, but also mixed, experiences from when his children were young, and when he still identified as a lesbian:

At the start when we moved in they were quite friendly…but when they clicked that [my] partner wasn't a bloke, then the whole thing changed, the whole atmosphere… You would think that being gay would be easier in a town, but no, not at all – if you were openly gay it seemed to give people the feeling they could abuse you in the street – verbally and physically. There were a couple of occasions when that happened, nothing too awful, but just things that made us uncomfortable and the kids questioning. But on the whole, it was a really good move… We moved the children to a different school that turned out to be superb. They had a completely different viewpoint and were incredibly supportive of Marcus and his needs, as well as the other kids, and there was no issue with me.

Clare, in Nita and Clare's story, described the impact of agency resistance on children waiting for placements:

When we set out to adopt in 1992 there were many social workers who wouldn't even consider us as adopters for children they were trying to place. There were children we would have adopted who were never placed for adoption with anyone and that was seen as preferable to letting us, as lesbians, care for them. Our second daughter's foster carers would not allow introductions to take place in their house because we were lesbians. Today things are much easier – there are civil partnerships and the whole climate is much more accepting of LGBT parents.

Most contributors in the current edition are bringing positive stories of support from professionals, their own networks, local communities, and even birth families. Jamie, in Jamie and Simon's story, recalls one birth parent's reaction:

The dad was a bit 'iffy' at first but eventually when he saw how much effort we were putting into caring for this child, he was very impressed. When we went to the looked-after children review the dad was quite emotional, and said he would rather his son stayed with us because we'd done such a great job.

Darrell, in Darrell and David's story, describes their experiences of acceptance in a small rural village community with a church school:

When we were on adoption leave together, we took [him] to a church playgroup and we were virtually the only men. There was one other man, who was a shift worker and brought his child because he was available then. He said he'd not known any gay men before, but he was very open and said we'd taught him something. There was no problem with anything at pre-school either, it was just 'of course he can do everything, we'll do cards for his grandmothers on Mother's Day and two cards on Father's Day.' We've not encountered any problems from the other parents at pre-school or playgroup, and we've been invited to all the parties and so on as a family.

In terms of agency engagement, of the 17 single and couple households contributing to the 1999 edition, all but one had been assessed by local authority agencies, whereas 3 of the 13 households in this edition were approved by independent agencies. This parallels an increase in the use of independent agencies in the sector in general and greater acceptance of lesbian and gay carers in some of those agencies, although it is also worth recalling here that the UK Equality Act 2006 and its associated Sexual Orientation Regulations (2007) exposed a number of agencies operating either tacit or explicit anti-gay adoption policies. However, the contrast between the two editions of this book also shows a significant change in the openness of most agencies to assessing LGBT applicants. Rob describes the straightforward way in which one local authority agency raised and dealt with his sexuality:

> I didn't have an issue with applying to become a foster carer as a single gay man. I went to a few different authorities, but I applied to [a London borough council] because they were so instantly welcoming. One of the first questions they asked me was if I was gay and when I said, 'Yes', they said, 'No, problem at all, that's great.' And it just went on like that; it wasn't an issue, they were very supportive. From my perspective I was very glad that they had mentioned it and made their support so clear.

Rob also highlights an important difference between fostering and adoption in terms of the impermanence of the family identity he creates with each new placement. This relationship has to be fluid and, ultimately, subjugated to the needs of the children temporarily placed with him, who may or may not be able to cope with him being out either as a gay man or as their foster parent:

He's told the friend's mum that I'm his uncle. He's not told them he's in foster care. That's the difference between fostering and adoption. I know quite a lot of LGBT adoptive families are very proud of their family identity and they promote it – this is who they are. It's not like that with fostering – you are there to support the kids and ultimately, it's about the children. You can't put them in a difficult position because you don't know what their futures hold. And you can't commit, because they are not going to be with you forever. That can make it difficult and hard as a carer because no matter how much you want to tell people, you've got to put that second to the needs of the child. That's really important.

The changes in the law since 1999, described earlier, have meant that going through the legal process has been relatively straightforward for couples adopting after 2005. Before that, unmarried couples could not adopt together in law, so one partner had to elect to be named on the order as a single adopter. Couples featured in the 1999 edition describe putting together complicated packages of adoption and residence orders under the Children Act 1989, with carefully worded wills to ensure the same guarantees of permanent parenting for the children they were trying to adopt, as Clare explains, in Nita and Clare's story:

> …we had to decide each time which one of us was going to be the named adopter on the adoption order and who would apply for a residence order at the same time. We never told the children who their named adopter was as we didn't want them to feel any insecurity about their ties to either one of us. When the law changed in 2005 we went back to court and adopted the younger two children in both our names. Lubna was over 18 by then so we couldn't change her adoption order.

All the contributors talk about the importance of good support networks and many have valued having access to LGBT-specific support groups, such as LAGFAPN and the Northern Support Group in earlier decades and New Family Social in more recent years. Lee says:

I was one of the first people to join the Northern Support Group for gay and lesbian carers. I wasn't at the initial conference, but when I heard the group was being set up I was there like a shot. I had come out by then. It was great for the kids, because that was the thing that I really, really wanted it for, so that they saw that there were other children who had gay parents. Seeing all those kids together with their mums and dads, mingling in and out, it was great. That group was hugely important to me, because you could go to the group and relax. It didn't matter what we talked about actually, if you were having issues or you weren't, or if somebody else needed your support. It was wonderful not having to explain myself to anybody.

Not everyone had found it easy to access appropriate support. For instance, Kath points out;

One of the problems with groups is that people can have such diverse experiences and attitudes, which can make them feel more isolating than the unifying factors. I think sometimes I spoke about issues without feeling safe. I think maybe the groups should have been called something different rather than 'support' as this can lead to so many expectations.

This is echoed by Elizabeth, in Elizabeth and Mary's story:

We did get involved with a LBGT support group and that gave a wider context to things – a lot of sharing of experiences, lots of people at different stages, most going through assessment. It wasn't particularly helpful, because so few people were at our stage, and we didn't want to put people off by focusing on problems.

However, Jamie and Simon's story highlights the fact that, for many of our recent contributors, online support and making contact with others via social media and the Internet has become increasingly important:

We also found support in the LGBT charity – New Family Social – dedicated to LGBT families who foster or adopt. With New Family

Social, we mostly talk online. We share experiences… (Jamie, in Jamie and Simon's story)

This point is also echoed by Dylan, who talks about having made an online video about trans adoption:

Since being approved I have made a video for agencies training others in how to assess a trans adopter – everyone needs to be aware of the Gender Recognition Act.

Barbara and Shazia found being with an independent agency a barrier to accessing any kind of support, either tailored or generic:

We're not in any support group actually. We did ask about other gay and lesbian couples or parents that were fostering, and we've not heard anything. But I think that's one of the difficulties with an agency, it's very hard to access that kind of support, and I think you miss out on a lot of support not being with the local authority. They don't know what other foster carers are in the area, not to mention, who's black, who's gay, who's got any disabilities. (Barbara, in Barbara and Shazia's story)

Many carers describe very positive experiences of support from friends, family, neighbours and local communities. When Barbara and Shazia's foster son died, they drew on a reservoir of lesbian and gay and local neighbourhood support that contrasted sharply with the inability of the social services department to acknowledge them as bereaved parents.

In 1999, no one interviewed for the book was involved in any other activity related to fostering and adoption beyond looking after the children placed with them. By 2018, eight of those interviewed were involved in social work education, training foster and adoption panel members or speaking to preparation courses for prospective applicants. One of the interviewees, who appears in both books, is now an adoption panel member, and another worked for an independent fostering agency and is now in a local authority looked-after children team. Given the disproportionately high level of professional backgrounds amongst this group of applicants, it is not surprising that some have gone on to be involved in professional education and training on the subject. It is maybe more surprising that only one has become involved in decision-making through becoming a panel member and this may signal that there is still some distance to travel before lesbian, gay, bisexual and transgender carers are proactively included in all decision-making on the approval and matching of heterosexual as well as LGBT foster and adoptive applicants and families.

Finally, the follow-up stories from 1999 contributors include accounts from two contributors, Lee and Kath, who are now grandparents, and document several fostered and adopted children who are now in their thirties. They look back both at how challenging it has been and how rewarding they have found making the choice to foster or adopt. Paul and Richard describe how Patrick's behaviour tested them, but nevertheless focus on the positives of their foster care and adoption journey:

> We didn't know that we would be able to cope with Patrick. We didn't know it was going to be necessary to cope and we're not always sure we have coped with him, but we're still here. And he's still here... We would encourage anyone thinking about it to adopt or foster. The success of the placement was that Patrick was eventually able to make a secure attachment to us, something he had not been able to make with anyone else. Would we do it again? Yes. Adopting Patrick is the single most worthwhile thing that we have done with our lives – so there is no doubt at all that we would do it again. (Paul, in Paul and Richard's story)

Conclusion

We are much heartened by the rise in research in the field of LGBT parenting, including foster care and adoption, which continues to ask new and important questions. We also welcome the publication of practice guidance by some social work and welfare agencies determined to better their practice with LGBT foster carers and adopters (Brodzinsky 2011; Brodzinsky and Goldberg 2016;

Brodzinsky and Pertman 2012; Hicks and Greaves 2007; de Jong and Donnelly 2015; National Resource Center for Permanency and Family Connections 2012a, b). Although such policies are by no means perfect, they do offer us hope for the development of better practice in the field of LGBT foster care and adoption in the future, and we hope that this book might also contribute to such expansion.

Julianne Pidduck has argued that there is something of an anguished relationship between forms of kinship and the LGBT experience, since this requires a relatedness 'forged not only on our own terms [but also] within conditions (and relations) not of our own making' (Pidduck 2009, p.446). We believe that the contributors to this book, and indeed those who added their stories to the original 1999 edition, all demonstrate such forging of new relationalities, sometimes in the face of heteronormative and traditionally familial expectations. We have been told many times in the past by social workers, trainers, educators, panel members and interested LGBT people that they all found the 1999 edition of this book valuable, helpful and, in some cases, something of a lifeline, and so we also hope that this new, revised edition offers as much food for thought as our original did. It has certainly been a pleasure to research and write, and we think that the great generosity of all those LGBT carers who have contributed their stories here comes across in their accounts of what, to them, is merely ordinary life.

ORIGINAL (1999) STORIES WITH 2017–18 UPDATES

NITA and CLARE
Two Mums, Three Daughters

Nita and Clare's approval as adopters was pioneering for their local authority in the North of England, which had not knowingly assessed any lesbian or gay adopters before, but was open and enthusiastic about assessing Nita and Clare. Following the adoptions of Lubna and Neelam within two years, they waited a further four years before adding Meena to their family. Now with Lubna and Neelam grown up and Meena on the verge of adulthood, they continue to be close to all their daughters.

We begin with Nita and Clare's original (1999) story, 'Arranged Parenting':

'What do you think about children?'

'Very nice.'

'No, you know what I mean. What do you think about having children?'

Nita turned over and snuggled her head into the hollow of Clare's shoulder. She let go the lingering threads of a dream and concentrated on the question. 'You mean giving birth?'

'Not necessarily, just being a mother however we might do it.'

'I'd love to have children, but I'm not bothered about having my own', Nita responded slowly. She had always assumed in a sweeping unspecific way that she would have children, but once she had come out as a lesbian the prospect seemed to become less likely; life was so busy and she kept thinking she was still young, there would be time enough later.

'I wouldn't want to give birth!' Clare was emphatic. 'All that pain and blood doesn't bear thinking about, and anyway, the world's already overpopulated. What is it they say? One child from the developed world uses ten times the food and energy and money that a child from the developing world uses?'

'Yes, and there are plenty of children already born that need a home; look at all the children in care, especially black children', Nita continued eagerly. 'Have you seen those posters on the bus stops on High Street? They're advertising for adopters and foster parents. I was thinking, we'd make good parents, wouldn't we? We could offer love and security.'

'Too right!' Clare responded and they were quiet for a while trying to imagine being parents and thinking of everything they had brought each other – warmth, love, laughter, a passion for India, a love of Scotland.

'You know Saira and Linda did it, didn't they?' Nita interrupted the silence. 'They had Sonia placed with them as soon as they were approved – it was incredibly fast.'

'But they weren't "out", were they? I don't want to lie – I'm not ashamed of my sexuality, and it's no basis on which to start a family.'

'Anyway, we're useless at lying. We'd just get ourselves in a pickle', Nita agreed. 'Look, we're middle class with loads of childcare experience, loads of support from our families, we're both teachers – we've got everything going for us. Someone has to be brave enough to be "out", so why not us? If someone had done it before us the door might be open already.'

* * *

Nita and Clare didn't tell a lot of people to begin with, just those who they knew would be the core of their support network, like Nita's parents, who live nearby, and close friends, some of whom had children they were closely involved with. Everyone was very supportive, although some were concerned that they might be disappointed or face a lot of obstacles and prejudice. Some were not sure whether or not to take it seriously at first.

* * *

Clare phoned her mother, Hilda, one Sunday afternoon.

'Hello. It's me, Clare. How are you, Mummy?'

'Fine. Your brother's just been round cutting the grass – it's like a jungle out there. He says they're all well. How are things with you and Nita?'

Clare decided to plunge in. 'Oh fine. In fact, we're thinking of applying to adopt.'

'What? A child?' asked Hilda in disbelief.

'Well not a humpback whale', Clare responded curtly.

'That's a big thing to do. What do you want to complicate your lives for? I thought you were both so happy?'

'We are and we want to adopt.' Clare was starting to feel frustrated by her mother's response.

'Well, I must say I don't think they'll let you', Hilda cautioned.

'We'll have to convince them, won't we?' Clare breathed deeply. I'm not going to get angry, she told herself.

'But you haven't got a garden. You'll have to move, won't you?'

'I think not having a garden will be the least of our problems', Clare laughed. 'Anyway, we've got a back yard. The thing is, they want adoptive parents to reflect a wide range of families, not just rich people with big houses and big gardens.'

'You know, Maureen adopted and then she and Clive got divorced and now Enid looks after the children more than Maureen. They're always with their grandma – it's not right, is it?' Hilda mused conversationally.

Clare counted to ten in her head. 'Well, anyway, we're applying to adopt. They'll be Asian or Asian mixed race children to match Nita and me.'

'Why does that matter?' Hilda argued. 'Children are children whatever their colour.'

'It's important for the child to feel part of the family where she's placed, and Nita's Indian and I'm white.' Race always was a sticky issue for Hilda, thought Clare.

'But Nita was born here', Hilda asserted.

'So? She's still Indian.'

'Mmm… Well, lovely to hear from you, Clare. I'll have to go, it's choir practice in a minute. Love to Nita. Bye.'

'Bye', said Clare, as the phone went dead.

* * *

Nita and Clare's first move was to ring the local authority adoption agency anonymously and ask what their policy was on approving lesbians and gay men for adoption. The reply was firm – the authority operated an equal opportunities policy and all potential adopters would be considered on their merits as potential parents. Armed with this knowledge, but aware of the emptiness of much equal opportunities rhetoric, Nita and Clare knew they still had to pick the moment to disclose their sexuality very carefully.

* * *

'So, what's all this I hear about you wanting to adopt?' Alia said curiously. Alia, a lesbian friend, was sceptical about whether or not Nita and Claire realised what they were up against.

'The grapevine works fast. Yes, I'm on the waiting list to be assessed.' Nita smiled.

'Have you told them you're a lesbian?'

'Not yet, but we're going to', responded Clare.

'What? Are you mad? If you do, they'll never give you a child, especially not an Asian child.'

'But we'd make good parents', Nita protested.

'No one's denying that, but be realistic. This isn't a political act, you know.'

'No, it isn't, but someone has to be honest and make a case for lesbian parenting', Clare argued.

'So, you two are going to take on the council, are you?' Alia smiled.

'If we have to, but it's not about that, not yet anyway. It's about us wanting to adopt. We've loads of skills, we're offering them two fully participating parents with lots of childcare experience, which is more than they'll get with most heterosexual couples. The only possible reason they could turn us down is on discriminatory grounds – if they do, then it'll be clear cut', Clare explained.

'Remember, no one who is out has ever tried to adopt here, so we don't know what they'll say', Nita joined in. 'Those lesbians who *have* adopted have been economical with the truth, to say the least.'

'Apart from Sue, and she was turned down', Alia reminded them.

'That was ten years ago and we don't know the facts of the case. It might not have been about her sexuality', said Clare.

'If you really wanted to be parents, you'd lie', Alia asserted.

'Oh yes, and spend our lives wondering who's going to tell on us? It's dishonest. I'm not prepared to pretend that Clare's just a good friend or a childminder', Nita insisted decisively.

* * *

Nita approached the agency initially as a single adopter and was sent on a preparation course for single black adopters that had a safe, positive atmosphere. After the course she told them she wanted to go ahead with the assessment and asked for Marcia to be her social worker, first, because she was the only black social worker and second, because Marcia had lesbian friends. The first assessment visit was one of the most difficult moments in the process, as Nita had to explain that she wasn't single and that her partner was a woman. Marcia was a little stunned but digested the new situation quickly and was happy to take on a joint assessment.

The assessment was long and intensive but Nita and Clare felt lucky to have Marcia as their social worker; she was honest, straightforward and very enthusiastic about the combination of skills and experience she felt they had to offer as adopters. However, she was fairly new to adoption and the department as a whole was nervous about taking a lesbian couple to panel. There were occasions when decisions about how the application should be processed were changed; for instance, originally the referees were two women friends; one was a single parent and the other was in a heterosexual relationship and had a child, although her partner was not involved in providing the reference. They were later asked to supply a third reference from a heterosexual couple with children, interviewed together, which they duly did. There were also delays in going to panel while the panel received extra equal opportunities training addressing the issue of sexual orientation, and the department waited for a member who was known to be homophobic to leave. Marcia left Nita and Clare to fill in the assessment form on their own initially and then used the answers as a basis for discussion and as the main body of the completed Form F, which is the name for the assessment report that was/would be presented to the adoption panel at the time. She was amazed at the reams written and satisfied with most of it as it stood. There were a few points on which they had a lengthy discussion, the most thorny being the male role models in their lives and whether or not they would adopt a boy.

* * *

'I want to ask you about what you've said about disabled children. I know you've ticked all these categories, but I think you need to really think about what you're prepared to take on. There's no reason why you should take a child with any disability at all. You've got as much right as any other couple to have a perfectly normal healthy child, a baby even. You mustn't think you have to accept anything you don't want to.'

'It's all right', Nita smiled, 'We're actually fine about some kinds of disability; we've got lots of experience of children with learning difficulties at work, and we really feel okay about the things we've ticked.'

'Well, I'm just saying I see you with an ordinary healthy little baby or toddler in a few months' time and that's what I think you should hold out for', Marcia insisted defiantly. 'Now I know we've talked about this before, but I think we need to return to the issue of you saying you'll only take girls and not boys.'

'We don't feel confident about parenting a boy', Nita explained.

'Is it that you don't like boys?' Marcia suggested, playing devil's advocate.

'No, it's not that. We have more boys in our lives than girls at the moment. Najma's got two sons, Shaheen's got three sons,

Ruth's got a son, and we look after them all. It's just that we know about growing up as a girl, but not as a boy. Other lesbians feel confident bringing up boys but it's not for us', Clare asserted.

'I'm sorry to push you on this, but I know it will be an issue with the panel. If you were offered a sibling group with a boy, would you take them?'

'No', replied Clare.

'Would you consider them then?' Marcia re-phrased quickly.

'No', Nita repeated, thinking this was getting farcical. 'It's not that we don't like boys, but we don't want to spend all our energy on them when there are lots of girls out there who need us and who we'd be much better at bringing up.'

'The thing about boys is you either bring them up to be sensitive and caring, which means they end up only relating to women while men beat shit out of them. Or, you bring them up to be "lads", which means football, aggression and everything we don't have to put up with in our lives at present', Clare explained starkly.

'I'm sorry to labour this point but I really do think it could be the difference between getting you through panel and not', Marcia insisted. 'If you were offered a sibling group with two girls and a baby boy, would you consider them – just consider?'

Wearily, Clare looked at Nita. 'I don't think so.'

'Okay', Marcia persevered. 'What about if you had two girls placed with you, you went to court and they were adopted, then a year or two later the birth mother had another child, a baby boy, the girls' brother, and he was to be placed for adoption. Would you consider taking him?'

Nita and Clare looked at each other again doubtfully and then Nita said, 'Yes, I suppose we'd consider that.'

'That's good', Marcia smiled with relief. 'I can work with that at panel. I can say you would consider a boy given the right circumstances but you'd prefer a girl or girls. Sex preference is not unusual in adoption.'

* * *

A year after the first contact with the agency, Nita and Clare were approved to adopt up to three children aged seven and under. They were the first 'out' lesbian couple to be approved by the local authority. They held a spontaneous party for friends and family, but in the midst of the celebrations they knew it was only the first step. Some people were still saying they would never be successful in having a child placed with them.

They began scouring the adoption publications for Asian and mixed race Asian girls under eight. Marcia brought possibilities from time to time and they rang up social workers themselves. As with many black and mixed race adopters, they were referred to the British Association for Adoption and Fostering (BAAF), that offer a computerised system for linking children with particular needs with suitable families across the country. Because the Asian communities in their area are small and close-knit, it was not appropriate for them to be considered for children from within their local community.

* * *

'Hello, I'm ringing about Rukhsana and Noreen who are advertised in *Be My Parent*. BAAF gave me your number. I've been ringing all week to speak to someone.'

'Yes, sorry about that, we're very busy. You know we're looking for an Asian or Asian mixed race couple for these sisters, don't you?'

'Yes, I'm Asian and my partner's white. Also, the area we live in is very multi-racial and has a big Asian community.'

'Good. These girls have had a lot of moves and their behaviour can be challenging. They're in separate foster homes at the moment, but meet regularly and we want to place them together. We're looking for energetic parents who can dedicate a lot of time and energy to them. Would you like to tell me a bit about yourselves?'

'Well, we've certainly got time and energy. I work part time and my partner is currently working full time but she wants to go part time if we adopt children under five, so that we can take equal responsibility for looking after them.'

'Sorry, did you say "she"?'

'Yes, my partner's a woman.'

'I see. We have had quite a lot of enquiries about these girls, some of which look like strong possibilities for linking, but I'll take your details in case the possibilities we're currently pursuing fall through. We'll get back to you if need be. Now, can you spell your name for me?'

* * *

Rukhsana was subsequently placed on her own and they are still looking for a family for Noreen, even though Nita and Clare could have offered them a home together. As Nita and Clare offer no specific religion and as Nita is not fluent in an Asian language, there were many occasions where they were told they were ruled out because an agency was looking for a particular religious and linguistic background for a child. They themselves also ruled out some children suggested to them because the children were older than they had been looking for or they were not sure the racial match was appropriate.

They enquired about another Asian sibling group who were in three separate white foster homes. They were visited by two social workers who postponed the visit twice before being directed to attend by a line manager, and who were visibly uncomfortable throughout their stay, in one case to the extent of not even taking their coat off or having anything to eat or drink, despite the two-hour journey to get there. Nita and Clare were eventually turned down by that authority's panel on the advice of their legal department, that said that, as lesbianism is not an accepted lifestyle in the Hindu faith, it could be argued under the Children Act that their 'chosen way of life' meant that they could not provide a suitable environment for the upbringing of these children. This was despite the fact that they had been told the children had a multi-faith background and were not being brought up in any particular religion. This interpretation of Hinduism was also challenged by a Hindu social worker from Nita and Clare's authority. The couple took out an official complaint and some recommendations for future practice were made. The report on the complaint investigation acknowledged that Nita and Clare had demonstrated that they could meet the cultural and linguistic needs of the children, yet found that the authority had acted within the spirit and letter of the Children Act and the panel decision could not be reversed. These and some other children they enquired about are still not placed, even though Nita and Clare were offering a secure and loving home.

As the months passed, Nita and Clare began to feel that they would never be seriously considered for a child they felt was right for them, and they began to lose heart. The helplessness and the not knowing were strange; they had always seen themselves as being in control of their lives and now someone else was choosing for them. The matchmakers were weighing carefully Clare's sprawling Essex family, Nita's Indian heritage and her family's migration from India, their friends, childhoods, work, holidays in Scotland and, inevitably, their sexuality. They had to be optimists, had to believe that someone would be wise enough and experienced enough to arrange a suitable match now that they had committed themselves to 'arranged' parenthood.

* * *

'I don't know why you're putting yourselves through all this. What's wrong with the turkey baster?' Sandra, a lesbian friend, admonished one day.

'Lots. What's going to happen to all these kids with anonymous donors as dads?' replied Clare.

'They don't need dads', responded Sandra.

'No, you're right, they don't. But everyone needs to know their roots – what did Bob Marley say? "Trees without roots can't grow." Especially black kids', Nita explained. 'Look at how long it took me to sort out my identity and I had it all there in my home.'

'Well, you could have gone for a known donor', Sandra argued.

'And how easy do you think it would be to find an Asian donor?' Nita countered. 'And what would we be looking for? An Indian donor? A Hindu? A Muslim? Because you realise I'd have to have the baby, unless I wanted to be the only black person in a white household. And then what about when the baby's born? Is it realistic or right not to involve the man in the child's life and do we want to artificially involve a man in our life like that?'

'But it's taking so long – it would have been quicker to get pregnant', Sandra protested.

'Well I've no burning desire to reproduce, I don't even know if I'm fertile. The thought of having a Jackson and recreating the genes of my parents fills me with dread – my family are bonkers', Clare intervened, laughing.

'It's not for us', Nita concluded emphatically. 'Anyway, the bottom line is we don't want to give birth, we want to adopt. We always talked about parenting in terms of adoption. It's a positive choice for us.'

* * *

Eighteen months after approval they finally saw Lubna's details in an adoption magazine. She was eight, older than they had generally been looking at, but everything about her leapt out as being a perfect match – her interests, her experiences, even down to her birth mother being from the same city in India as Nita's father. They were just about to go to India on holiday so they didn't do anything immediately, but Lubna's social worker had seen a letter about them that their social worker had sent round a number of local authorities. On their return they found that Lubna's social worker had already contacted their social worker and wanted to visit them with a homefinder and a friend of Lubna's family who was supporting the adoption. Nita and Clare were very nervous, but as soon as the visitors arrived they knew this was going to be very different from their previous experience of a visit by children's social workers. Everyone was relaxed and positive, and by the end of the visit it was apparent that the social workers wanted to proceed to the matching panel.

Two months later, Nita and Clare were matched with Lubna. She had been with the same black foster parent, Thelma, for nearly four years, which could have been very difficult, but Thelma was wonderful and totally supported Lubna in feeling good about the move. Nita and Clare were terrified of meeting Lubna because they had been warned that she was not positive about adoption, but they had made a video and a book about themselves that she saw beforehand. She knew from the beginning that they were lesbians and she knew about lesbians from the soap operas on television. By the time she met them it seemed as if she had already decided she liked them. From then on it was a dream come true, everything they could have hoped for and more. It was love at first sight. She bonded with them immediately and was starting to pack her things up to take to her new home at the end of the first week. The introductions spanned a hectic two-and-a-half weeks, at the end of which she moved in and they all started their life together, just over two years from the day Nita and Clare had been approved to adopt.

Nita and Clare have always been joint parents and Lubna has always been adamant that they should be treated equally, both coming to school for concerts and parents' evenings, all three doing everything together as far as possible. The school Lubna goes to, just around the corner, has a very mixed intake, with children from many different black communities, other children who are fostered and adopted, children in single-parent families, children living in extended families and other children from lesbian households. Lubna is assertive about fending off what she regards as nosey enquiries, but she has also not found herself particularly unusual in a very cosmopolitan inner-city environment. She has grown in confidence in defending the family and insisted on attending Gay Pride this year. On their return she could be heard lecturing her friends on the meanings of key words such as heterosexual and homosexual and testing them on their understanding!

It took 18 months from placement to reach the final adoption hearing due to legal complications specific to Lubna's case, but the case was finally heard in the High Court. The application was for an adoption order in Nita's name and a joint residence order giving both Nita and Clare parental responsibility for Lubna. This is very important because it gives Lubna the security of knowing that both Nita and Clare are equally responsible for her and committed to caring for her together.

* * *

'Good morning, Lubna. I'm your barrister, Angus Mackenzie.'

'He sounds like Nigel from the Archers', whispered Lubna.

'Can I speak with these ladies for a moment?' He took them aside. 'Well, it's 60-40 in our favour. This judge is new – reward for serving on some government quango – but he can be picky, he may want to make something of the…errr…' he shuffled uncomfortably, '…the same sex thing.'

'Ladies, he called you ladies!' Lubna giggled as he moved away to speak to the court usher.

After a nerve-wracking two-hour wait, the barrister, official solicitor and *guardian ad litem* all went into the court. Nita and Clare smiled at the judge through the courtroom's glass doors, hoping he'd see they were human beings. Then they were called into court leaving Lubna happily playing pontoon with their social worker.

Everyone was smiling as they entered the court. Angus spoke. 'My Lord, Nita and Clare have been in a stable relationship for the last seven years. They have provided Lubna with a secure and loving home. You will have seen from all the reports, my Lord, that Lubna is flourishing.'

The judge responded enthusiastically, 'These reports are some of the best I have seen and the court is thankful for all the hard work that has gone into them. Be assured they are read and much appreciated.'

The social workers beamed at the compliments being bestowed upon them. As the words droned on, Nita and Clare realised the enormity of the moment. This man was God – he could make or break their dreams.

Angus concluded, 'Therefore, my Lord, I move that the adoption order be granted in the name of Nita and a joint residence order be granted in the names of Nita and Clare.'

'Absolutely', replied the judge, 'And I'd like to meet the child – the most pleasurable part of my duties – if you would bring her to my chambers.'

Nita and Clare hugged as everyone congratulated them. Then Clare leapt up and ran out of the court. Lubna was still happily playing cards with Sue.

'It's all done, you're adopted!' cried Clare. 'The judge wants to meet you.' Lubna frowned mistrustfully but she was reassured that it was just a formality. In his chambers, Lubna played with the judge's wig produced specially from a black tin box.

'She seems an absolute delight!' the judge enthused.

'She is!' Nita and Clare chorused.

Postscript, December (1997)

When Lubna was placed, she was adamant that she didn't want any siblings, but two years later, and after the adoption had been to court, she changed her mind. She was ten by then and decided she wanted a much younger sister. We began looking again and soon saw Neelam's details in an adoption newsletter. She was described as a ten-month-old mixed race Asian baby with moderate hearing loss, and they were looking for a family with at least one Asian parent and possibly other children. She had been in care with a white foster family since she was a few days old.

Once again, we were preparing to go on holiday to India! Two social workers from the authority where she was living visited us a fortnight before we went away. They had been considering another couple, but after the visit they were very keen on us and said they would wait for us to get back from India. Once we got back, everything happened very quickly. We were re-assessed as a family to take a second child and Lubna was interviewed separately, which she enjoyed. Our local panel approved us to take a second child and the panel in the city where Neelam was in care matched us with her without any problems. When she finally moved in she was 16 months old and she settled incredibly well. She's an absolute joy and she and Lubna have great fun together. Clare is now on adoption leave and, in the future, both Clare and I will work part-time in order to share being at home to look after Neelam. Clare will be the named adopter when it goes to court and we will apply for a joint residence order directing that she live with both of us, as we did with Lubna. We've already started thinking about a younger sister for Neelam!

NITA and CLARE (2017)

Soon after adopting Neelam at 16 months, we realised she needed a sister closer in age to play with than Lubna, who was ten years older. We had originally been approved for three children so when the local authority that placed Neelam with us asked if we would be assessed as one of their families, we agreed. It took longer than we had expected, but in 2001 we adopted our third daughter, Meena, then aged seven months. She was placed from a different local authority, so in total we have been approved by two different agencies, one of them our local authority, and have had children placed with us from three outside agencies, none of them our local authority. That was a lot of different social workers and panels to prove ourselves to!

Meena was accommodated by her local authority from the day of her birth and her birth mother was involved in the choice of adopters. Meena's birth mother had a kind of person spec for the prospective adopters of what she wanted for Meena, including wanting Meena to have siblings and to grow up with books and learning. She was presented with our family profile and a profile of a heterosexual couple and she chose us as an adoptive family because we offered two older sisters for Meena and parents who were both teachers and also a writer and an artist. The fact that we were also a lesbian couple didn't seem to concern her at all.

The adoption process

The concept of a lesbian couple had posed the local authority some challenges when they were first assessing us as adopters. Their processes were based on rather conventional and conservative notions of relationships and family. Some of their assessment questions were loaded with assumptions about gender roles that many of my feminist heterosexual friends would have taken issue with.

When we were being assessed, we had to supply an eco-map with all the males and females in our network. Males were considered much more important than females, as our social worker felt that the panel would be looking out for a dearth of males. Consequently, we put down as many men as we could think of, even if they weren't really that significant. When it came to referees, it was usual to provide two, which we did. One was a single Asian heterosexual woman with four children. The other was a mixed race heterosexual couple with two children. Our social worker was asked by her manager to provide a third reference from another heterosexual couple with children. We delivered!

As a mixed race couple we had always been clear we wanted to adopt Asian/white dual heritage children and that was always fine. As we adopted pre civil partnerships, we had to decide each time which one of us was going to be the named adopter on the adoption order and who would apply for a residence order at the same time.

We have never told the children who their named adopter is as we didn't want them to feel any insecurity about their ties to either one of us. When the law changed in 2005 we went back to court and adopted the younger two children in both our names. Lubna was over 18 by then so we couldn't change her adoption order.

Our daughters

Our eldest daughter, Lubna, was eight years old when she was placed with us and is 31 now. She settled in very quickly. She had not wanted to call us 'mums' as she had lived with her birth mother till she was nearly five and remembered her clearly. So we told her she could call us by our first names, and that made everything much easier. She knew we were lesbians and understood what that meant as there were lesbian storylines on Brookside and EastEnders at the time, which she had seen. She was proud of us being gay. We lived in a diverse inner-city area where her friendship group was unfazed by her having gay parents. We often gave her the choice of one parent coming to her school for things like parents' evenings, but she always wanted us both to come. She has always referred to us as 'the parents' and still does so to this day. She had a gap year in India and went to university in Scotland when she was 19. She lives in London now and works for a national charity supporting trafficked children. She's still close to her siblings and visits as often as she can. She's planning to move back to our town next year, after taking unpaid leave to go travelling for a few months, and we're looking forward to having her nearby again.

Our second daughter, Neelam, was 16 months old when she was adopted and is 21 now. She studied Animal Care at college, worked on a city farm for two years and is now working as a support worker with young people with special needs, which is a huge achievement given that she has had to overcome her own disability and learning difficulties to get to where she is now. Neelam has worn hearing aids since being a baby and was later diagnosed with an auditory processing disorder and dyscalculia. We have had to fight to get our daughter's needs met throughout school and college and into an apprenticeship, and are still supporting her now she is in her first job.

Our youngest daughter, Meena, was seven months old when she was placed with us and is now 17 and studying Art at college, which has always been her passion. When she first went to school and was in the reception class there was some confusion amongst the other children in the class that she appeared to have two mums, but when this was confirmed they thought it was really cool. She has had her own challenges with learning, medical problems and mental health issues through secondary school and college and has had some excellent professional support thanks to a really good GP and to us keeping on top of her constant stream of appointments. She and Neelam still live at home, but Neelam is planning to move out soon now that she has a job.

Bringing up our daughters

Bringing up our daughters, we were always positively out with other adults and children in our local schools and community. If there was any animosity, it never reached us. We chose to live in a part of the city that was diverse, alternative and most likely to be accepting of many different versions of family. Our arrangement was only one among a multitude of step, extended, foster, adoptive, same-sex, grandparent and other families that filled our children's primary school classrooms. As a stable couple who have remained together throughout our children's lives, we were unusual amongst the parents of our children's friends, many of whom were living apart. We have structured our working lives around our daughters. We have mostly both worked part time so that there has always been someone at home and we've not had to depend on childcare, and we feel this has been a major factor in creating a safe and secure environment for our daughters.

We have a great relationship with all three of our children. We have always been open and honest about everything to do with their adoptions, birth families and questions about sex and sexuality, and have encouraged them to be open with us. The difficulties we have had have not been around their being adopted or our sexuality, but the more usual stresses of adolescence – tensions between independence and safety, freedom and responsibility that characterise most relationships between young people and their parents – and no more or less serious than friends and family have had with their birth children.

Contact with birth parents

Letterbox contact was agreed for all three girls. On three different occasions while Lubna was growing up, we took her to spend time with her birth mother in India. In a more limited way she also met her birth father, half-siblings and birth grandfather in a different part of India. We did this because Lubna had lived with her birth mother until she was four-and-a-half, and they had lived in India for a year when she was a toddler. She retains a strong attachment to India and has continued to return there independently as an adult, spending her gap year there before university. As a child she benefited from seeing that her birth mother was safe and settled, and also from being able to assert her own identity as the same person in a new family that she was firmly attached to.

Neelam's birth parents participated intermittently in the letterbox contact set up by her adoption agency, and Neelam spent a lot of time thinking about them and worrying about her birth mother, who she knew was not well. In recent years she has had direct contact on a couple of occasions with her younger birth brother, who is a full sibling and is also adopted. Since her 18th birthday, she has not taken up the opportunity to explore meeting her birth mother and doesn't seem to feel ready to pursue this. She has enough challenges in the present embarking on her adult working life.

Meena's birth mother has never used the letterbox contact that was set up and social services have not had an address for her for a long time. Meena has expressed some interest in her birth family, but only occasionally. Her best friend at school is adopted and her friend's brother, adopted with her, found their birth mother on Facebook; they went through some turbulent times as a family managing the resulting contact. This seemed to prompt Meena to search for her birth mother and siblings on Facebook. She found them, but has not had a response to her contact, and this has been quite hard for her as she has just had to leave it. She talked to us about it as she was doing it and we tried to support her.

Extended family and support

We have had a lot of support from friends and family in bringing up all three girls. We see my family regularly, although they don't live nearby, and when we first adopted Lubna, Nita's family lived barely a 15-minute drive from our house. Before our youngest daughter, Meena, was placed with us, Nita's father was diagnosed with Parkinson's disease, and we took the decision to combine our households. We moved to a new house on three floors and Nita's parents came to live with us on the ground floor. Having grandparents on hand to engage with her on an adult level was very special for Lubna when the house seemed to be dominated by the needs of a baby and a toddler, and she was very close to them in her teenage years. Growing up with their grandparents was also important for Neelam and Meena. At the same time, the constant comings and goings of a young family kept the older members of the household busy and entertained!

We used to attend the Northern Support Group and a local authority support group specifically for lesbian and gay foster and adoptive carers in the early years of adoption, but they were as much about supporting others as ourselves. As teachers, we often gave advice to others about how to challenge and get help for their children in school and how to navigate local authority systems. We were also interested in raising awareness and helped to organise a couple of national conferences for lesbian and gay foster and adoptive parents.

The group meetings were particularly supportive for Neelam as she met her best friend outside school through the Northern Support Group. Her friend is also dual heritage and is also adopted by a mixed race lesbian couple like us, so she regarded this friend as her soulmate for many years.

Nita continues to be proactive in supporting adoption by the LGBT community. She is a trainer and has spoken at national conferences and delivered training courses with social work teams and adoption and fostering panels in different parts of the country on behalf of the Northern Support Group. She also spoke at a preparation group in our local authority and a single woman participant came out to her in the break. She was able to tell her about the Northern Support Group and the woman went on to adopt a child as a single lesbian adopter.

Changes in attitude

Things have changed enormously in the last 20 years. When we set out to adopt in 1992 there were many social workers who wouldn't even consider us as adopters for children they were trying to place. There were children we would have adopted who were never placed for adoption with anyone and that was seen as preferable to letting us, as lesbians, care for them. Our second daughter's foster carers would not allow introductions to take place in their house because we were lesbians. Today things are much easier – there are civil partnerships and the whole climate is much more accepting of LGBT parents.

Therapeutic support

We were never offered any therapeutic support for ourselves or for our daughters. Our eldest daughter, Lubna, had play therapy at a reputable psychodynamic institute in London before she came to us. Her therapist advised against placing her for adoption, and was particularly alarmed that she was to be placed with lesbians and predicted the placement would break down in adolescence. Fortunately, the social workers did not agree with the therapist and the placement went ahead. I don't think our daughter feels she gained anything from the therapy; she just remembers being confused by having meanings ascribed to her play activities that didn't ring true for her.

Our youngest daughter was referred to child and adolescent mental health services (CAMHS) as she has anxiety issues. She was only seven months old when we adopted her, but of our three daughters, she seems to be the one who has most difficulty in understanding and processing her adoption. However, this is part of a bigger issue for her as she finds it difficult to express her feelings and struggles with academic work, despite there being no apparent or diagnosed difficulties. She is now awaiting an assessment for Asperger's, after years of us saying she needed help and her being under everyone's radar, as often happens with girls who cause no visible issues for anyone else.

Family ties

We remain a close family and are rapidly absorbing our daughters' three steady boyfriends into the wider sphere of our family. Lubna's boyfriend is moving north with her next year, after their globetrotting adventure; Neelam is moving out with her boyfriend and their friends as soon as his course finishes in the summer; and Meena's boyfriend spends a lot of time at our house as his apprenticeship is round the corner. His single mum actually went to the school I taught in for 20 years and I remember her well as a student, which we both laugh about now. We know Neelam's boyfriend's parents through a host of teaching and community connections as well. The girls have grown up as a family and are now forging new ties and communities of their own. They display all the usual sibling rivalries alongside caring deeply about one another and consider themselves sisters, and us their mums, in every possible way. The challenges of bringing up three very different daughters have been worth it a hundred times over, and we are very proud of all three of them.

PAUL and RICHARD
A Complete Life-Changing Experience

Paul and Richard are a gay couple, now turning 70. They have been together as a couple for about 45 years. Paul was a financial consultant and Richard an independent social worker. Patrick, who came to live with them on a fostering basis aged nine, was eventually adopted by the couple, and is now 32 years old. Despite the challenges they faced in parenting Patrick following his adoption, they remain in close contact with their son.

We begin with their original (1999) story, 'Out of Step', written by Richard:

I have a clear memory of when it hit me as a teenager that I would not be able to have children of my own. Embarrassing as it is to admit it, I remember crying about it on one occasion in bed at night. It seems amazing now, more than 30 years later, that I could have had such a clear perception at that young age. Like a lot of teenagers, I was struggling with issues of 'abnormal' sexual feelings and sexual identity 'problems'. They sound more manageable and reasonable when phrased in these objective, adult terms but carry none of the horror and desperation that I can remember feeling at the time.

It must be better for young lesbians and gay men growing up today. The misinformation and the void beyond have surely been replaced for most youngsters, with much more information mixed with the misinformation. Do some young people who are 'different' sexually still think they are the only ones?

Anyway, back to the subject of children. I decided that even if I couldn't have my own children, I would be able to work in the childcare field. (I am sure some readers will groan about this, but there are a lot of lesbians and gay men in social work for good reason.) I had the considerable asset of a loving family and a secure home background to draw on. Even though, whilst at university, I decided that my religious beliefs were a sham, I retained 'do-gooding' ideas. I met other gay people for the first time and at 24 met the man I've been living with for most of the last 25 years.

I trained as a social worker and, being sufficiently 'long in the tooth', I even saw the tail end of one of the old children's departments that existed before social services departments were set up at the end of the 1960s. Foster carers, or foster parents as they were called in those days, were more scarce than today, with many more children's homes in existence. I almost always enjoyed visits to foster homes, whilst secretly envying the foster parents' freedom to care for other people's children.

Fostering and gay rights

I'm not sure when it first dawned on me that I might one day be able to join the ranks of foster carers. I suppose there were two parallel developments going on in the world, one to do with fostering and adoption, and one to do with the identity and expectations of gay men and women. Both ended up affecting me very personally.

The early 1970s and the developing 'gay liberation movement' very fortuitously coincided with my reaching adulthood (21 in those days). I became involved in the Campaign for Homosexual Equality and dragged my partner in as well. I remember taking my courage in my mouth and asking work colleagues, including my boss, to support a vote at the AGM of the British Association of Social Workers (BASW) to include sexual orientation in a non-discrimination clause of their code of ethics. Although risky in those days, it was quite a satisfactory way of 'coming out'.

In 1976, I was a member of a small national group of Gay Social Workers & Probation Officers (GSWPO) who had signed a letter in a social work journal. Those names were obviously burned on the memory of the assistant director of the department I next applied to work for. Before being offered the job, although I'd not breathed a word about GSWPO at my interview, I was told by my future boss that I'd better be careful not to use any work time on such organisations.

After sampling the 'joys' of a managerial post for a number of years, I decided to go for a post in fostering and adoption. The developments in family placement, as it was now termed, had also been considerable. 'Catch-all' foster homes were being replaced by a plethora of differentially defined family placements. There were not only short-term foster homes but also task-centred foster homes. Children and young people who had not been considered suitable for placements with families were now being given that opportunity. Teenage and professional fostering schemes were being set up. The orthodoxy of transracial placements was being challenged by schemes to find black families for black children. Permanent placements were being heralded as the right of all children and young people in the care system. There was even a change in the law to allow single men to foster. The latter rang a particularly personal bell, as you can imagine.

The two parallel developments finally came together in 1987 when a London-wide working party was set up by the London Strategic Policy Unit, the rump of the old Greater London Council. The task of the working party was to look at fostering and adoption policies and practice throughout the capital, as they affected lesbians and gay men. My boss in the Family Placement Unit, not surprisingly, asked if I wanted to represent my authority on the working party. It produced the first account in this country of issues on this subject – *Fostering and Adoption by Lesbians and Gay Men* edited by Jane Skeates and Dorian Jabri, published in 1988.

Applying to foster

Just prior to this, Paul and I had already started telephoning agencies that were seeking permanent foster carers or adopters for particular children. It felt like we were doing something unacceptable and you had to take more than a few deep breaths before dialling each number. Mostly we had embarrassed responses. One outer London council said that they had difficulty enough getting their fostering and adoption panels to accept single carers let alone gay carers. Another council wanted us to explain, when we responded to an advert for a particular boy, why we were interested in fostering boys. She had agreed that we wouldn't be considered for girls! (Although Paul and I had done a lot of caring of a relative's daughter.) Quite often we were told that the child concerned wouldn't be able to cope with having gay carers on top of everything else they had experienced in life.

Fortunately, after about a year of 'banging our heads against a brick wall', we got an offer to assess us from one of the few boroughs that had a statement of anti-discriminatory childcare policies. We received a general assessment with no particular child being considered. A year later, in August 1988, we were finally approved for a permanent placement of a child aged nine years and upwards. We felt that this was a major achievement in the climate as it was then, and thought our 'approval' would stand us in good stead for being accepted as suitable carers for a particular child. We should have known better.

The authority that had approved us did initially go ahead and consider us for a possible placement of a much younger child. However, when the child's mother was asked what she would think of her son being placed with a gay couple, she gave us the 'thumbs down' and their legal department didn't think we stood much of a chance in a contested court hearing. After that the authority never approached us again.

We hung on for some time waiting to hear from them, but eventually 'got the message' and realised that we were going to have to approach other agencies if we were going to stand any chance of success. For the next two-and-a-half years we touted ourselves around 15 or more agencies, following up adverts for particular children or asking the agencies to consider us generally.

We finally agreed to take a homeless teenager from The Albert Kennedy Trust. This is an organisation that specialises in placing lesbian and gay youngsters with older settled gay people. Richard (he had the same name as me) decided that he wanted to come and stay with us after visiting from Manchester. However, once we had helped him get a job he started disappearing more and more into London, and eventually decided he wanted to go into bed and breakfast accommodation. It all happened within a period of two months or so and left us, and particularly me, feeling pretty drained. Paul concluded it wasn't the sort of placement we had sought anyway, and that we should go back to focusing on a younger child.

At around this time I was asked by a female friend of mine if I would consider becoming a sperm donor for her so that she and her girlfriend could have a child. Although there was the expectation that Paul and I would have a part in the life of any child who was conceived, I knew that this would be insufficient involvement in parenting for me. Also, I wasn't wanting to bring another child into the world when I knew there were so many children in need of substitute homes. Thus, Paul and I continued our search.

Some agencies gave us a reasonable consideration and at least met us. Most didn't. However, as a former fostering worker (I use the word 'former' as I had by this time moved on to work in a Family Centre) I knew that many, many couples flog themselves around agencies asking to be considered for particular children. Most of these people, though, would be restricting themselves to very young children. There are few such children compared to the number of people offering them a home. Paul and I were offering ourselves for the so-called 'hard to place' older children, where potential homes were few and far between. Nonetheless, it seemed that a children's home was preferable for some agencies (and probably for many more if the truth was known behind the reasons they gave) than taking the chance of placing with a gay couple.

What was the chance that they would be taking? Mainly, I think, facing the prejudice of a hostile, sensation-making tabloid press. The Government had set the tone with Clause 28 of the Local Government Act in 1988. Even reasonable people in social services departments, or on their fostering panels, didn't believe that they could look at the situation after that with an open enquiring mind.

Back door

At the end of 1991 we again considered doing something that wasn't what we had been approved for. One agency that had responded more positively to our general enquiries asked if we would consider doing some respite care. Basically, as many people will know, this is providing a break to carers of difficult and/or demanding children and young people. The child concerned was a six-year-old boy called Patrick who had recently been placed with his sister in an adoptive placement and was giving his carers 'hell'.

Paul said that this wasn't at all what we were looking for. However, I was equally determined that if no one was going to ask us to do anything else, at least we could help out someone and not go completely to waste. Paul reluctantly gave way, but he had been right. We made lousy respite carers. We ended up not providing the support that the prospective adopters needed. I had the benefit of my training and work experience and understood what I was meant to be doing. Paul didn't stand a chance. He took to Patrick like 'a duck to water'. He is a bright boy and Paul really enjoyed everything about him and tended to minimise his problems. As a result, the prospective adopters thought we were critical of them.

Paul realised on one level that he shouldn't be getting emotionally involved. However, when Patrick went to a specialist residential establishment with schooling on the premises and no plan that he should return to his former prospective adoptive home, the inevitable had already happened and Patrick's move changed the basis of our involvement. The community home and Patrick's local authority kept us at arm's length about what the future might hold. However, they did encourage us to become 'social uncles' to Patrick, and we were allowed to take him out for the day once a month.

Patrick gave us a hard time, as he always had done. He was angry with everyone in his life. Fortunately, he was receiving a lot of intensive help from the staff of the residential establishment. Contact was re-established with his mother, and he began to understand more about all the separations in his life, even if he did not really come to terms with them. Our contact was eventually increased to a weekend once a month when we stayed with Patrick at a flat belonging to the residential establishment. The local authority also updated our assessment report and we were then also approved as foster carers by Patrick's local authority. We were not, however, approved as *his* future foster carers.

Patrick had been at the community home for two years before that decision was finally taken by his local authority. During that time we had to deal with a lot of resistance from one key manager in the local authority and some homophobic attitudes from a residential worker. It felt like a constant battle for a long time. It is arguable that the two years of uncertainty was justified whilst plans were worked out for Patrick. However, for us, it was very painful. We gave an enormous amount of our time and emotional energy to Patrick and all the meetings connected with him, and there was always the possibility at the end of that time that he would be placed with someone else. Our relief and pleasure when the decision was finally made was literally a dream come true.

Foster carers at last

Six months later, Patrick came to live with us on a permanent basis. He was upset at leaving the other children and staff he had become attached to, although he said it was different from other separations in that he was moving to familiar people and a familiar place. (He had, by then, been visiting our home for some time.)

It certainly hasn't been 'plain sailing' since then, although the sense of fulfilment for both Paul and me has been enormous. As a child who had had difficulties at school, we had to get Patrick 'statemented' and get a school to accept him. He had been six when we first met him but he was nearly ten by this time, and had four more terms to do at junior school. More recently, getting a secondary school to suit his needs was also a struggle. However, he is now successfully coming to the end of his first year there.

He has now been with us for over two years. He has decided that continuing to see his mother just gives him grief. He does, however, still regularly see his sister with whom he was previously placed. Like her, he now also wants to be adopted and we are about to embark on negotiating this with the courts.

General issues

Turning from the personal to more general issues, I'm sure that a lot of people will question how appropriate it is for a gay couple to adopt a child as young as Patrick. However, issues to do with our sexual orientation have not been to the fore. The struggles we have had have been much more those of any couple taking on the task of parenting a child in care with all the problems their past brings with them. We are part of large extended families, and Patrick has also been settling in as part of our families.

Generally, I think male parents, whether straight or gay, face much more suspicion than female parents, who are regarded in society as 'natural parents'. Thus, men seeking to parent alone or together are still likely to be scrutinised more closely or rejected more quickly than lesbians in a similar position.

There is also a vulnerability that you feel as a male parent. The issue of men showing affection to children has been hedged around with so much media suspicion that you need a lot of confidence in your own ability to nurture and care for a child to counteract this. As a gay male parent there is the added pressure to put all sexual activity 'in the deep freeze'. One focuses so much on being accepted as a parent that you feel added pressure to minimise that part of yourself of which society disapproves.

I don't think that Paul and I would have persisted in trying to become foster carers, and finally been successful, but for my knowledge and experience of social work. Nor would we have had the enormous amount of time to devote to the whole process but for the fact that I was working part time and Paul was self-employed. There must be any number of potential gay male foster carers going to waste because they don't have the 'know-how' to challenge the system or all the necessary time and energy to devote to the struggle. More importantly, there are a lot of kids in care who are missing out as a result.

What has been the reaction of other people to Paul and me fostering? One reaction that has surprised me in particular has been that of other gay men. Many have been interested, if surprised, that we have finally been successful. Some good friends have been very supportive. However, we've met more hostility than I would have anticipated, and I think there is a good deal of self-oppression within the gay community. 'Gay men can't be trusted to be parents', because that's what we've been taught.

However, people's attitudes have generally been much better than we feared. We have taken the line of expecting to be accepted, and neighbours, other parents at school and school staff have generally been positive, although sometimes it would have been interesting to know what was being said behind the scenes.

Patrick asked us years ago, when Paul and I were talking about our first holiday together, 'Why were you such good friends? Are you "gays"?' When we told him we were, he looked a bit worried and I asked him what he had heard about gay people. He said that he'd seen something in a sex education book he had looked at, at the children's home. He didn't seem to want to talk any more about it at the time. This was a year or more before he came to live with us.

Since that occasion, when there has been the opportunity, we have talked of how some people are attracted to members of their own sex, although most people are attracted to the opposite sex. Patrick understands that Paul and I love one another. We have always thought it important not to hide our affection. We will give one another a cuddle or a kiss as the occasion warrants, as we would do in front of members of our extended families.

Patrick himself is an affectionate child. He wasn't when we first knew him, but he has become much more demonstrative over the years, more confident that he is loved and is lovable.

Greater coverage in the media about homosexuality has helped and it has hindered. It has helped in so far as there is more about people being gay and more acceptance. For example, it was Patrick himself who related the news about the age of consent debate in Parliament in 1994. However, the media also reflects, and to a certain extent perpetuates, the prejudice and negative views about lesbians and gay men. As Patrick says, the term 'poofter' is a term of abuse at school (as it is in society at large). How do we help him with this?

Patrick is happy to bring friends home from school and is learning confidence that name-calling from other children will be dealt with firmly by school staff, as it was on the two occasions it has happened in his present school. It is complicated in that issues often get mixed up. For example, on one of the occasions another child had made fun of the fact that Patrick had, as she conjectured, been rejected by his mother. However, she then went on to imply that his mother couldn't have thought much of him, leaving him with 'two gays'.

Paul and I have put in a lot of work to ensure that the school staff will not allow discrimination to go unchallenged. We have taken time to make get ourselves known at both Patrick's schools, joining the PTAs (Parent Teacher Associations) and school events as well as getting to know school staff. Paul has also got himself elected as a parent governor. It has helped that Patrick has always had a helper in class because of his statement of educational needs. This has been the person with whom we have had the most direct liaison, and it was the current helper who ensured that the year head spoke to the children involved in name-calling. One of the children, who had previously been friendly with Patrick, apologised directly to him as a result.

Concluding comments

We are generally hopeful that with a good solicitor and the backing of Patrick's local authority, both of which we have, we will be successful in our adoption application. This is particularly as it is in line with Patrick's wishes. With the present state of the law, only one of us can adopt, but we will also be applying for a joint residence order so that we both have parental responsibility.

The fact that an adoption order was granted to a gay male couple in Scotland in 1996 must be a good precedent, with emphasis being placed on the needs of the child. However, it would be reassuring to know if there are any similar cases in England that have managed to avoid publicity.

A final concluding comment that both Paul and I would like to make is on the general acceptance that we have found. Our experience has been that, when faced with the reality of a gay household with children, people are much more ready to accept us on our own terms than the worst tabloids would have you think. We feel that it is now the Clause 28 Tory MPs who are totally 'out of step' with the everyday reality of our experience.

PAUL and RICHARD (2017)

We finally adopted Patrick in 1999, three years after he moved in with us as his foster parents. Considering all the challenges we had faced when trying to become foster parents, the adoption went through smoothly, without aggravation. At the time we couldn't adopt as a couple, so one of us adopted Patrick but we applied for a joint residence order.

When we were originally applying to foster, it felt very much like we were pioneers. In the mid to late 1980s the whole gay thing was viewed in an unpleasant way – gays and lesbians were treated by the press in unpleasant terms. And it was the period of AIDS – the whole atmosphere was that lesbians and gay men were not acceptable. Social workers sometimes made us feel as if we were really being off the wall suggesting that a gay couple could foster a child, as if we were being rather unreasonable, going too far. Even when we were fostering Patrick we did face prejudice, particularly from one social work team leader. In the end we complained and things changed almost immediately.

But by the time we adopted Patrick attitudes had already begun to change. Now being gay or lesbian is a non-event. People are coming out all the time, people in the public eye. And obviously that means it's changed the attitude of the powers that be in determining whether gay people can foster and adopt. Society has changed much more quickly than we ever thought possible.

Patrick's early life

We first met Patrick when he was five years old and he spent time in our care consistently thereafter. He came to live with us when he was nine years old on a fostering basis. We adopted him when he was 12 years old. That is what he wanted. He didn't take either of our names, because he didn't want to; by that time he was too old to want that and too independent.

Patrick's early life had been extremely traumatic. His relationship with his mother was fraught. He was removed from her care when he was six months old, after she had shaken him when she was drunk and he had to be admitted to hospital. The tragedy is that he wasn't placed for adoption at that point in his life. It wasn't until he was five years old that he was placed for adoption along with one of his five half-siblings. But by then he was a really disturbed child – he tried to hang himself at school when he was just five years old and spent six months in a children's psychiatric unit. His sister went on to be adopted by the couple with whom both children had been living. Patrick was said by the psychiatrist to be much too damaged to ever settle in a family, and so they placed him in a therapeutic community, and it was from there that he came to live with us.

Patrick never knew his father and his father doesn't know he exists (we have no photo of him). Patrick's main blood relationship is with the half-sister with whom he was first placed for adoption. They are in regular contact and see one another as often as they want. She now has a son and daughter although she doesn't live with either of the children's fathers. We all went to her son's Christening. It was a very happy occasion. Patrick was in his early 20s by this time. Although he is two years younger than his sister, Patrick is the bright, intelligent one, and you might think that he was the elder. Patrick hasn't wanted contact with any of his other half-siblings, although he has met three of them.

Bringing up Patrick

We did find that it was important to be involved in Patrick's schools. When he finally came to live with us, he had another one-and-a-bit years to go in the local junior school where, because he was statemented, he had a full-time helper. This was not because he had a problem academically – he is very bright – but because of what he had been through psychologically. Because he was statemented, we were allowed to select the secondary school Patrick went to. We put down one of the local schools – it was a grant-maintained school – and Patrick was immediately rejected on the grounds that we didn't fall within their catchment area. We told them that was irrelevant because Patrick had a statement, but they kept refusing. We finally got the local authority on side and they wrote to the head teacher, but the head teacher still said, 'I'm not under your control, we have our own policies.' Eventually we spoke to somebody in the Department for Education and they said, 'Well you're right, we'll contact the school.' The school was still stonewalling, hoping we'd go away, and eventually an under-secretary at the Department of Education wrote a letter to the school saying, 'The Secretary of State is minded to instruct you.' And Patrick then got in on appeal. We don't think the refusal had anything to do with us being gay, though we have become less sensitive to things like that.

It was important that we got involved and kept involved with the school. One of us was on the Board of Governors of the school for the duration of the time Patrick was there. We needed to make sure that Patrick wasn't singled out, because the head teacher could be very difficult. But there were no teaching or staff problems with Patrick, as far as we could tell, except for his behaviour occasionally. He did tell us a couple of times about homophobic comments from other pupils, but Patrick was always pretty tough, and you don't argue with Patrick too much. What things would have been like if he had been a timid child, we don't know.

We were very involved in his junior and secondary school. As well as being in the PTA and on the Board of Governors, we did the car boot sale on Saturday mornings and all that sort of thing.

It was important to be very much there for him, ready to pick up on anything, should it happen. We didn't go around with a badge saying, 'I'm a poof', but a lot of people knew that we were gay and nobody ever commented. It's so important that others get to know you as people – not just as the boy's parents or as a gay couple – and at the time we were, as far as we knew, the only gay couple with a child at the school.

Therapy

We did have psychotherapeutic help for Patrick which the local authority paid for. That helped Patrick and also helped us. Patrick still has a good relationship with the dramatherapist that he saw. She's a lovely lady and it's good that he's still got that link. Therapy helped him when his mother died when he was 13. His dramatherapist helped him with his sense of identity and he had some bereavement counselling. He also had an assessment by a psychiatrist on one occasion. As an adult he has had help from the local drugs and alcohol treatment agencies because of his problems.

Patrick in his late teens and 20s

Patrick always wanted to be in the army – that was his big ambition – but he does crazy things. When he went for his interview to be a soldier, he was doing press ups on the train. Then he realised that he was about to miss his station, so he jumped off the train as it was moving and arrived for his interview with a broken arm. That's Patrick. He would have done well in the army. When he went down to the Army Recruitment Office he filled out the application form and did an exam and the Recruiting Sergeant said, 'You're not going into the infantry my lad, you're going into the Royal Engineers, because they take the smarter ones.'

He enjoyed the physical side of the army and that kept him going for the first two passing out parades. We were so proud of him at those passing out parades. But once he was at Chatham, in the classroom, nine to five, he started coming back in the evening to see his old mates and went back to smoking skunk (marijuana). He was caught three times and the army finally said, 'enough is enough'. At the end of his army career he took an overdose. It was a cry for help because he made sure he survived – he contacted the health helpline himself, which was just as well, as if it had been up to the army, he would have been long dead. He was in hospital having his stomach pumped out hours before they knew he was missing! He is a survivor.

It's just such a shame. Two things are a shame. First, it's a shame that he hasn't benefited from the education system, as he could easily have gone to university and would have got a good degree. He is working at much lower ability level than that of which he is capable. He achieved nine GCSEs at grade C and above but then started using drink/drugs heavily. Second, it's a shame that he didn't stay in the army, because he'd then be a qualified engineer. And it is a shame, too, that he spends all his money on drugs and alcohol and doesn't give any priority to getting a girlfriend.

At one stage in his early 20s, Patrick was on cocaine and he would come here and there were real dramas, or they seemed real, about guys out to get him because he owed them money, and one of us would go down to the cash machine at 10 o'clock at night and draw out £200. But it didn't solve anything; he just used it to buy more cocaine. We gave one lad £500 to get him off Patrick's back, because Patrick was terrified he would kill him. Over one nine-month period we paid out about £6,000. Another time he had a gun. Somebody had told him to keep this gun, one of his mates. And we told him the gun had to go – straightaway. But he was afraid to give it back and we ended up driving him to the estate where this person lived and he put the gun on the wheel of their car. It was pretty scary stuff.

Patrick's involvement with drugs and alcohol has been very difficult for all of us. He's an alcoholic and has only very recently been able to address the issue. He smoked marijuana to an excessive extent, so that all his money was going on booze or drugs.

His mother was an alcoholic and you wonder if it's in the genes. He's not on cocaine any more. Now when he's drunk, he's maudlin. His mother had that dependent personality, so the odds are stacked against him, really. But he can be absolutely charming. I remember the psychiatrist saying that he had a borderline personality disorder, but since you can't do very much about that, it's not a very helpful diagnosis.

Patrick is now 32 and he hasn't lived at home for many years. As a late teenager he had to leave, as he was stealing stuff and selling it. We tried tough love and he was sleeping on buses or in friends' sheds. We've tried paying for his accommodation but he has been kicked out of more rooms than you've had hot dinners. He was at the YMCA at the end of the street for quite a while. He was always getting expelled for causing damage or getting high and causing scenes and so on. In the end, a couple of years ago, we purchased a studio flat nearby for Patrick and he lives there rent free.

He's driven us to absolute distraction. There were times when either or both of us would have a shouting match with him and he would be shouting at us. We've had to have the police here. He's never physically threatened us, he's never physically harmed us, but in his early 20s, his sheer presence when he was having a shouting match was incredible – the damage to doors, the damage to the house, terrible, but he is a lot calmer now. He used to feel persecuted and that it was everybody else's fault and that we were bad parents. He often used to tell us that we should've done things differently.

One of his jobs was in the warehouse of a beverage company. He lost this because of not turning up for work. He had a driving job delivering to shops in London. He lost this job because of being stopped by the police for drunk driving. It's not easy to get a job when you have a criminal history – alcohol- and drugs-related – for instance, he would steal things from us, and from other people, and pawn them and cause criminal damage. He was even in prison once for a few weeks because he failed to complete a Community Service order.

He can't manage his money, or doesn't want to manage his money. So we are always being asked for money. We've tried looking after it for him. It started out by him saying, 'Here's £100, so that you can give it to me gradually,' but then the following day he'd say, 'I want my £100 back please.' And you'd say, 'But…' and he'd say, 'No, it's my money, I want it now.' So, we don't even try to manage his money for him now. On one occasion the doorbell rang and it was Patrick; 'Quick, quick, take this bag, take this bag.' So, and it was a couple of carrier bags, we took them and he immediately ran off. Five minutes later the doorbell went, two big burly blokes from Tesco; '…We believe that somebody has left some stuff here that belongs to us.' So, we had a look inside the bags, and there were bottles of gin and vodka and brandy and stuff, which we immediately gave to them and they went away. On another occasion we were out shopping with him, getting him some food and loading the car, and a security man came up; 'Would you mind accompanying me back to the store?' So we said, 'We've paid for everything.' We went back with the bags, Patrick, carrying the bags, and I noticed, but the store man didn't notice, that a bottle came out of one of the bags and went onto a shelf. The bags were checked and of course it all tallied up. We could've been arrested.

When we are in Spain – where we go a lot, as we have a house there – until very recently we used to get these desperate phone calls – we used to dread them. When he had credit on his phone, he used to keep phoning until you gave in. He wanted money of course. When he was a teenager we used to take him to Spain with us. However, that stopped because of his behaviour when under the influence of skunk. He wanted to be a fitness instructor and we paid for a course, for his training – PE was one of his best subjects at school and he was going to do it at A level. This was after he came out of the army. And we thought, well, that's a job he's going to enjoy and it's got good prospects. But sadly he lost the two jobs he got at a gym: first time he was photographed with his hand in the till, second time he had an argument with a customer, probably because he was high.

He was befriended by a much older woman, of whom he is still very fond. She is a bit of a mother figure as well as being someone with whom he had a sexual relationship. She was very good to him and helped him get two jobs, both of which he lost. He went to Cambodia with her. She had lived and worked there and had a flat in Phnom Penh. However, they both returned after a year because of his use of alcohol and drugs. She arranged treatment for him with his alcoholism but that was unsuccessful. Another time he wanted a job on a construction site but he needed a certificate – quite basic – and we paid for that but he never turned up to the exam.

Patrick in his 30s

We are very pleased to say that two years ago Patrick finally engaged with a local alcohol and drugs treatment agency. He attended there on a daily basis for 18 months in all. This was a major development. He has been abstinent from alcohol for the last year. Even more recently, and it's still very early days, he has stopped using marijuana, which was taking all his money – prior to this, he would rather have had the drug than feed himself.

He now has an office job in a very small wholesale spectacle firm. He works on the computer and manages orders and supplies. He has been with them for 18 months. He got this job through a friend. He wants to move on to a better-paid and more responsible job, but he needs to leave the firm with a good reference, so the longer he stays, the better.

As a child and teenager Patrick was an integral part of both our extended families. He lost most of these relationships in his late teens and 20s because of his behaviour and the fact that drugs and alcohol always took first place. The one relationship that was maintained was with one of our relatives who is an alcoholic. In his 30s Patrick is attending family occasions again, and very slowly he and they are beginning to repair the extended family relationships.

Keeping in touch with Patrick

During his 20s, contact was on the basis of, if he needed something, he would contact us. Often he would say, 'I'd very much like to see you', and make an arrangement but fail to turn up. Generally we would see him once a week, but he was on the phone an awful lot – 80 per cent of the time for a handout. He's the most accomplished liar you've ever come across. He could persuade you that black was white. He's very good at talking and arguing. He's a bit head-in-the-sand – if a problem arises he'd much rather hope it goes away than deal with it.

There was a conference where the Professor of Social Work from East Anglia University was talking about research that he'd done on people who adopted older children and what their experience was 10 or 20 years later. By and large, for most of them, it was a bit of a struggle to say it had been rewarding; they'd all been given a pretty hard time. That would be true for us as well. From when he first came to live with us until his mid-teens, it was rewarding, although difficult. He certainly made an attachment to us, which is quite an achievement considering the age at which he came to live with us. The main challenge of adopting Patrick was parenting him. It definitely needed two of us and for us both to be male because of his history. However, he sorely tried our relationship to the point where once we even thought of walking out on one another – it didn't happen, though, even for one night.

Bringing up Patrick did affect us mentally. Richard suffered with a depressive illness (partly due to Patrick's behaviour) and never returned to work, retiring early on health grounds. During the last few years we have gradually seen a change for the better in Patrick. He has joined us in Spain at Christmas for the last three years. This last year he bought us both Christmas presents. He has never given us presents that he has paid for before. Recently he has become more trustworthy. He is very dependent on us and contacts us on the phone every day, usually talking about work. He has meals with us regularly. If anything, he is much too dependent on us. He needs to make more good friends. He needs to get a girlfriend. He is often talking of having children of his own and recognises how much he needs a female partner.

Looking back

Despite everything, looking back, we would do it again – and we'd still have Patrick. He was such a lively, fun-loving little boy, full of beans. We took to him straight away when we were doing respite care (when he was placed elsewhere for adoption with his sister). We didn't know that we would be able to cope with Patrick. We didn't know it was going to be necessary to cope and we're not always sure we have coped with him, but we're still here. And he's still here.

We often say that we're very pleased that Patrick isn't dead, because he tried to hang himself at school and tried to commit suicide when he was in the army. So we don't worry about him like we used to because he's a survivor and he will look after number one, one way or another.

Societal changes

Things have changed enormously for the LBGT community in the past 20 years. I mean, we were around when being gay was illegal! We were the first on the register in our local authority when we became civil partners – we got council champagne in plastic glasses! We also married as soon as this became lawful. In the 1990s we didn't even imagine that these things would be possible. Things have changed so much.

We would encourage anyone thinking about it to adopt or foster. The success of the placement was that Patrick was eventually able to make a secure attachment to us, something he had not been able to make with anyone else. Would we do it again? Yes. Adopting Patrick is the single most worthwhile thing that we have done with our lives – so there is no doubt at all that we would do it again.

LEE

They Always Come Back Eventually

Lee is in his 60s and is a trans man, currently undergoing gender transition. At the time of the first edition of this book, Lee was a lesbian called Barbara. When we originally followed Lee up in 2014, he had changed his name from Barbara to Helen and was still living as a lesbian. But now, Lee identifies as a trans man. Lee is a social worker and has fostered 63 children and adopted five. They are now all grown up and living in their own homes, and his eldest adopted son, Sean, has four children of his own. Lee keeps in close contact with two of his children. While he was fostering, Lee started to train as a social worker and, once qualified, worked as a family liaison officer in a school and then trained foster parents and social workers. He worked for an independent fostering agency before moving on to a local authority looked-after children team.

We begin with Barbara's original (1999) story, 'The Eye of the Storm':

Before fostering, I worked with young people in youth clubs and then I was unemployed. I was interested in fostering, but I almost ended up doing it by accident! I went with a friend to a meeting about fostering organised by the social services department in 1983. I didn't think they'd consider me because I didn't think single people could foster, but I ended up getting approved as a foster carer that same year! Initially I started fostering teenagers, and the first one came for six months. He was called Ian and he came from a children's home. I was approved to care for up to three long-term foster children at any one time. My motivation at that time was that I wanted to offer young people a home until they were able to move on to their own independence.

When I made the application to be a foster carer, I didn't tell them I was a lesbian and it was never talked about, although the social workers were well aware of my sexuality. This was in 1983, and my local authority didn't have any other gay carers then that I knew of... Anyway, if I'd have come out then, it would have been a big problem to the authority. As it was there were no problems with my approval. The social workers did talk to me about my past relationships, but I only told them about relationships that I'd had with men.

I had been fostering for about one-and-a-half years when Susan moved in as my partner. We had a new social worker then, called Rachael, who was aware that we were lesbians. Susan made a separate application to foster short-term. This was in 1984, but again nothing was said about our relationship, even though we were living together. I often look back on that and think why, why didn't they discuss it with us?

Although some of my social workers had always known about it, four years ago I came out as a lesbian to the social services department. The social workers just said, 'We already knew!' That was actually very disheartening for me because I'd really worked myself up to telling the social workers and facing them with the truth. The director just wanted to know if I had faced any prejudice, and that was that. But it was a really big issue to me, and they all just said, 'fine!' Maybe things are very different now... The authority has four sets of lesbian or gay carers now, that I know of.

In 1987, Sean and Matthew came to me as a long-term placement, with the view to their being eventually placed with another family for adoption. About a year later, they were still here and we all felt that it would be a good idea for me to adopt them. My approval to adopt them was very quick and the social workers just upgraded my Form F for the adoption panel in 1988.

I adopted Sean and Matthew because it seemed the right thing to do and because they wanted me to. Later on, I adopted another boy, Marcus, who has cerebral palsy. He came to me five years ago as a 'hard to place' child. The plans were for him to be adopted, but no carers could be found despite advertising. Marcus was seen as having very great needs and the prognosis for him was very poor. They said he'd never sit up, that he was totally deaf and that he'd never walk. When I said I'd adopt him, the social workers made it very clear to me that I was very lucky to do so because they wouldn't normally allow single people to adopt! They had no other options for Marcus, needless to say. Anyway, we've proved people wrong because he is doing great now. His communication is good, he walks fine and he now attends a mainstream school. He's seven years old now and probably functions educationally at about four years, but he's doing really well.

I asked the social workers to re-approve me again, for various reasons…because I had come out as openly gay and I was now single again after Susan and I split up, but also because I had adopted three of the boys. But the social workers just said it was too much work to resource. When I went to the adoption panel about the boys, I didn't come out and the social workers advised this because of the panel itself! This was in 1988. The only thing that was really checked out was with my referees, who were asked whether the adopted children would be clear that I was their mum. Again, things are different now, and someone has gone through the adoption panel as an open lesbian.

The fostering panel was a different story and has always been very open and welcoming to me. When Susan and I were together and both fostering we were used a lot…we've fostered over 50 children, and we took a lot of sibling groups that are very hard to place. These were groups of about three or four children. We did a lot of work to reunite children with their families, bringing sibling groups back together again, preparing children to be adopted and taking children from placement breakdowns. We were a bit like a rescue service! I remember one Christmas we had nine children! They often came in groups of three siblings and so we had to get a minibus! Susan took younger ones, and in 1986 I changed to take short-term placements of children up to eight years old. Susan was approved to take up to three short-term placements up to age eight. I think the hardest thing we had to do was introduce children to their new adoptive parents when they had to move on. We did a lot of this, but I always found it hard to see them go, and I always worried that no one could look after them like I could!

Susan preferred younger children and babies, and I wasn't into that to begin with as I had always taken older ones. I remember one time when we had to take some premature twins, a boy and a girl, and I was terrified! It was awful and we had to do night feeds every two hours between us…but it was incredible and this eventually gave me the confidence to handle babies, so I got used to them. Those twins stayed for about five months and then moved on, mainly because Sean couldn't cope with having them around. I remember another baby boy that we collected straight from hospital who stayed for seven months. Part of our work with him was to reunite him with his siblings in preparation for adoption. We cared for about five newly born babies, at different times, and many more aged up to two years.

After that, we started to take older children, and I have always found it easier to take boys, maybe because I grew up in a family of brothers…so I've always taken boys. I was happier taking boys, and felt I had more to offer them in terms of experience and things that I was into. But just recently I've taken a brother and sister, Rebecca and Paul. Susan was the one who always dealt with the girls, but I was approved for either sex. Now I am approved for one or two long-term placements of boys, but now that Susan and I have split up, we still do some co-care and we support each other…we live next door to each other!

When I said I wanted to care for boys, the social workers made a thing out of saying I had to provide male role models. Actually, I think that's rubbish because the boys get loads of male influences in many areas of their lives. However, the social workers wanted me to name some specific men that I knew, but at the time all that I was able to say was that I would find them 'godfathers'. The social workers said that they needed to say all this to get me through the fostering panel, and so they just said that I was aware of the gender issues and would address it. Otherwise it's never been a problem with boys, and I've never felt uncomfortable with it. Two years ago my fostering review made the decision that I should be approved just for boys, but they've since broken that rule when they placed Rebecca and Paul here. Now some people in social services have been saying, 'Is it appropriate for a lesbian to care for a girl?' and, 'Why do you want to care for her?' That is just awful and it makes me sick!

There is a shortage of carers here, and social workers still phone me and say, 'We've got so-and-so, can you take them?' and sometimes they do overload me. This is a general problem with all carers who tend to get overloaded with placements, and this can lead to breakdowns and allegations. I'm involved in supporting other foster carers here and I attend the Fostering Liaison Group (with the director, assistant director, fostering officers, etc.) to represent my area (there are three areas). I'm also involved in carers support groups, so that means I'm very involved politically, and people come to me if they have allegations made against them. My role is to support the carer against whom allegations have been made, and to make sure the process of investigation is fair, whether the allegation is true or not. I've been doing that for eight years and I have been the vice chair of the local Foster Carers' Forum.

Have there been any problems about my sexuality? One or two social workers have questioned whether it is safe to place children with me, and the fostering officer told them that was ridiculous. Some social workers have refused outright to place children with me. Others have just been downright rude and that is just to do with their prejudice...no one has ever said my childcare is poor! Many regard me very positively, and some social workers actively seek to place children with me or with Susan.

I have had an allegation of sexual abuse made against me by a doctor, but it was dropped when he found out I was gay. He said that a boy in my care had been sexually assaulted, but he withdrew the allegation at a case conference when he said that the evidence was of penetration by an adult male penis...as it turned out there was no evidence anyway, but the whole thing was awful. No one supported me and it made me question everything about my care of children… I know how people feel when they have allegations made against them.

I've also had a problem recently with a principal fostering/adoption officer who was recruiting people to assess carers for NVQ (National Vocational Qualification) awards. I said that I'd like to be an assessor for the scheme and she said, 'You do realise that it's a sensitive thing going into people's homes to assess them…' She wouldn't openly say that she had a problem with my being a lesbian, but I think that's what it was.

I've also been doing training for foster carers, especially around protecting children who have been sexually abused. We used videos and case studies, and one of these was about a boy who had been systematically abused and was questioning his sexuality. There was so much homophobia from foster carers on the course, which really hurt me personally because they all know me and they must know I'm gay. Also, it's very worrying because they're caring for teenagers. We referred the issue to the department and their response was to drop me from doing the training! The training is now done by a fostering officer and one of the male carers who was so homophobic! The issue just has not been dealt with. The department deals with all other child protection issues but not gay ones. Also, my carers support group has got five gay people in it, but this is never mentioned!

I came out to my boys four years ago. I felt it was probably obvious to them, but also there were some issues to do with school, so I decided to tell them I was gay. We just had a normal discussion about it and about sexuality generally. One of the boys said that children at school had been saying that I was gay but he didn't tell me because he didn't want to upset me. There's never really been any trouble at school about it, but I remember the first day that Sean went to high school one child said, 'Your mum must have a lot of sex to have all those children!' Matthew was also at that school and I was worried that, because Matthew can be very difficult sometimes, he might use the fact that I'm gay to get at Sean or create trouble for him at school, so I went to see the school bursar to explain about myself.

From that point, Sean's teacher refused to make eye contact with me and he stopped communicating with me… I remember when they did sex education in Personal & Social Education and they discussed homosexuality in detail and Sean got distressed. I went to try and talk to the school about how to be sensitive about it but they wouldn't discuss it with me and just said, 'Is there a problem at home?'

The primary school is very different…it's Church of England and I went to see the head to explain I was gay. He was fine and said thanks for letting them know. They're very supportive, and the head has actually helped me deal with some of the personal stuff that affects the boys. That school has taken all my kids and they even have a Carer's Day instead of Mother's Day for my children and they ask me how to approach stuff about 'the family'. That's great! The boys themselves don't say that much to their friends about me being gay, and they deal with it themselves in their own way. One has chosen to say, 'My mum is divorced.'

My fostering placement worker has just retired and they've just left me to get on with it! That's not very good really because they still give me loads of kids to care for I will speak up when I need help, but that's not the point really. When I asked for my re-approval, which, as I said, never happened, the social worker talked about what would happen if I got another partner in the future. She said it was just for information and she said, 'if I'm being too personal let me know!' and that was fine… That social worker has had three gay carers so she's used to it!

I have a new partner now but she's not involved with the care of the children. So I'm still registered as a single carer. As a single carer it can be hard because you don't get so much support. I had a support worker and social worker and some friends who were also fostering, but they were all in couples. I never went to a support group and I had no idea there were groups for gay carers. I certainly wasn't keen on the idea of going to a support group that was all heterosexuals and me! When I found out about the Northern Support Group, it was great. I read about it in the gay press, and I really enjoy going. It's nice to meet other gay carers, and some of us have been away on holiday together with all the kids, which was good fun. Also, it's nice to get out of my local area and meet up with others and talk about the problems and the good times.

Why do I foster? I just do it because I love the kids to bits; I'd have hundreds if I could! And if you get a social worker who is prepared to work with you, we can do marvels really, whatever the children's problems. We've been able to get some kids far more accepted by their peers even despite them having huge emotional problems. And sometimes the problems have been huge! I have had to deal with some very difficult and sometimes violent behaviour, and at times the house has been in turmoil. There's a saying, isn't there, about 'the eye of the storm', which is the really calm part amongst all the chaos and destruction. It's the centre that holds everything together, that drives the whole thing, and that's what I feel like sometimes…

HELEN (2014)

When we last spoke, I had three adopted sons, and Paul and Rebecca were living with me as foster children. Their social workers tried to move them on through *Be My Parent*, but there were no takers. In the end, I said, 'Look, this is plain silly. As much difficulty as they were giving me, you can't have that insecurity for that length of time.' So, I said, 'I'll have them.' So, a brother and sister for my three other adopted boys. Once I'd taken on Paul and Rebecca, I didn't have any other kids coming in. As my original story shows, I had done a lot of both long-term and short-term foster care, but now I felt the family was complete.

When the children were young, we had a fantastic Church of England primary school, but a terrible high school. The boys were bullied there, homophobic bullying, so they changed to a different school that was more supportive. They still had problems with other kids, but I think that happens at secondary school – your parents just have to be different in some way, not necessarily gay or lesbian, for you to get picked on. Each of them dealt with it in the way they wanted. Sean just told people it was none of their business but could resort to emphasising this with his fists if they did not leave him alone! Matthew just denied it all; one weekend I went away and they went and stayed with friends – and his whole thing all weekend was, 'Mum's gone away to get married, mum's gone away to get married.' It was a complete fantasy. He lives in a fantasy world that can be dangerous, not just for him, but to anyone he involves in his fantasy. As an adult he has come out as gay and has worked within the gay community, but he is no longer in contact with me, which is really very sad, though he keeps in touch with my ex-partner. I appreciate that he needs to sort himself out and we need to give him the space to do that.

I live in a town now – part of that was because Marcus, one of my other adopted sons, has a disability. Little village schools are great but they don't have the facilities of bigger city schools, or the number of staff. We could afford a beautiful, big house in town where the children could have their own rooms. That was better for all of them to have their own rooms, but particularly important for Paul – he had been sexually abused by a sibling and needed to have his own space. What we hadn't banked on was the more closed nature of the town: in the little area where we live there is one family that is very dominant – everyone is related and that sort of creates a culture. At the start when we moved in they were quite friendly because one of them was a builder and did some work for me. I had told them I had split up with my partner, part of the reason we had moved, but when they clicked that this partner wasn't a bloke, then the whole thing changed, the whole atmosphere. So that links in a bit to the school because a lot of their kids went to the school. You would think that being gay would be easier in a town, but no, not at all – if you were openly gay it seemed to give people the feeling they could abuse you in the street – verbally and physically. There were a couple of occasions when that happened; nothing too awful, but just things that made us uncomfortable and the kids questioning. But on the whole, it was a really good move.

We moved the children to a different school that turned out to be superb. They had a completely different viewpoint and were incredibly supportive of Marcus and his needs, as well as the other kids, and there was no issue with me. In fact, once I had completed my Social Work degree my second job was working for them, carrying out family liaison within the school. That school was very open and very accepting; it supported the kids but didn't put up with any messing about. One of the things I remember is Marcus getting upset because the parents of a girl he was friendly with wouldn't let her come home with us for tea because of me. And of course he couldn't understand that and it was really very difficult and it caused a bit of trouble in the playground, but the school stamped on it and supported us. And at the high school, when they went to the high school, there wasn't any difficulty at all because there were other kids with same-sex parents.

Looking back at the piece I wrote before about my experiences, it is interesting to see how society has changed. People have become much more accepting of same-sex couples having children. I mean, when I first moved to town all the lesbian women I knew were either having their own children or adopting girls; that was seen as 'right' – lesbians had girls. So I didn't fit, I didn't integrate very well because, of course, my children were all boys, except one, and she was not the best behaved, it has to be said, bless her. And the kids had a little bit of a reputation, so we didn't get invited round to places, plus there were five of them so inviting five in is a bit different. Each of the children had different people that were interested in them, took them out and spent individual time with them, which helped.

I think today I would challenge people's views more. I feel more confident about doing that. I would question people's insensitivity. But 15 years ago I would not have felt confident enough to do that, even though I was vice chair of the Foster Carers' Forum. Although I was sort of accepted, there was still that institutional homophobia, and that did affect how people behaved. I would be a lot more direct today and ask what I could have done that would be so offensive. It still worries me that I wasn't direct in questioning homophobic attitudes.

I come across prejudice in my role in the independent fostering agency when assessing carers, as I hear some terrible views expressed about people from a different culture; I feel sad that these levels of prejudice still exist. Why is that still happening? Why are you still worried about that? What is causing you such offence and upset? It doesn't sit well with me and Marcus is the same, and you'd think, bless him, with his disability, he wouldn't notice, but he's very sensitive. He can't fathom why people are so rude and dismissive to wheelchair users. And I can feel that sort of inside me, it feels uncomfortable and that just adds to any uncomfortable feeling I get from people who are homophobic. But it's the same with racism and things like that. And then I come across a couple and they are also looking at a prejudicial comment or act with equal surprise and I think, 'Oh thank god for that, I'm not on my own.'

Quite recently I came across the adoption officer, who I talked about in my original story, who was definitely homophobic and had an issue with my becoming an assessor. She plays golf and there was a competition and I went and talked to her, we had a bit of a heated discussion; her views still have not changed. Luckily I wasn't paired with her! But that gave me a bit of closure because I'd actually stood up to her. For me, the overwhelming thing about prejudice is sadness. It blocks things, misses things out. It's disappointing because she was a social worker, and a senior one at that.

I went into fostering and adoption because I wanted to give children a better start than I had, and I wanted to protect them because I hadn't had any protection. When I was a child I had no idea about fostering and the fact that you could be taken away from your family. Perhaps that was the era we lived in then. I think everyone today, including children, has a better idea and knows that children should be protected. There is so much more about that kind of stuff in schools today. But there is also so much abuse going on that people are not aware of.

I have moved on to work in a looked-after children team now and work with children going for adoption, those placed in foster and residential homes on a long-term basis. I find it more interesting as I can work directly with children, which I really enjoy. I remember thinking when I was fostering that I had got beyond being shocked.

But every child who comes into care has a shocking story about what has happened to them or what was alleged to have happened to them. The ongoing amount of neglect and abuse is just shocking. And there is child exploitation, too; I think that has always gone on, but I don't think it was really recognised until recently. So we must do as much as we can to help them.

Kids are resilient, but the abuse that happens to them can damage them for life. All my children are damaged to different extents. Before Marcus came to me he had almost been written off by the authorities – they said he'd never sit up, he'd never walk alone and that he was in the process of going deaf. But that lad – all you had to say in a really light whisper was, 'There's a sweet in the corner Marcus.' And it didn't matter how much noise was in that playroom, and there was a lot sometimes, he was over there like a shot! So far as his physical development is concerned – walking and running and everything – he wanted to play with the other children, and you can't get a stronger motivation than that.

When he first went to primary school he got really upset in the playground. The teacher asked him, 'Whatever's the matter?' and he told her, 'They keep running away from me.' And she just said, 'Well run after them then.' And you know, he fell down and cut his poor little knees, ripped to a shred, but he did, and he chased them and he caught them and he's done that all his life at different stages. He has no hearing impairment whatsoever, but because of the palsy he has one side that hasn't developed like the other; one of his legs hasn't developed properly so he has an unsteady gait; even his eye on that side, his pupil, is smaller. But the real problem is his heart and one lung are on that less developed left side, so everything is smaller than it should be. So his heart beats faster than it should, just to keep the circulation going, and he gets very bad fatigue, which is his main physical problem. He still can't work out his money, but he reads a bit, and smartphones have revolutionised his life. He doesn't have to try to spell any more! He does try to read before switching on the voice reader, which is just superb as it's building his reading up. And electronic tablets – he's technology mad; computers have made his life better, he loves communicating online. Technology has made such a difference to his life, it really has. It's brought him on, it's given him interests. He's an absolute delight and his personality is just as super as it always has been.

Coming out

I think people do still have to come out, I'm sorry to say. One thing I say to students at college is, 'Would you all like to come out, heterosexuals please?' And, you know, they're aghast and don't understand, so why is it that gay men and lesbians have to 'come out' and what have you? So yes, it is still important to come out, but I don't think it's an issue with respect to being a foster carer; I think it's more accepted. In a way, it's the novelty factor, and agencies that have same-sex couples fostering almost see it as a badge of honour. And that worries me. But for some agencies, you're the carers and that's it. There are a huge number of independent agencies now – that's a change, as when I started there was just the local authority and the newer agencies are more inclusive.

In a way I wish I had come out at the beginning, when I first started fostering. But I suppose in another way I don't think it would've been quite as acceptable at that time. I think most people were accepting, but if it had been in their face I think we would probably not have been allowed to foster in all honesty. They'd have found a way, or something, that would've stopped us fostering. Foster carers reacted in different ways – they were either completely and utterly hostile or they weren't bothered; there was no in between. I suppose in the end it was just a relief that I'd actually said it and that the world didn't fall down. And then I just sort of shrugged my shoulders and got on with it.

I was one of the first people to join the Northern Support Group for gay and lesbian carers. I wasn't at the initial conference, but when I heard the group was being set up I was there like a shot. I had come out by then. It was great for the kids, because that was the thing that I really, really wanted it for, so that they saw that there were other children who had gay parents. Seeing all those kids together with their mums and dads, mingling in and out, it was great. That group was hugely important to me, because you could go to the group and relax. It didn't matter what we talked about actually, if you were having issues or you weren't, or if somebody else needed your support. It was wonderful not having to explain myself to anybody. And that's a relief.

I've been involved in many groups and I've been what I suppose I'd call a 'straight lesbian' in lots of ways, because I was usually in groups with lots of heterosexual people, and that's the world I've sort of been in and that just is how it's happened. It certainly wasn't by choice. So, to actually be in that lesbian and gay group was just such bliss. I knew I could go in and nobody was going to ask any silly or awkward questions and I could say 'she' when talking about a partner or ex-partner and there was no concern at all. The kids were just superb and just accepted everybody; they weren't fazed, and it was just brilliant, it really was.

I think one of the challenges still facing adoption and fostering agencies is not so much understanding people's different sexuality but understanding people's differing lifestyles, whether a couple is homosexual or heterosexual. All the carers in the agency I work in are currently heterosexual, but there's not one that's got the same sort of family lifestyle as another. I go in knowing nothing about them, new to the situation and make no assumptions, though I think when same-sex couples are assessed, assumptions are made about them. So there's still the old, 'there'll be a masculine one and a feminine one' as far as lesbians are concerned, and gay men, too, to be honest. And I think, 'Oh please, if you just only knew the range.' When interviewing carers, I ask all sorts of questions including questions about their sex lives. Being open and listening instead of making assumptions is proper assessment and takes away the opportunity to make assumptions or judgements.

There used to be an emphasis – which is not necessarily correct – about ensuring female carers have male role models for the children in their care and *vice versa*, a belief that they needed these role models to become well-balanced people. But even when I had a partner, when we were going through the adoption process for Paul and Rebecca, I felt it wasn't about the roles that we had as a partnership or the roles taken within the house. The boys were taught to cook as well as Rebecca, the boys were also expected to help with the cleaning and they also did 'boy' things in the garden, like climbing trees, but then so did Rebecca. So I think there was a realisation that there were no defined roles, and that they were still well-balanced people.

Fostering

We fostered all sorts of children. We had a black African Caribbean lad, a super little boy, who was fostered at the same time as a white British lad, and they had been foster brothers in a previous situation. Both boys had suffered abuse. The boys were here for about two years and then social services started to look for permanence for them. They wouldn't let us have them because they felt they were too close to my boys in age, which was very annoying. So the black lad had to go to a black family – he was so distressed at leaving me and my partner that he actually picked all the skin off his fingers to try and see if he was white underneath – it was horrendous.

But we have had all sorts of children, young Asian kids as well as black African Caribbean and white British children. Race didn't seem to be a problem, and we helped write a book for the local authority about where to go to get different health and skin products, the hairdressers and barbers that knew how to braid and cut hair properly etc. There just weren't enough carers from different ethnic communities for them to be matched to.

That has changed. There was always some success at recruiting African Caribbean carers, but independent fostering agencies have been successful at recruiting Asian families and Eastern European families. Local authorities are now catching on, realising that if independents can recruit families from these communities, so can they. That is pushing independent agencies into specialising in finding carers for the hardest to place children, those with really, really challenging behaviours or who have had multiple moves.

The agency I worked for recently took on the case of a nine-year-old who has had multiple moves – he's a beautiful little kid but no one will take him any more, and he's only nine.

I suppose I am middle class now. I'm almost ashamed of it to an extent, but I know where I have come from. I'm middle class from a working-class background. A lot of the kids – and the carers – are from working-class backgrounds.

Adoption

I adopted Sean and Matthew to begin with – they were the first. Then Marcus, then Paul and Rebecca. Rebecca was two when they came to us and she must have been 11 when I adopted them both. It was just before legislation came in allowing same-sex couples to adopt together. It was just as well, really, that it worked out that way as my partner left me shortly after the adoption, and if we had adopted them as a couple, it would have been much more complicated.

The judge couldn't have been nicer and asked the kids, 'Are you happy?' and they were both giving it, 'Yes', with a kick of encouragement under the table! It all went through lovely and it was like a celebration. I was just trying to think what year we actually adopted them, but I can't really think. What is she – she'll be 20 now, so nine years ago, nine or ten years ago. Sean is nearly 32, Matthew is 31 in May, Paul 28 in August, Marcus 28 in October and Rebecca 25 in July. That's frightening, isn't it?

Sean, the eldest, is the only one with kids, so he's got a ten-year-old daughter, an eight-year-old son and a five-year-old daughter – they're all siblings – and then a half-sibling of four. It all merges. They are delightful. I enjoy being a grandmother. I actually delivered my grandson because they didn't get to the hospital quickly enough, so I was the first one he ever saw! But they're all special. They are just all delightful, bright, eloquent little kids, you know.

All of my children have turned out differently. Sean has found his niche working in the food industry as a chef. He's always loved food and cooking. He's sometimes struggled to find work. He's now acknowledged some of the problems he has with attachment. He went through a period when he was younger of assaulting me. But bless him, he went for counselling and it's really helped sort him out. He has no issue at all about me being gay and his only issue is, 'Mum, why haven't you bothered to get a girlfriend?' I say, 'Don't you think I've got enough to do seeing to you lot?' And he keeps looking out for me, bless him. I went to a big lesbian music festival in Shropshire last year and he's going to come with the children this year. He's so well adjusted, it's just amazing. I'm incredibly proud of him.

Matthew has been more difficult. He never accepted my sexuality. He struggled with family and without family and he always had to be the best. My ex-partner was quite academic and he aligned with her and thought she was more cultural than I was. And although he aligned more with her, his attachment issues are huge, so he's struggling. He's accused me of physically assaulting him and all sorts of stuff; he's very, very bitter about his childhood. He always saw his birth mother as Sean's birth mother, not his, so he was very disassociated. It's very worrying and very sad. He was and is a beautiful, beautiful boy, absolutely stunning and intellectual and intelligent.

Matthew came out when he went to university, even though he's had a huge issue with my sexuality. I think it's because he doesn't really like his sexuality, I think that's it. I kind of hope he's getting more and more into his own skin and then he may well accept mine. But no, Susan, my ex-partner is his mum, he tells everybody now, not me. And I think, 'Well that's alright really.' I just hope he can be happy, as he lives in this fantasy world and I worry that if he gets very badly hurt, or let down, or physically gets very ill or something, it will crash down and his vulnerability will be exposed and he will have no one to support him. Whilst I don't worry about it often, when I'm thinking about him I think I'd rather he lived in his fantasy world than crash, because, whilst he wasn't very abusive as a child, the only time he did get aggressive was when he faced reality. He doesn't want to see me, because he can't, he can't cope with me, because he knows I know who he is.

Paul, well, he's a bit of a wide-boy. He's always going to be okay. He gets by, he was doing waiting on tables at big events, you know the events and they hire the waiters and waitresses in. He was a bit of a wild teenager, a bit of a shoplifter and a bit of a bully boy. But he was seriously affected by his stint in youth offending, he was so appalled by the injustice of it all, and he's never going back, he said; well, he's never been caught again, whether he's done anything I don't know. But I think he's going to be okay – every now and again he opens his Facebook and lets me have a little look to see what he's doing, especially around his birthday, of course.

Rebecca is really, really troubling. Bless her – the fact that she's even functioning on any level after what had happened to her is amazing. I'm very, very impressed with her. Again, every now and again she sort of invites me to be on her Facebook so I can see what she's up to. She seems to be reasonably well adjusted, everybody knows her locally and she hasn't got pregnant yet, and frankly I think that's an absolute success story. So she's functioning, she has a job and a partner and appears to be happy in her own little world, and what more can I ask really.

Marcus is amazing. I am so proud of him. He struggles a bit with his mental health, he gets depressed quite quickly if he's not out and about doing things. He doesn't like the fact that he's got a disability. His whole dream is to get married; not sure about kids yet, and when he sees the grandchildren he says, 'No, thank you very much.' And I tell him, 'Yeah, I think that's the best idea really, love.' He's got himself a girlfriend at the moment who also has a disability, and she has a nice family who are accepting of his disability. So Marcus wants to get married, have his own little house. He has lots and lots of aspirations, only held back by the fact that he has a disability and can't live independently. And for that, I'm sorry. He is now living in his own bungalow with a good staff team supporting him so has a lot more independence.

Marcus is fiercely heterosexual. He'll say, 'I'm definitely not gay', and that's okay because he's not saying it out of prejudice. He's stating his identity, 'I am heterosexual.' He has no problem with me and when I've got a girlfriend and stuff, he's more than happy, that's not an issue. And he tries to keep in touch with a previous partner, Jane, who he was extremely close to but, because she's got another partner, it is not often – but he gets the odd birthday card and he's still fiercely in love with her. His thing is now, 'I won't let her get away, she can't ignore me.' He's gorgeous, gorgeous.

I am sorry I don't see them as much as I would like. But they always come back eventually. I always keep the same phone number so they'll always be able to get hold of me. The positives are that none of them have committed murder, thankfully none of them have committed suicide and all are maintaining good lives. They are all doing pretty well, functioning on one level or another within society, and for that I'm absolutely delighted.

But despite that, looking back, I sometimes wish I'd never done it; there's been a lot of pain, and it's taken up my whole life. But on another level, even if we don't look at how fantastically they've turned out, if we look at me and my development, it has led me into training as a social worker, for good or bad – I think for good. That has led me into social work education where I hope I've been able to influence lots of other social workers and it's led me to this job now. I've developed beyond anything I imagined. I could never have imagined getting a university education and a degree – that was a shock to me. I never had that aspiration, my mum didn't give me that aspiration, but these children – my foster and adoptive children – gave me aspiration. I was encouraged by other social workers I met through fostering and if I hadn't started fostering, I don't know what I would've done. And I think it's made me a more tolerant person, taught me not to be judgemental. It's made me really think about people and be a lot more compassionate.

And you know, even now, when we've got trouble finding respite for some of the kids we've got, I still keep thinking, 'I wonder if I would just get approved, so I could have them?' And then I think, 'Don't be silly, you've got your house to yourself and your cats, you can come and go, everything's where you left it, sadly including the washing-up.' But you know, nothing's getting pinched anymore, because I mean – god only knows the amount them little devils have cost me, bless them. And Sean every now and again says,

'I'll repay you one day, love.' And I'm thinking, 'I know you won't, but you're still loved.'

I think society has changed a lot since I first fostered and adopted. Society is a lot more accepting. There are still the bigots who think, 'Right because you're up and open about it, we can have a go at it', but that isn't going to change. Because there'll always be some, but I think it's just so much more accepted. And do you know, research is showing that kids from gay and lesbian parents are much more tolerant and well adjusted. That's fantastic, and I think it's because when you're with a group that's been oppressed you understand that being intolerant is not acceptable, whether they are birth children, adopted or foster kids, they are such lovely people to meet. So, looking back, it's been an incredibly journey and I wouldn't have been without it.

LEE (2018)

Since being interviewed I have moved on incredibly and 'come out' as transgender and am on another journey to finally be me – I have been living as a man for the last three years, and it is brilliant. Sean and Marcus know and they are accepting; Sean asked me why it had taken me so long – that explanation is for another book, maybe!! My friends, family and work colleagues have been very supportive and I have received less discrimination than when I came out as lesbian – now that is a sign of society changing!

ELIZABETH and MARY

Expect the Unexpected

Elizabeth and Mary have been together for nearly 30 years and are in their 60s. In the past they provided respite care for Peter for seven years, and went on to be approved for a permanent, full-time placement of a child of primary school age in 1994. A year later Daniel came to live with them, and their original story reflects this time. We then followed up with them 18 years on, with Elizabeth and Mary looking back at the challenges they faced in bringing up Daniel. They also reflect on the relationship they have with both Daniel and Peter today, now that both boys are adults.

We begin with their original (1999) story, 'A Special Mothers' Day Card':

It seems a long time ago that we made the decision that we wanted to adopt. We had talked about wanting children from the time we got together. Our first thoughts were to 'grow our own' rather than to get one 'off the peg'. We did put some energy into thinking of inseminating and joined a self-help insemination group. We found the whole process of meeting donors very strange and stressful. Only one of us could try inseminating and we were both pretty freaked out by the whole thing, and especially the uncertainty and stress of waiting for a period and for fertile times. We just didn't have the stamina to go on for more than a few months.

We first approached social services as a general enquiry. One of us rang the advertised fostering number. She'd been feeling fed up with work and wanted to get on with other parts of life, like being with children. We were sent a pack of information. We'd also seen a piece in the first *Out on Tuesday* (Channel 4) series on television about respite care, and this seemed the right thing for us at that time. When we rang back to tell them we were interested, a social worker came to see us the following week.

We didn't 'come out' straight away, although we were clear that we were both interested and committed to living together and we owned the house together. One of us applied as a single carer with the other also involved. The social worker set up meetings with us, with specific topics to discuss at the meetings. These included discipline, food, money and other issues. She also asked us to write down our life stories for her. That's when we 'came out'. The social worker knew that the council had an equal opportunities policy that covered sexuality, and thought it would be all right. She said she would check with the boss what was involved because she was new. She came back the next week and asked us about our attitude to men and variations around that question.

We didn't know any other lesbians who had been through the assessment process openly as lesbians. We did know one carer who is a lesbian but had not been 'out' when she was assessed. She knew others and one woman set up a support group. She was very active in the Foster Care Association locally so she was able to get their support. There were about five single lesbian carers or couples involved in that early support group but none of the others had been 'out' when they were first assessed. Some of them did an enormous amount of difficult work with many children.

We were questioned about our attitudes towards men during our assessment. There weren't many men in our circle at that time. We emphasised that we weren't antagonistic to men and that we weren't separatists – but the social worker didn't know what that meant! We said things like 'We get on well with male colleagues at work', 'We get on well with our brothers.' We had both lived in women's houses before moving in together.

Our social worker didn't offer any apologies for asking these questions and we laughed about it in between the sessions, wondering what she would come back and ask next. The rest was so positive we just took it in our stride. We asked her to assess us as two individual carers (who were each out lesbians and in a couple) because we didn't trust the confidentiality throughout the department. We didn't want to be 'Miss A and Miss B' on all the files, making it really obvious, although we were happy to be out in the small print inside the files. She colluded with this.

I don't remember her asking about 'role models' but she did ask about the way we divided household tasks. Sometimes we were not sure what was going to go in the report and what was the social worker's personal interest in comparing our life with her married life!

We were each approved. We began respite care in the name of one of us. We didn't 'come out' to the child's family although we didn't hide our close relationship and they accepted that we were both equally involved. With hindsight, it might have been easier to be 'out' from the start, but we had decided not to be, as we usually only expect to tell friends once they know us and understand our lives. In fact, the family has been very supportive and we are still caring for Peter now, seven years later. The original arrangement was for one weekend a month and one week of the summer holidays, and we have maintained that level of involvement.

One of the difficulties of being assessed separately was that they had one of us on the books with no child placed. They approached us to take another. After some time, we had another child on a different weekend in the month. This was an older girl with very different needs. We found it difficult that we had not been out to the family and doubted that they would have accepted the placement if they had known. This was a tension. We found this second placement too much and had to withdraw. Again, the social worker was very supportive and helpful about the way we felt in letting the child down. After that we asked them to more formally recognise us as a couple caring for Peter.

Later we joined a support group concerned about the issues for lesbian and gay foster and adoptive parents. Through the group we learnt a lot more about what was involved in fostering full time and the extent to which lesbians and gay men were being accepted.

We were already providing respite care to Peter, and we finally decided that we were ready to apply for full-time fostering. At the first interview we thought the social worker was really trying to put us off. We accepted that it was not because we were lesbians; it was because she wanted to be sure we knew that taking on 'damaged' children would be challenging and that they had very few young children. We still said we were interested.

We waited several months and were then given only one week's notice of a course over six weekday evenings that was the next stage. We felt that other carers there had perhaps had more preparation for the course than we had. There were about 16 people in the group – two single carers, six heterosexual couples and us. We had not met the social workers leading the course but we were pretty sure they knew about us. Our sexuality was not concealed but it was also not openly discussed in the group as a whole. Sometimes it was not clear which group we should join when we split into smaller groups. Did we both go with the women (which we did), or would it have worked better if we had split up as a couple?

The classes were not part of the assessment but you have to attend the classes before they will start your interviews for Form F. We enjoyed the sessions on child development, including a graphic illustration of the long-term damage that missing a stage in development can cause. There were also discussions about sexual abuse, and what it is like for the birth parents and for foster children moving to a new home.

We waited some more months before our assessment interviews started. Our social worker was very open and willing to learn from us about the way we lived and our relationship, and we were open with her from the start.

We had a tricky time discussing the gender of the child we would want. It had not been an issue when we first decided to do respite care. It turned out that one of us (who had brothers and had provided care for a friend's boy) had a preference for a boy and the other (who had sisters and nieces and had cared for a girl) preferred a girl. Our social worker thought it might be more difficult to get approval if we specified a girl because of our sexuality, but was willing to talk it through. In the end we said one or two children of either sex. It was also a factor that the authority had far more boys than girls to place.

We were shown the full write-up of our interviews before it went to panel, and were told straight away after the panel meeting that we had been approved. It had taken a year from our enquiry to approval. We had not told many people except close friends about our application until we were approved. It was good to tell people that we were planning to adopt, and our families were supportive although concerned about what we were taking on.

It took another year before we had a child placed. After we were approved we were in line to take a girl, and although we had not met her, we had moved her in in our heads when her circumstances changed and she was no longer available to be placed. That was a blow and we needed to grieve.

We considered other children suggested by our placement worker and also looked at the adverts in the NFCA (National Foster Care Association) and BAAF (British Association for Adoption and Fostering) papers. We rang up about one young boy from another authority. We came out to the placement worker on the telephone and she was enthusiastic. Later, another social worker left an answerphone message to say that the child needed a father. We now know that he was placed with a single woman. That experience put us off dealing with other authorities. Even within our authority we had the impression that some social workers dragged their heels in providing information to us about possible children. It didn't feel like we could do anything about that.

We did consider several other children and talked to their social workers. When we decided that they were not the right child for us, usually because they sounded too challenging, we were not put under any pressure to agree. We were also sometimes disappointed when a child we had been asked about was not available. At least once this was because a family from Catholic Rescue had come forward. We didn't try and compete! Each time we were thinking about a child it was very stressful. All we knew about the children was a summary of their situation passed on by our placement worker or their social worker. We were never shown photos, but we still felt very involved.

We did feel that the social workers pushed our limits. We had said primary school age. The children who were suggested were in the last year of primary, and we realised we wanted a younger one, so we told them to adjust our age range to eight and under. (The child placed with us was seven years and eleven months!)

With regard to telling others about our sexuality, we have just told school and other authorities that we are both his parents without any further discussion of what that means. Informal situations can be difficult as there are so many complications. The simple question on the beach, 'Are you here with your mum and dad?', has so many complications for Daniel that the enquirer gets a confused picture, of which the two female parents is only a small part!

Daniel's social worker was interested in the respite placement we already had because he knew Daniel needed two actively involved parents. He accepted that was more likely to come from us than many heterosexual couples, and felt it was demonstrated in our care of Peter. Other factors he was looking at included how we (and he) would explain that Daniel had two mums, how Daniel would adjust to a non-traditional family (he thought better than many children) and the male role models issue. He seemed to be really trying to work out what type of placement would suit the child and whether we fitted the bill. On the other hand, he had not had any other offers!

Daniel has had mixed reactions to having two mothers. He doesn't call either of us mum – we use our first names. His school has been supportive. When he did his first 'Mother's Day' card at school it was a teapot. His had two teabags in while everybody else only had one! In our circles he probably gets more hurtful teasing from children about being fostered than he does about having lesbian parents. That may change as he gets older.

ELIZABETH and MARY (2017)

Daniel joined us when he was nearly eight. He has learning difficulties. Actually, he had the mother of all learning difficulties! We never really knew how much of that was inherited. But before he went into the care system, which was three years before he came to us, he had suffered four years of neglect. He had a very violent and painful upbringing, and nobody knew how those things combined.

He was due to be placed as an only child and they thought it was positive that he was placed with women because his relations with men were bad at the time. His father had been very violent, beat his mother up. And Daniel did continue to struggle with male relationships for some time. He would react so much more quickly if it was a man telling him off. We were so concerned that when we realised he was going to have a male teacher at primary school we discussed Daniel's possible reaction with the school. By the time he came to us he'd been identified as needing to go to a special school and that as well as learning difficulties he had some unspecified developmental delay.

Actually, he wasn't always on his own at first as, when Daniel first came, we were still giving respite care (one weekend a month) to Peter, who had profound learning difficulties. At first the two boys were alright together, then as Daniel got bigger it ended up with one of us looking after Daniel and one of us looking after Peter in order to meet their different needs. We're not sure what we would have done if Peter's family hadn't moved away soon after Daniel moved in. Long term we couldn't have coped with Peter and Daniel.

We still keep in contact with Peter – birthdays and Christmas. Today, Peter lives in a communal house with support workers near his mum and his brother. Last year we went to see him. He's 30 now, but we hadn't seen him since he was about 15. He was so unchanged: he still had all the same behavioural mannerisms and he seemed to know who we were and that was lovely. When we saw him, we wanted to just put our arms around him, like when he was a little boy, but he is a grown man now.

We gave Peter respite care for seven years. Although he was seven when we first had him he was more like a one-year-old in his abilities. During the years he came to us, he learnt to walk and to feed himself. He made real progress. I think that's the thing about children with learning disabilities – even when they are adults they continue to learn. People say, 'Oh what's his mental age?' And that's not right because they are never stuck in one age. We had a very strong bond with Peter. And it was because everything went so well with Peter that when we applied for long-term fostering or adoption, we said we were happy to take on a child with disabilities, and as a result Daniel came to live with us.

Daniel was a lot more challenging than we expected. We were told there'd be a honeymoon period and after that some of the issues would come out. But I don't think we had a very long honeymoon period at all.

Daniel went through the special school system until he was 16. We had a lot of issues. He was always, even when he was very young, a 'need you/don't need you' person. He was constantly saying to anyone coming to see him, 'I don't want to be here', but his body language clearly indicated that he did. He refused any therapeutic support, so we went on his behalf. We learnt coping techniques, most of which were helpful, some less so. But what was very helpful was that it resulted in a couple of NHS assessments of him by a psychologist. The assessments concluded that he had an unusual profile. On the lingual scale it showed he was quite low cognitively; he was verging on severely disabled in his cognitive understanding through language. But on the other end of the scale, for the equivalent of motor skills and processing information through visual clues, he was near to average.

When he was small, Daniel did seem to enjoy the sort of comfort that came from having family around. He was able to interact with our parents and family up to his late teenage years and there was no issue with our being lesbian. But later he became quite rejecting of one or other of us. He'd say some terrible things. I think that was peer pressure. He couldn't take comfort from us. Strangers didn't recognise us as his parents because of his attitude, like sitting at the other end of a waiting room, but he did need us.

He continued to be given contact with his birth family throughout and that was a trigger for some difficult behaviour. We were encouraged to let these visits happen and we felt obliged to support them. We used to tell the social workers that he found it traumatic. We kept showing them the pattern of how his behaviour changed after a visit. But he didn't refuse to go, although it was very, very confusing for him.

He could see the difference between the two families. Until he was 11 we went to play centres to meet his birth mother and siblings. We were a very awkward little gathering, no social worker present. We were encouraged to sort of 'adopt' the mum, make her part of our family. His birth mother was quite young when she had Daniel and there was an idea that, as well as being good for Daniel, it might also help her parent her other children. But it wasn't what she wanted. We'd meet in this indoor play centre and the kids would run riot. We just hoped we didn't meet anybody we knew! We wonder whether these meetings would have been seen as important if it hadn't been us, if it had been a straight couple rather than a lesbian couple? We think the meetings were, in some respects, to stop his birth mother kicking off, to keep her happy.

There was a big change when Daniel was 11 and went to secondary school, because the social worker who had worked with him for a long time wasn't part of the teenage team. Different policies came into place. Contact with his birth family changed. It was suddenly decided that having us at the contact meetings was a source of conflict, so a social worker would collect him and take him to these meetings. The previous social work team had known his mother. They had worked with her and supported her to keep her other children and knew the type of relationship she'd had with Daniel. But that understanding of the situation went out the window when the team changed. In some ways that's when things got worse. He felt the impact of the change, but of course he couldn't vocalise any of this; it all came out in aggressive behaviour towards us. The therapeutic support he received didn't agree that the contact was beneficial and should continue. But it wasn't in the therapist's control and it wasn't in our control. I suppose we hid those views from Daniel, rather than create a difficult situation for him. We tried to be as neutral as possible regarding his birth mother.

Daniel wasn't released for adoption at the point he was placed with us. So this became a key issue, and when he was 10 or 11 there was talk of Daniel finally being freed for adoption. We had taken Daniel on as a long-term fostering placement with a view to adoption. Because of this, we were told to tell Daniel we were his 'forever family' and he was to see the placement as adoption. However, his mother then challenged the application to free him for adoption. In fact, she and her solicitor decided to challenge the care order altogether! Daniel was 12 at the time, maybe 13. We didn't know what to do. We got advice from a solicitor, who said, 'Don't do anything that could be seen as inflammatory', like applying to adopt before the freeing process was complete.

The hearings and the whole process went on without involving us. A *guardian ad litem* interviewed Daniel and represented him. We were told by social workers that his birth mother didn't want us there. She thought it would inhibit Daniel, so the social workers decided that it was probably a bad idea. The *guardian ad litem* came to see us after the hearing, along with Daniel's social worker. It was clear from the things they told us that Daniel's birth mother and her representatives were making an issue of our sexuality. The social worker kept telling us, 'If only they could meet you they would realise that you don't have three heads.' We don't know whether the homophobia thing was used against us as an argument. We heard everything third hand, which made it difficult. You don't really know who to trust in these circumstances. You don't know what will be used against you.

In the end, Daniel wasn't freed for adoption but stayed in care, and we were asked to let things carry on as they were. Daniel's legal guardian told us that Daniel had said he wanted things to stay the same. So they took that as meaning he wanted to stay with us. And we were advised that Daniel's needs – and our needs – may be better met if we didn't adopt him, because in those days there was very little support once you had adopted, if any. We were told that his birth mother had no chance of having Daniel's care order rescinded, that he wouldn't be going back to her anyway. His mother agreed to drop the case if we agreed not to change anything. So it stayed the same and social services issued a certificate to show that he could stay with us. When he felt unsettled, we would reassure him with it, but his birth mother has since told Daniel, 'Oh, I stopped them adopting you.' He told us that. If we were to give one piece of advice to anyone looking to adopt we would say, 'Make sure that the legal stuff is done before you start.' The reality is that we all make decisions based on what we know at the time.

Daniel finished school when he was 16. Then he went to a special needs unit within a mainstream sixth form. That was very rocky. Daniel found that very, very hard. Thankfully there were very good professionals around then, and the head of the unit really engaged with the fact that he wasn't in the right place. So, with their help, he went to a residential college that could meet his needs. It was a college specialising in creative arts and crafts where he could use the skills that he had. His manual dexterity and fine motor skills are good. He did a whole range of crafts that you would never have imagined. And his reading improved because he was with a lot of young people with Asperger's who read, whereas in the special school his friends didn't read. His functional literacy improved, as did his confidence. They had a brilliant 24/7 curriculum. He got entry-level certificates in different subjects. Most importantly, they taught him independent living skills. They gradually moved him from a room in a shared house with support staff to managing in a 'granny flat' in the garden of a support worker's family home. They didn't have microwaves, so he learnt to cook oven chips! He played five-a-side football with local people and also learnt to go to the pub to watch football. For each activity, they gradually encouraged greater independence. Changes happened incrementally, and that gave him confidence.

He was 19 when he left, and the learning disabilities team in social services found him a flat near here, but offered nothing educational – just a flat with care workers. He's 27 now, but developmentally, he's still like a teenager. Because of his learning disabilities he still has a social worker who he is rude to, as he always was, but who takes it. He lives on his own and manages his washing and cooking. We won't say cleaning. He manages his money and we sort out his benefits for him, as he would find that hard to manage. We make the applications and put an allowance into his bank account twice a week so that he doesn't have to budget over a fortnight.

We think of him still as part of our family. We've absolutely no idea how he would have coped if we'd treated him as a foster placement and said, 'You're 18 now, off you go.' There is hardly any system to cope with a disabled child who hasn't got a family. His social work team does continue to involve us and that is really good. But one of the more difficult things for us is that Daniel has in many ways now rejected our family. We invite him to family occasions but he doesn't come. He made a little speech once about, 'Well you're not my family, but you're my adult friends.' And since his last year at school, he hasn't been accepting of us as lesbians or as a couple. It's slightly better now, but there was a period when he was very rejecting. I think it was partly because we'd got more confidence and were a bit more together and he and a friend once saw us holding hands. When he was younger, we remember him saying, 'Why do all your friends…' and we were waiting for it, and he said, '…wear glasses?' Things changed as he became more aware of his own sexuality. Some of his peers at college were very homophobic.

Since he has had his own flat, he doesn't come to our home. Never drops in. But we talk to him every week and we go to see him about once a month, but mostly we meet him in the car or in the car park. We've only gone into his flat if it's a special occasion. He won't go anywhere with us. We recently said, 'Well, when you're 30 we think you'll want to go for a drink with us.' And he seems to have picked up on that and I think he thinks that when he's 30 he might.

He's very lonely; he hasn't got much. He's a young man who's got a flat and nothing to do so he draws and watches television. He's got some friends, but we're not sure they're a good influence. He's had girlfriends, but we're pretty confident there are no offspring anywhere! He has an older friend we've not met who he goes to the pub with and he's occasionally been to football matches with them. So that's good – and he still keeps in touch with one of the care workers from his college who he got on really well with – and it turns out she's a lesbian, so he hasn't carried on being homophobic. He finds it difficult to get close to people because he worries he will be rejected. He finds it difficult to give. It's very unusual the odd occasion when Daniel does think of us. We remember comments like, 'I'm going to put ten quid on Euro Millions and if I win I'm going to live in Australia and you can both come to Australia too.' That was pretty unique. One year he drew a picture of a cat and framed it and gave it to us for Christmas – that was very special because he doesn't do presents or cards or say 'Thank you.'

He doesn't see his birth mother or siblings any more. His father beat up his mother repeatedly and he still wonders whether he should go and beat up his dad. He would like to find him and ask him why he did it. He found an ex-girlfriend of his father's on Facebook, but we think, thankfully, he hasn't found him. We wonder if it is because he is not really interested. It's a real difficulty that you can't control contact anymore. Bringing Daniel up was a struggle – very, very difficult. He found it difficult to control his reactions and sometimes he could become violent. But it didn't break us apart. If anything, it brought us closer to each other and to other members of our family – sisters and their children.

During all the time we had Daniel we both continued to work. Work was a sort of respite, or that's how we looked at it. Working helped to hold us together as people – home wasn't always the haven it is supposed to be. Now we are both in our early 60s, so no longer working full time. We see our role now as being there for Daniel, being non-judgemental. He likes to know we are nearby. He's surviving in probably a very scary world for him, one that he doesn't really understand but where he passes as understanding more, until you have a conversation with him. Our favourite is when we were talking to him about going to a soul night at the pub. He said, 'It's not about the music.' And we said, 'Well it's about soul music.' And he said, 'Well, when it's a singles night and they just play singles.' He makes his own sense of things.

We love Daniel, you know, but maybe you do want something back, so perhaps there is some disappointment. When we were assessed for taking on Daniel, the person assessing us knew how disabled Peter was and thought, 'They love him and enjoy having him even though he can't give anything back.' But actually, in many ways, Peter gave back a lot more than Daniel.

We think Daniel is a success story; nobody thought it would work, but he's coping, living on his own and not in trouble with the police. And we got through it, we're still together. And there have been lots of people who have helped along the way. We've had some very good support, sometimes without us being aware of that support. Lots of different people have helped. We found some conferences and some books helpful. We've been doing some clearing out and found four copies of a photocopied pamphlet or study called 'The Effects of Early Trauma' that Adoption UK produced. Lots of different resources were useful, and sexuality doesn't matter; these resources are useful for everyone.

There was a time that if you talked more openly as a couple about a problem, people would be thinking, 'Oh it's because he's been placed with a lesbian couple.' Whereas we hope that's a bit easier now. It was our fear that people would judge us as lesbians; that's inhibiting, it stops you discussing things openly. We did get involved with an LBGT support group and that gave a wider context to things – a lot of sharing of experiences, lots of people at different stages, most going through assessment. It wasn't particularly helpful, because so few people were at our stage, and we didn't want to put people off by focusing on problems. But overall, we are glad we fostered. We don't regret it.

KATH

On to the Next Generation...

Kath has a background in social care and the voluntary sector, and is an adoption panel member. She continues unfolding the story of her growing family of children and grandchildren, and reflects on the attitudes and assumptions she encountered on her journey.

We begin with her original (1999) story, 'Matched':

I always knew I didn't want to have my own birth children; I had a number of friends who had babies quite young, and the struggles they had dispelled any illusions I might have had about having little babies. Also, I feel there's something about the state the world's in that means if there's a child there who's got a life already, who I can offer something to, I would rather do that than go through the whole process of having a baby. I had a lot of relationships with children in my life and I knew I could offer a lot to a child and could gain a lot from having a child in my life. I also knew there were a lot of older children around needing families, and I felt confident that I could attach to an older child, and in some ways would prefer that. I felt that as a single lesbian I wanted to adopt on my own and I could be clear about that.

For a long time I knew it was something I wanted to do, and I kind of worked towards it by choosing to live in households with children before moving to my own place, but for some people it was still a surprise. Some people were really positive and others were protective of me, like my mum, who was quite concerned I might not be approved, although once I was approved she was right behind me. Some people who were parents themselves were worried at what I was taking on. Others were worried about the game I was going to have to play not being out through the process. I had lots of struggles about that myself, but in the end, as I was on my own, I felt that what I was presenting more than anything else was a single parent. I felt the social worker assessing me might have had her suspicions from the start and was almost warning me off saying anything to her directly because of what she knew about her particular agency.

The assessment itself did have its difficulties because I felt quite vulnerable, but generally it felt empowering and my social worker was very supportive; she was quite astute and I really enjoyed our discussions. You could say she didn't do her job as well as she should have, but I suppose I pre-empted some of her questions, answering them before they were asked in my thinking beforehand and sometimes in practice as well. Sometimes I felt she was playing the game, but it turned out later that that wasn't the case at all. From the beginning she was quite clear that she thought I was worth getting through the process and she was going to do her best to get me through.

When I first went into it, I considered a range of family options and children with different special needs, but discussions with my social worker clarified that it was more likely to work with one girl, and she was always pushing the strong, single woman model. In the end I was approved for one girl aged between five and ten.

Where I live there's a lot of poverty and it's a very mixed community. I have very close relations with my neighbours, including Asian families in the area. My social worker saw this and my relationships with their children as very positive, both in being good experience for me and also networks for a child coming to live with me. But when children's social workers came to see me I received some very negative feedback about the area. Although I knew this was their problem, it still had a big impact because of the power they had in choosing families.

There was a lot of pressure on me to demonstrate good support networks because I was on my own, and some pressure to provide male role models. But although there was some brief mention of limited contact with men on my Form F, both my referees were women single parents and the support network I presented was very female.

It went through panel with no problems and the whole assessment was very quick, less than five months. But looking for a child took much longer and the waiting was excruciating. After a few months I was approached about a child, but there were lots of potential problems regarding the child's birth family. This child was around in my life for a long time and I really took her on board emotionally, but in the end I said I didn't want to pursue it. I followed up one or two adverts for children in newsletters and was approached about another child. Often huge assumptions were made about me based on very little contact, and it was hard not to take this personally, especially being on my own with it and in the vulnerability of not being out. At the end of the day I think this was down to the inexperience of these social workers in assessing families for the children they had to place, and their own agendas. I certainly felt in a couple of instances that there was little understanding or sensitivity to my situation. By one social worker I was described as 'strong, but lacking in humour', by another, 'lovely, but not sure she'll be strong enough'!

Then there was an ad in one of the newsletters for Rosie. The write-up appealed to me immediately and they were clearly not looking for a family where men were a big presence. I also remember Clare from the support group ringing me up and saying she'd seen this child in a newsletter who was just for me! There was quite a lot of interest in her, but they picked out my form and came to visit me.

The next step was when I went to see the foster carer, who was very positive about me. Different people seemed to have very different views of this child. I think I'd say to anyone, get as many views as possible of the child and don't take any of them too seriously; remember they'll be different with you. The sort of things the foster carer described to me about Rosie were quite different from how she was when she came to me, and a lot of this was about the carer and the kind of household it was. Any doubts the social workers had were dispelled by the meeting with the foster carer, and it was decided to go ahead to the panel. There were a lot of delays around that and I felt I had been hanging around a long time waiting for her. We were matched at panel and then discussions about introductions started, which they envisaged being quite a long process; they just weren't committed to speeding things along. I ended up writing a letter of complaint. This was well responded to and I got what I was asking for and we went very quickly into introductions.

Again, I was in the position of playing a game because Rosie's social worker was certainly wondering about my sexuality, and possibly the foster carer was too. During some chat with the social worker, I was talking about having friends in Huddersfield and she said, 'Oh is that so-and-so?', who just happened to be a lesbian couple. There were suspicions and there seemed to be a message that it was all right, but for me to have actually come out would have been quite difficult. I found that whole experience of not being able to be open and suspecting that everybody was colluding didn't sit very well and I wish I could have felt able to be out in the first place. If you're in a system where you as the potential adopter are playing the game, and it's only you playing it, that's one thing, but the fact that a lot of people working in the system are playing it as well, it just seems even more ridiculous.

The other controversy was about how the introductions would be done. Because Rosie had had so many rejections in her life there was an expectation that I should go along at first as a friend just dropping in, not as the prospective adoptive parent. But I was very clear that I wanted to be introduced as her adoptive parent and that she should see the album I'd made about myself first to get an idea of me before she met me. In fact, that worked really well. They were terrified about broaching the subject with her, but she was over the moon when she saw the album. The actual day I met her was absolutely wonderful, I would never have imagined it could be like that; there was an immediate something and it felt quite easy, even though I was terrified. One good thing was that I was able to move into the foster home to some extent, even staying there for a weekend, and I got to know the other children there a bit and got a real picture of where she was living.

The introductions were incredibly tiring because of all the travelling, and emotionally it was a complete whirlwind. It took about three weeks. I did feel quite fearful that if a child came to me and had particular problems and outed me to social workers, that was a vulnerability hanging over me. But it was never an issue with Rosie because from very early on she was introduced to my lesbian friends. Whenever we talked about anything around sexuality or families, I was very clear that some of my friends are lesbians and that if I ever intended to go out with anyone it would be a woman, and she took that on board quite easily. I think that was partly because she was watching things like Brookside; it was a time when lesbian relationships were on the television and there had been a shift in children's awareness because of that.

Rosie had had a lifetime in care and she'd had enough of social workers; it was agreed they wouldn't come very often after she was placed. They were very supportive of the placement and very happy for me to go for the adoption order quite early on. I didn't feel particularly that I had to prove anything once she was placed with me, but now we have had some time post-adoption, Rosie and I feel a kind of liberation.

It was about 15 months from when I was approved and about six months from first seeing Rosie in the newsletter to her moving in. The adoption process was a bit drawn out and there was a problem with the court because, although there is a new court here, like several other new courts there's no facility for keeping parties apart in the family court. Otherwise it was very straightforward – the actual hearing was quick and we went home and had a party afterwards.

There was a lot of pressure before the adoption. Because Rosie had had so many moves and had had pre-adoptive placements before, the adoption was a huge big deal for her, and it was something else she'd not been through with another family. She went through months of saying I was going to die when I was 40, which I worked out was when she would have been with me two years, which was the longest she'd ever lived with anyone. So in some respects it gave her some sense of security to feel that the way she thought I was going to go was to die, not to shove her out. She has incredible fears and insecurities; they don't come out now in the same way, but they're still going to be there. It has been quite hard, and it has felt like an enormous responsibility because she has had so many upheavals and a catalogue of bad judgements and mistakes made about her care, and it sometimes feels like you've got to make up for it all and you can't, you can only do what you can do.

I'm absolutely besotted with her and we have so much fun together. I couldn't in my wildest dreams have ever imagined a better match – I think she's absolutely incredible. But I don't think I expected to feel quite so overwhelmed by her story, and that's partly because I am a single parent and partly because there is so much in her story, and I had to be clear who I was going to talk to about some of the things in Rosie's past. You can make plans for that but then things change, like friends starting relationships or other people who've got a real commitment to Rosie having a hard time in other ways, like a relationship breaking up, so I've protected them from some of the things I've needed to talk about. I think support is quite difficult because it doesn't matter how much you plan for support, you can never really envisage what you're going to need and it's never going to be exactly what you think it might be.

The biggest thing for me is having someone to share the pains your child goes through. Every time something happens to Rosie that's painful for her in her life now, in my mind there's this whole big scenario behind it and I feel like saying, hasn't she been through enough? There are lots of people who care about her but they're not able to share that feeling in the same way. If I was going through it again, I would seek out one other person who would be given all the information, whether a friend or my mum or whoever, so that there was someone else who has the same kind of background information on the child's story. You can end up taking on so much, and at least if there's someone else who's done that you've got someone to share it with and you don't have to go over old ground or explain yourself. I'm lucky that I know some other people who have adopted and I've got a lot of support from friends and family, but the load is spread a bit and it's having one place to go that would make a lot of difference.

She felt safe with me very quickly and transformed from this child who had been described as 'biddable' to testing me out in lots of respects. She is very strong-willed and very strong physically. We have periodic episodes of violence, which are incredible power struggles; they don't happen very often, but when they do they are extreme and aren't very manageable. Thankfully, I have people I can ring and sometimes they have come down, and just having someone else there can change the emphasis. When I talk to her about it she says she feels she could have stopped things in her past happening and there's anger there and the feeling that she was responsible, and that comes from having had so many rejections. She can't quite handle the dependence she feels upon me and she needs so much reassurance. I know there aren't any easy answers; you just have to do what you can to get through it and talk about it afterwards. Although there are odd times when I feel out of my depth, these are fleeting, and my experience of professionals has led me to believe they are generally more out of their depth – usually they have not dealt with some of the things that I have.

There have been many occasions where I've had to take risks and push for Rosie's needs to be met and sometimes my own. I think you have to be prepared to do that – if you're clear about what you want and what you think is right, you've got to be prepared to push, to write letters of complaint, challenge social workers, write to the court about their inadequate new building, request financial help, whatever it takes. Through contact with other people who have adopted, I know I'm more fortunate than some. Before my child was placed I was told I'd have times when I would wonder what I'd done adopting a child – I haven't! I was prepared for a tough time and I know there are tough times to come. But what I receive from Rosie and our life together is much more than I've put in, and that's a lot. I think what I provide Rosie with more than anything is total commitment. Children's needs do differ, but in this case, as someone once said to me, 'What children who have been in care really need is someone to stick to them like glue.'

KATH (2017)

I found it strange reading my previous contribution after so long. I didn't recognise the voice somehow. So much has happened and I've learnt so much.

Rosie is now in her early 30s and is married with a six-year-old boy. She left school with a good set of qualifications and, after some time in further education, has been working in hospital admin for ten years. She has been in the same relationship for a similar time. My grandson, Derae, is thriving. I look after him a lot when both parents are working and sometimes he stops over or we go away together. He is so bright and an absolute delight. I was anxious during his first year and sometimes beyond. Parenting will throw up challenges for us all, but I think Rosie's own vulnerabilities have been far outweighed by her desire and commitment to being a good parent.

When Rosie was 14, I adopted again. We both wanted another child in the family and by then we felt ready. Chloe was six when she moved in. She is soon to turn 24 and has a four-year-old daughter, Bella. Chloe's relationship with Bella's father ended recently, but they still see each other most days to share Bella's care. Derae and Bella adore each other and are like siblings in many ways, with a healthy balance of falling out and ganging up together cheekily.

Four years on, I left my job and adopted Mia, who was about to turn seven. She is now almost 21, and after living with her boyfriend for over a year has recently moved back to live with me.

All three of my daughters have very different, complex stories and extensive birth families. They all have experience of being separated from significant siblings. I have supported contact with different birth family members, including reunions with some birth parents, and my daughters have also explored birth family independently. We have experienced many challenges and joys as a family and I am very proud.

The relationships I have with each of my daughters are all very different and we have been through different processes of attachment and struggle. They can all come to me with concerns and for support, though not always straightforwardly. They can also challenge me, sometimes very articulately, which I feel is a good thing. I frequently tell them I love them and two of my daughters frequently tell me they love me. The other has been less demonstrative and can find it harder to be close, but is proving to be a committed and loving mum. Her own reflections on being a parent and my relationship with Bella have brought us much closer. We all talk openly about birth family with each other, and the connections they have with their birth families are important to them and to me, though they have also needed to create distance from some of these relationships for themselves. Humour has often been at the heart of our connections and we all seem to laugh loudly.

The one-to-one relationship I had with Rosie was extremely important for both of us, but after some time we both wanted other children in the family. I also increasingly felt some sort of responsibility for the wider community of looked-after children, especially those with more complex stories who were deemed hard to place and particularly vulnerable to disruption.

It is probably quite unusual to be assessed and approved by three different adoption agencies. One of my daughters was an inter-agency link, so I have experience of several different agencies, which is interesting to reflect on.

I was not out for my first assessment. My social worker stressed that as a single adopter I would be a challenge for that particular panel. I was not in a relationship and didn't have significant relationships to hide. I approached a number of agencies, but at that point didn't really know if I would be able to adopt. The first social worker who visited was so positive about my potential – she saw my strengths with enthusiasm. Looking back, her faith in me has been fundamental to everything that followed. She did challenge me and guide me too; it was just that her affirmation and support helped me have confidence and resilience. I suppose I might have gone with another agency and been out, but with different consequences. I have learnt to learn from every experience and to use this learning in some way. This worker was also able to advocate for me in a way I don't think I had ever previously experienced. This has helped me advocate on behalf of my children, knowing how it feels having someone onside.

It never occurred to me not to be out for my second assessment. I went to another agency that professed to be supportive of lesbian and gay adopters in their literature. Whilst I had at times felt judged by others for not being out in my first assessment, this didn't appear to be an issue at all for the agency, though I did experience some complex difficulties with the social worker, who was openly lesbian herself. Whilst it became understood that the difficulties for the most part came from the worker's own vulnerability at the time, I cannot help but wonder if our both being lesbians wary of homophobia made the situation stickier somehow.

For my third assessment I went to yet another agency. Although the difficulty had been resolved with the previous agency and they had placed a child with me, I felt my experience was tainted. This third assessment was positive and managed to both address and leave behind those earlier issues.

The first preparation group I attended included 22 heterosexual couples and me...a not out single lesbian. There were a number of social workers involved and this was an exceptionally big group, to deal with a backlog across the county. From the outset I felt isolated and found many of the small group discussions uncomfortable. But once we got beyond the initial session looking at losses due to infertility (it was 25 years ago), I found the content thought-provoking and my social worker was very supportive. I was not expected to attend the preparation group for my second assessment, though in hindsight it may have been helpful because I may have felt more of a connection to the agency.

For the third assessment, I was expected to attend (I had recently assisted in the preparation groups for another local authority).

It was a very small group and I had absolutely nothing in common with the other participants who were all first-time adopters. There was another single prospective adopter and it was assumed we would link up, but I had so much experience as an adopter it was hard not to feel out of place. I received feedback that my participation was helpful, but I really didn't feel I gained anything. I would have been very happy to attend something more geared to my needs and the manager did acknowledge this would have been more appropriate in my assessment report.

After my third assessment I was able to attend panel for the first time. This was a very positive experience in that I was presented to the panel by the social worker as an exceptional adopter and the chair gave me direct feedback to this effect. All the questions they asked me were those I had foreseen – largely about managing three sets of needs. Whilst it is always good to have affirmation, I was, however, uncomfortable being labelled 'exceptional', as I feel all I have done is to learn from the children and respect them. 'Exceptional' can also mean 'different' and 'other', rather than someone whose experiences can be learnt from. Maybe my experiences are not seen as a model for others because I am a lesbian and my perspective is presumed to be irrelevant to the majority of heterosexual adopters? Sometimes people tell me I have different perspectives because adoption was my first choice, but the children's needs are still the same.

I entered adoption as a single parent and I am still a single parent. For the most part I have chosen this and I consider it would be very hard to find someone who could have committed to my family in the same way. I have also been so stretched for much of my parenting life and have not had the resources to consider someone else's needs. When I was first approved, I encountered a lot of assumptions and rejection in terms of children I tried to explore through Be My Parent etc. I was often told the children's needs were such that they needed two parents. For my other assessments and links I don't recall any particular focus on my single status and both agencies quickly found links for me. One worker even put forward her interest in me for a child whom she had previously thought needed two parents. I had assumed that over the years the assumptions made about families and the need for two parents would have changed; however, I understand this is not really the case.

In one conversation I had with a manager a few years ago, she inferred that I may experience less homophobia as a single lesbian adopter; however, in the same conversation she told me that at the national register of adopters, lesbian and gay couples were second in popularity to heterosexual couples for children needing placements, leaving single adopters, and presumably lesbian and gay single adopters, last in popularity?

I would maintain that whilst it can be hard and lonely being a single adopter at times, for the children, having a single parent can be less complex and confusing. I have had conversations with some adopters in relationships who have actually felt lonelier than I have, because there have been so many tensions in their relationships as parents of children who had experienced trauma and, of course, some relationships end.

I was fortunate that all my daughters came to live with me apparently feeling very positive about the prospect, though of course they would also have been extremely scared. Chloe quickly tested me by attaching herself to Rosie and often rejecting me, but in many ways that was what made it work. I didn't find it hard to make connections with any of my daughters. I think in part this was because I worked very well with the foster carers during introductions and beyond. I even stayed in the foster carers' home during Rosie's introductions and Rosie and I stayed in Chloe's foster home for hers. I am very different to these foster carers and parent differently, but we all accept these differences. One had very open views about the child needing either a single woman or a lesbian couple. One had a lesbian sister in a long-term relationship and another came out soon after the child was with me. I know some lesbian and gay adopters have experienced homophobia from foster carers during introductions, but for me, this was clearly not the case.

I am white British and would describe myself as middle class with working-class heritage. I don't think we give enough consideration of issues of class in terms of placing children. In my first assessment, there was a brief discussion about whether I might be able to provide a home to a dual heritage child in exceptional circumstances. This was put forward by the social worker as a way to discuss the issues, as when I explained my limitations as a white British woman, and particularly that I hadn't experienced racism in a white British dominant society, she was wholly in agreement. All my daughters came from generally very white areas and two of them in particular found coming to live with me in such a culturally diverse area quite challenging. I never considered myself as having any disabilities when I was assessed, though there were features of my childhood that touched on disability. Later, in supporting one of my daughters with her specific learning difficulties, I discovered that I have dyspraxia, which gave me insight into quite a number of things I had struggled with through life, but also gave me an insight into how specific learning difficulties more generally can affect children, particularly in school, where children's needs are often overlooked and misunderstood.

I was a founder member of the Northern Support Group for Lesbian and Gay Foster and Adoptive Parents and I also attended a local lesbian and gay support group for a while. I did find the Northern Support Group very supportive when I was waiting for my first placement; however, once my daughter was placed I didn't really experience groups as supportive, though I did get something from attending in terms of group identity. One of the problems with groups is that people can have such diverse experiences and attitudes, which can make them feel more isolating than unifying. I think sometimes I spoke about issues without feeling safe. I think maybe the groups should have been called something different rather than 'support', as this can lead to so many expectations.

For 13 years I had one-to-one support from a woman, Millie, also a lesbian. She was a counsellor with a lot of experience regarding trauma. We never found an appropriate label for the support she provided, agreeing that it wasn't counselling or therapy, though there will have been some elements of this. Quite often I would just sit and go through a verbal diary of the events of my week, and often there wasn't really time to explore feelings. Just having a safe place to describe my day-to-day life somehow placed it in the world and made me feel less alone. No one can get it right all the time but we had a very similar understanding of power issues and also of vulnerability and resilience. It was a particularly safe and empathic place for me to explore my daughters' struggles with discrimination in the wider world. I so often had to be a rock, not just for my daughters, and Millie was my rock. When she retired I found another source of support from within my wider network. This was different and helped me through the loss of my rock, but I still have Millie in my head when I face difficulties. After so many years it isn't so hard to imagine what she may say in certain situations.

I used to be strongly in favour of diversity policies and their importance in any organisation. Unfortunately, as a parent I have come across many people, professionally and personally, who seem to say the right things but do not necessarily follow through. We don't seem to talk about power any more. We don't seem to live and work in places really open to challenge and learning in this target-led, compliance culture. Challenge is often met with defence, and of course everyone is so busy, meeting targets set by others. There seems to be a lack of dynamism, and as one worker said to me, they are 'working to the whims of others'. Sometimes organisations can become complacent when they do have policies in place. I would much rather we live and work in environments where we can be reflective and open to exploring issues and learning from each other.

I think it is far easier for lesbians and gay men to adopt now. I sit on an adoption panel and many lesbians and a number of gay men have come through this agency very positively. I think some of the younger prospective adopters have no idea about the struggles that have gone before them. Having said that, I am sure there are other agencies continuing to struggle with this issue, and I continue to question and challenge assumptions and examples of homophobia within this agency. For example, one previous panel member stated that she thought lesbian couples offered so much because there could be 'two very nurturing parents'. One assessing worker stated that it wouldn't be appropriate to place a child known to have experienced sexual abuse with a gay male couple as the family would be more vulnerable to allegations and social stigma. I don't know where this came from, but I wasn't the only panel member to pick up on this. It is interesting that workers talk about the need for positive role models but are clearly confused about what this really means.

The issues around transracial placements, identity and racism are still not grasped by many. I despair that we seem not to have learnt from stories of transracial adoption. Often there has been some exploration of how adopters may help children with their heritage and identity, but this seems to focus on quite a simplistic understanding of multicultural identities. Rarely, if at all, have the workers explored with adopters how they would support the child or children when they experience racism. There have been examples of placing children of multiple heritage with white lesbian couples, partly justified through their having their own experience of oppression. Of course, there are also adopters who are more aware, who recognise the issues and their own limitations themselves. Recent governments' own adoption agendas and changes in legislation and guidance have really not been helpful, though I am also aware of more challenge to this emerging over time.

It is 25 years since I first embarked on the adoption process. I had worked with people in various settings and entered the world of adoption with some knowledge and my own thoughts on the complexity of human experience. I had always been wary of labels and cautious about making assumptions about others' responses to distress. Whilst I believed various theories were helpful as tools in terms of understanding how people may respond to life, and there are people who have benefited from professional therapy, I also saw therapy as potentially risky, and wanted to believe in more political responses to people's struggles. Having personally experienced some brief contact with various therapies, I was very uncomfortable about some practice and exercises of power that can so easily become problematic.

In terms of adoption, I was aware early on of various theories in relation to the children and I was aware of the 'attachment disorder' label, which I chose not to use. I have chosen to be an observing bystander who parents with empathy and with a broadly therapeutic parenting ethos, drawing from theory that may help the process, but primarily focused on learning from the children. I have tended to think in terms of the children's trauma and survival processes. In some ways this may have been easier for me, because all three of my daughters had experienced complex trauma throughout their early lives and this was evident. I recently heard that some prospective adopters are now more cautious of adopting very young babies, because of all the unknowns.

I think attachment theories, when they are properly understood, have been useful in helping us to grasp how very young children, even pre-birth, have experienced trauma and can be affected for years to come, and have also given us positive ways of helping these children within parenting relationships. They have also helped our understanding of neglect as trauma and the complex impact of this. But people, including myself in the past, so often have limited understanding of attachment theory and hook onto simplistic meanings, because of the label, especially in terms of adoption. I've felt much more reassured by the growth in understanding and use of the language of *trauma* in more recent years. Whilst I have mixed feelings about labels, 'developmental trauma' seems to me one that does at least place children's struggles in context and at the same time points out that trauma experienced during childhood will also affect development.

I really worry about a tendency to see therapy as offering solutions for children who have complex needs. All my children had experienced some sort of therapy prior to living with me. They were all adamant they didn't want this again. I think this says something. It can take a long time to really understand a child's trauma through complicated processes of building trust and safety. One therapist told me, on placement of one of my daughters, that she, 'would not attach and you will be back within three years'. Another therapist had worked with another daughter, aged six, to see herself as different versions of herself and to leave one version of herself – the most traumatised – behind when she moved to her last foster placement. This seems to me contrary to building a positive sense of self. It is my experience that young people who have experienced trauma do have a tendency to experience the world through a fragmented sense of self. A 'healing' process would be one that over time helps a person integrate their sense of self with increasing coherence. I continue to believe that children and young people need considerable time to work through their trauma and they may have learnt strategies for survival, which can be challenging to others, but it is better for the young people to be able to express and work through their experiences within the support of the adoptive family.

Support networks are always important. My own have changed considerably over time. In some ways the more responsibility I took on, the more isolated I became, though I have always been able to explore different ways of getting support and life outside the family. I have stalwart friends who have been very important, just knowing they are there even at a distance. They have different lives and families, but they have an unerring trust and faith in me as a parent. Sometimes support comes from surprising places. There have been neighbours who I might not have assumed would be so understanding. There are times I have had to involve the police for different reasons and for the most part – and I have heard other adopters say the same – they have been supportive. I have found the police to be straightforward, open to challenge and even bring humour into some situations, which has been helpful. I suppose they enter into so many seriously risky situations every day, they are not thrown into over-thinking the situation of an adoptive family that is doing its best. On the other hand, I had expected the fields of education and health to be more aware and onside, only to experience much frustration.

I had great ongoing support regarding contact from one local authority; however, I do think the success of this was dependent on the positive long-term relationship I had with that worker. I have sought support at other times from other agencies, specifically for help in either establishing or maintaining contact with birth family members, and have been very disappointed. My elder daughters were adopted prior to the establishment of statutory post-adoption services and, to be frank, I think this may have been a blessing.

I therefore expected very little in terms of support from agencies and, as mentioned, found my own sources of support. I am very worried about much of the support that has evolved for adopters in a fragmented, piecemeal way without proper evaluation or accountability. I feel there is often such limited understanding and experience. There are examples of adoptive families in crisis being tipped over the edge by inappropriate support. I have heard post-adoption workers describing themselves as providing 'therapy' to children and families without registration or even training and proper supervision. I have heard of services misinterpreting and misrepresenting some adoptive families, and even examples of families being taken through care proceedings to then be found to be exemplary parents by the court. Trauma is complex, and I believe that secondary trauma can go beyond the adoptive family to potentially impact on extended family, immediate neighbours, future partners and professionals in organisations, who do not really grasp this complexity.

I think all of us who want to help others, whether professionally or otherwise, need to acknowledge and consider our own power. If we are going to really use the language of trauma, we also have to address our own power within this. Some professionals are more self-aware and able to do this than others. We want to help and therefore do not like to think we may be doing something potentially harmful. Children are removed from harmful situations, usually within a birth family, but then what follows can also be harmful. Systems and processes in place to protect can also compound or cause further trauma. If we are open to reflect on this we will be better placed to help. Much of the adoption process actually seems to minimise the real experience of the child and misunderstands the lifelong nature of loss and displacement.

I have been sitting on an adoption panel for nearly ten years. This has been a largely positive experience. I have been able to input not only into decisions, but also into thinking, learning and attitudes. Sometimes this is a slow process and I have learnt more in later life about revisiting issues in different ways to help people understand. On my CV, I had listed my involvement in organising a conference for lesbian and gay adopters and foster carers, but I suppose I see myself primarily as an advocate for the children and didn't come out explicitly to the panel for some time. Interestingly, one of the professional panel members then came out alongside me, but most other panel members were so busy talking about the many strengths of lesbian adopters, they didn't seem to hear!

I have assisted with training adopters, professionals and panel members. I have also written papers to help others' understanding; for example, regarding contact, identity and helping children with very difficult stories. A few local authorities have used some of my writing for training. I presented a seminar with one post-adoption worker regarding contact, based on a piece of my writing, which was video-recorded to go onto their secure website, and I also have some writing on another secure website. A while back I was a keynote speaker at a conference for social workers about contact. I have also taken part in local consultations and responded to some government consultations. Briefly, I became involved in some of the more recent 'Adopter Voice' activity, but feel it will take some time for many professionals to genuinely open up to this. I identify strongly as an advocate for the children and rarely raise my sexuality. I used to quietly get on with my parenting role, but in recent years have shared my learning more openly and use any opportunity. I think there are many stories of adoption out there from which we could all learn.

I have made many mistakes, sometimes the same ones over and over. A perfect parent, if there were such, wouldn't be any good to a child, because how would they learn to reflect on their own mistakes? But we can also learn from our successes. Feeling an outsider, having experienced discrimination, injustice and loss in different ways has informed my parenting, and helped me develop my own understanding of vulnerability and resilience. But I am ever mindful that my daughters' experiences are different again, and I hope they continue to grow with the strength of their own voices.

Last Christmas the family dinner was hosted at Rosie's in the house they bought last year. This was a joyous experience and everyone got along very well. Of course, it is not, and has not, always been like that. There have been times of tension, conflict and estrangement, which can shift within the family. But the really important thing for me, about times like this, is that my daughters can plan together and work supportively as a team. One of the most joyful times of my life was being alongside Rosie and her husband at my grandson's birth and cutting the cord. It is also joyful to me that Rosie was later able to support Chloe and her partner through Bella's birth. There have been times in the past when I have really worried about what might happen when I am no longer here…but my daughters have shown they have not only developed individual resilience; they also have the resilience of a family.

NEW STORIES

JAMIE and SIMON (2015)

We Never Thought We Couldn't Be Parents

Jamie and Simon have been together for 10 years. Simon is a recruitment consultant for a financial insurance company. Jamie worked as a human resources consultant before being made redundant three years ago. Both in their late 20s, Jamie's redundancy kick-started their decision to become foster parents. They have found that their youth was a greater obstacle than their sexuality. Jamie tells their story.

We always said we wanted to have kids in some capacity. We had thought of other routes, but we decided on fostering because we also had a passion for wanting to help someone and we felt we had a lot to give. We never thought that we couldn't be parents; that never crossed our minds. We felt that as foster parents we would be trying to make a difference. It is emotional because the children do have to move on, but it's also made us who we are, made us stronger. We've learned from it.

As children, we were always taught that life was about getting a decent job, and enjoying the simple things in life, things like that, but I'd also been told by my parents, 'As long as you're happy in whatever you do, we will support your decision.' They always encouraged us to go for something if we wanted it – if it didn't work out, at least we would have tried it.

Getting approved – the assessment

We were approved through a private foster care agency. When we initially contacted the agency, we were worried that they might say no because we were gay, so we decided to be up front and came out straight away. It was fine; they were keen to take on a diverse set of carers and we were up for the challenge. We filled in an online form and within days they rang up with questions about why we wanted to become foster carers, what we thought the challenges would be and so on. And that was basically it. We had an initial meeting with a social worker who came to the house to look around and see the kind of environment we lived in and to discuss what we felt fostering would be like. After that conversation, she referred us to start the assessment. It was very quick.

We were first sent on a three-day course, called 'Skills to Foster'. It gave an overview of what to expect, the kind of situations we'd be dealing with, things like that. It was for people like us at the beginning of the assessment process. We were the youngest couple there and the only same-sex couple. Basically, everyone was fine about us. Maybe one or two older people questioned our being there, but I don't know whether that was because of our sexuality or because they thought we were too young. Nothing explicit was ever said. The course was an eye-opener; it showed the reality of what we were about to go into. We had worried that it would be harder for us because we hadn't got any kids ourselves. But actually, because we were not set in our ideas about parenting, we could start to build the blocks to be the right kind of parents for these kids.

I remember one of the other participants saying that, when they had a foster child, they were going to get them to do gardening because that's what they enjoyed doing themselves, but I thought I would do what the child wanted to do and build from that. We got the vibe that it wasn't about experience; it was about how you were going to approach fostering. At the end of the three days, written feedback was given on all the people in the group. We got a glowing report! I guess because of our energy and interest in finding out more, questioning more and challenging the status quo.

They seemed to like the sense that we were flexible. Once we had begun the process, they didn't want to let us go; they thought we would be good parents and saw our sexuality as an added bonus – we were expanding the diversity of the carers on their books.

After the course, the in-depth assessment began. The whole process took about eight or nine months. For both of us, it was very therapeutic because it is literally talking about yourself, how you'd been brought up, what kind of role model you would be, what expectations we had about the children coming to us, how we would cope with stress, that kind of thing. The assessor did talk very briefly about our sexuality. The question I remember was about how we would explain our sexuality if a child asked questions or didn't understand that we shared a bedroom. But that was about it. There is a question about your personal relationship in the assessment and it came up then. But there was no sense that they were trying to catch us out. They did ask us what we felt made us unique. Neither of us specifically mentioned our sexuality and she asked us why and we said, 'Well, that is not our identity.' We didn't discuss the challenge of parents who would react negatively to us as foster parents because of our sexuality. It was more about how, if there was contact with a child's family, we would deal with parents who reacted to our being a same-sex couple.

We asked about the children who would be put in our care and were told we could get anyone – boys or girls. We did say at first that we would prefer younger children, but they thought that was too restrictive and persuaded us to go for all ages, 0 to 18. We find we usually get slightly older boys, as there seem to be a lot of older boys in foster care.

During the assessment, they were also interested in race and ethnicity. Both Simon and I are white British and born in the UK. For us it would not matter if a young person was the same or of a different ethnicity or race – all we were focused on was providing the best environment for them to live and develop in. They wanted to know what our faith was, if we had any, and if, for instance, we had a problem with taking a child to a Sikh temple or a Catholic church and so on. It was really about our flexibility, our willingness to adapt to whatever situation we were put in. We know another same-sex couple who had a little boy placed with them whose birth mother was Roman Catholic. That relationship has lasted for ten years. The agency tries to consider all these things, but their prime concern is the child – if the child is happy, then there isn't a problem.

Looking back, we wished they had talked more about how they prepare a child for placement, what they tell the child about us, whether they prepare a child for going to stay with a same-sex couple. A lot of the time the fact that we are a gay couple goes right over the children's heads, but sometimes I think they need to understand that there is more than one kind of sexual relationship, not just your typical white mum and dad with 2.4 children. But you could say that about children from or going to a couple who are from a different ethnic group.

And I suppose we also hoped that they might have used more real-life examples of care. You hear about other people's experiences afterwards – good and bad – but I would have liked to have known more before. Fostering comes with many challenges, and it would be great to hear from more carers about some of the things they faced, from starting out and on gaining experience over the years. Things like setting up self-employment with the tax office and the mountain of records that need to be kept from both a financial and professional point of view.

At panel our social worker went in first to talk about us and then we went in and they asked us various questions about how we would deal with certain situations. It was very brief. They asked us a few questions to see if we had thought about things, but our impression was that they'd made up their minds before we entered that room. Then we went out and within about ten minutes they came out and just said, 'Yeah, we'll make a recommendation.' And that was it. They didn't ask us anything about being a same-sex couple. And within days of being approved we had our first foster child.

We are approved for respite, emergency and short-term care. These all have different time spans, from a day to a couple of months, but a maximum of two years. Respite care is usually planned, but most of the children coming to us are for a short-term placement. At our next annual review we are hoping to be approved for long-term care so that a child can stay with us until they are 18.

We've never felt that, as a same-sex couple, we have been treated differently by the agency – it's just been, 'You're a carer and this is your job.' They do tell the kids and their families that they are going to a same-sex couple. Nowadays, it's not about same-sex couples – it's more about social care and changing the attitudes of parents who have to understand that carers come in all shapes and sizes. The agency does have other LGBT carers, but not in our region. For them, taking us on is diversifying, but they are keen to keep us on board. We have had no problems with the agency or the local authority. I think an advantage for our agency is the fact that we don't have any kids, we've got two spare bedrooms, we're young, and we can take on almost any placement that comes through.

Our children

We currently have a 15-year-old, who was meant to be here on respite for a week but who has been with us for nearly four weeks. You quickly learn that plans change – what you're told is going to happen doesn't happen. We've looked after three children since being approved. The first child was in the process of getting asylum. He was literally here for a few hours and then he ran away! So, when he came back he was moved somewhere else.

The next child we fostered was a seven-year-old. He came to us straight from school, so we had to start from scratch, including clothes, bedding, the lot. Obviously, we explained at the beginning that relationships come in all shapes and sizes – that my partner and I would sleep in the same bedroom, things like that. But I think it went straight over his head. He had fun here, so he didn't think of anything else. At first there was no contact with his family and then he saw his dad. The dad was a bit 'iffy' at first, but eventually, when he saw how much effort we were putting into caring for this child, he was very impressed. When we went to the looked-after children review the dad was quite emotional, and said he would rather his son stayed with us because we'd done such a great job.

Our social worker was impressed that something like that had happened so quickly. The mother was a different story. There were seven children and they had all been put into care. She just wanted to sabotage any placement. I don't think she would have liked any same-sex couple, but I also think she wouldn't have liked someone who was in any way different – a different colour or a different religion. She was very pleasant, very nice, but you could tell that she wasn't happy. She felt that we'd stolen her child, so she was prepared to do anything to try to break down the placement.

Our current foster placement is completely different. He's 15 and he's told his mum where he's staying but there has been no reaction. He's about to meet her for the first time in seven years. He wasn't meant to have any contact with his birth family, but he has been in touch with them indirectly through Facebook. He's naturally anxious about that meeting. He smokes and he wants to give up – we don't encourage him but we don't criticise him either – we just say he can't smoke in the house. Since this meeting has been planned, he's been smoking much more and he's told us he's worried about it. Unfortunately for him, he's been in care since he was five years old – we're his ninth set of carers. At 29, neither of us is that much older than him; I think that works for him and he's even introduced us to his friends. He accepts us. So there are some real positives. There are also some negatives, but that goes with the territory.

If we are worried about any behaviour, we refer it to someone else and they advise us. For example, the 15-year-old lad has autism. The social workers don't tell you much about it and we had to find out some of the information for ourselves. The trouble is, when a child first comes there is no involvement with the mental health services or any rehabilitation programme because the view is that the child must first settle in. That's great, but when you're dealing with these problems on a day-to-day basis, it is difficult to help if we don't have access to any resources. It's a struggle sometimes.

Fostering is about the child, making them as happy here as they can be. The social worker tries to have a catch-up every few weeks. They want to try and get the lad into a residential unit now because he's been moved around so many times. But the system is weird; his school, his previous carer, and even his social worker, none of them think a residential unit is for him, yet somewhere along the line someone is putting it through, so he's going to go there. It's a kind of lad's lad environment, and he's more of a follower and that's the worry there. Who's to say how long he'll be with us? If he were to stay short term, that would only be for two years, and then he'd be leaving care anyway. We keep reminding him that he's not going to another carer, that he will be going into residential care or he'll stay with us. And if he starts having a bit of teenage attitude, we just ride that out. To us, it's challenging but it's about never giving up on them. With most placements, you seem to go through a honeymoon period and then a sort of the downward spiral, and then it levels out and it all goes steady and everything is okay.

It's interesting that we have had both a seven-year-old who was just coming into the system and now we are looking after someone who has been through a long journey in care. When we have younger kids, one of us needs to be around the whole time, but at the moment with this teenager, although looking after him is my main job, there is time, so I am slowly edging my way back into part-time work. We'd actually said we wouldn't take the 15-year-old because he sounded so challenging on paper; apparently he'd made various allegations about different people – and then he came to us as a day care and it was the opposite.

You do have to be flexible; it's about the child. We're going on holiday in June and, if our current foster placement is still with us, we'll just take him along. You've got to want to put kids first, you've got to realise the journey that they're on and take it from there. We get a lot of referrals but we don't accept them all. Sometimes you think, 'I can't do that', particularly when we are told that they've done things like flooded the house they've been living in or made allegations against people, and sometimes ones where they even like to start fires or run away continuously. You have to think if you are ready to take on that bigger challenge.

Dealing with false allegations

We have been trained to cope with false allegations. They didn't talk specifically about same-sex couples – more about allegations being made against anyone and everyone. The training looked at safer caring, protecting the child, protecting yourself. We were given simple guidelines, like never go into their bedrooms, knock and say you want to see them, things like that. It's guidance for safe caring. There were two classes on safe caring and for each child there is a safe care policy – as well as all the risk assessment and tons of other policies on smoking, on everything you can think of.

But if an allegation is made against you, there must be an investigation – and although we know we would have support from our buddies/fellow foster carers and our social worker, we would still have to go through that investigation. I think that does put people off. It is a very scary thing. I remember during training one foster carer told us that a false allegation had been made against her husband, saying he had been getting in the bath with the child. It was completely unfounded, but there was that fear and there was an investigation. She said that they came out of it stronger because she knew that it wasn't true. And it helped the child because rather than getting rejected, they knew that, whatever they said, these foster parents would still be there for them.

If an allegation is made against a child you think, 'Okay, maybe it's something we can help with', but when it's the foster child making allegations about the carer, you think, 'Are they going to do this to me?' And you have to kind of be selfish in that respect when considering whether to take a placement. You have to consider whether this could be traumatising to the point where you wouldn't want to continue fostering.

Ongoing support

We do get regular training with our agency and there are support groups that meet every other month and we have regular one-to-ones with our social worker. Even when we go to fostering support groups, being gay is seen as part of the norm. Everyone expects there will be a variety of carers. There doesn't seem to be as much of a stigma attached to being gay these days. We're in our late 20s and we're one of the younger couples in the support group. Usually the same people turn up to these events. A lot are in their 40s and 50s, and we have come across a few foster carers in their 30s. We haven't met anyone really young within our regional support group or amongst other LGBT carers.

For the first year, we are part of a buddy system set up by our agency, to help get us on our feet. Our buddy is another foster carer who has been fostering for years, and she's literally just there if you want to ask any questions or to meet up and talk through things. We are also part of a support group that meets every other month, also organised by the agency. It's within our region, and we all have a catch up about how we've coped, what's happened and sometimes different people come to talk to us. And then there is our social worker who is on hand 24/7 if you just want to rant and rave down the phone, but is always there. And there is continuous training – online as well. We go on a lot of courses – we take anything we can get, because you can never have enough knowledge, so we're always expanding that, and the more experience we get, the better we become really. One thing our agency offers after you've been there two years is the National Vocational Qualification (NVQ) as a foster carer.

We got in touch with the LGBT adoption and fostering group through the fostering agency once we had been approved. There weren't many books or forums or groups out there for families like ours. There was a book called *Proud Parents*, and we read it while we were being assessed – it was a real eye opener and it showed that yes, there are challenges, but there are also a lot of positives. We also found support in the LGBT charity – New Family Social –

dedicated to LGBT families who foster or adopt. With New Family Social, we mostly talk online. We share experiences, though the bias is on adoption. We'd love to see more foster carers get involved. We're trying to get our agency to link with them. There is this whole new policy about 'foster to adopt' coming in, and that will have implications as well. It is better for the child to have a special guardian or to be adopted – it's more stable. I think if anyone of any sexuality is interested in fostering, they should just pick up the phone and ask the questions: no question is too silly or too small. You soon realise if you have the skills to foster, if it is the right thing for you.

Making a difference

Your primary role as a foster carer is to look after the child. Beyond that, it is up to each individual how much they invest in it. For us it's a career. Already we've been recognised positively. We had good feedback from our own social worker. Even with that first placement, the boy who ran off, when he came back we let him stay the night because we felt that was the right thing to do, but they were really grateful for that; apparently he should have just gone with the police. It's simple things that can make a difference; for instance, the seven-year-old, after he began staying here his teachers and social workers noticed that he started to have manners at school – he was saying, 'Yes please', and 'Thank you', along with getting 'star of the week' awards. For us that's just what you do, but it made a difference to how people saw him. And the good thing is that these changes are recognised by our agency and social worker, even if they are small.

If anyone is thinking about adopting or fostering, it can be worth going on a course just to see if it's right for you. It's a different world and it is challenging and exhausting at times, but sometimes, you know, it's very rewarding. Like this 15-year-old lad who is with us at the moment is fantastic; maybe we could really change his life just within the next year or so if he stays around. And he's talked about some of his previous carers and they have made an impression.

It's about what you put in. We were fearful at first that maybe we were too young, but we just did it, and so far we can honestly say it's been a massive learning experience, but the best one.

And there are times when you wish it was just the two of us, but then wonderful things happen, like one day when I went to pick up the seven-year-old at school he was just so excited to see me, because he had to show me this award – the 'star of the week' award – and for him it was that someone actually cared, someone was picking him up from school and was happy for him. It's small things like that. Of course, there are bad days and you get resistance, but it's all about how you deal with that and the support you get. There is a desperate need for more foster carers.

We can't honestly fault our agency; obviously there are benefits in terms of pay, we get a Christmas hamper, we get birthday and Christmas cards – they do summer and Christmas events for the kids; they care. And we can say no if we don't feel a placement is right for us, and that is not possible with some local authorities that want you to take whoever they ask you to take.

It's not always easy. You know, we've been shouted at, screamed at, strangled; but when you think, 'Why are they doing this?' you know, it's because of what's happened to them. For a split second, you think, 'Oh, I want to get out of this now', but then you step back and you think, 'Actually, I'm going to change this.' And yes, they do test our relationship with each other – sometimes they try and create a crack there. But I think, if anything, it's taught us that we're stronger together, and made us realise we're doing this for a reason. They can try to get under our skins, but we're here to stay.

JAMIE and SIMON (2017)

We still foster, and the 15-year-old lad remained with us. Then, at 18, he decided he wanted to stay further and is now with us under the 'Staying Put' arrangements until at least the age of 21, which again is another new development that we thought we would never take on. The residential unit was tried out; however, this didn't work out and at the request of the young person he was placed back with us. Alongside this we have had numerous other respite and short-term placements in quick succession, and one of them has also stayed with us; so we now have another 14-year-old boy who will remain with us until he is 18 as well.

For Simon and me, we are still together and stronger than ever. We have grown as individuals and have developed further skills of patience, organisation and empathy that we didn't think we would need or learn. Simon continues to work at the same place of work on a full-time basis, juggling both fostering and his recruitment role. For me, having teenagers has allowed me to go back to work on a part-time basis whilst continuing with my care duties. Working within the world of hospitality/hotels as a human resources officer has further developed my skills of communication and confidence, which in turn allows me to develop my fostering role.

We have moved house with our foster children, which was a positive change for them, and life continues to move forward. Having moved to a bigger house, we now have another spare bedroom where already we have taken on a further two respite placements. Who knows what the future holds, but we know it involves fostering and a chance to support and develop the young people who come into our care.

DYLAN (2015)
Being Positive About Difference

Transgender man, Dylan, always wanted to adopt. The one serious hurdle in his assessment was a negative report from the medical adviser, but persistence by an authority enthusiastic to take him on as an adopter won out. He has since produced a video about trans adoption.

I always knew I would adopt, even as a child – it seems a waste to produce more children when there are already children needing loving, safe families. My dad was an industrial chaplain and we were always political. My parents always talked about the world and difference.

I started transitioning at 26 and I'm 43 now, so it's been a long journey. As a young person, I started off as straight; I fancied blokes but I felt uncomfortable being treated as a girl. I was always attracted to androgyny in men and women. After a short relationship with a man at university, I decided I was probably a lesbian and had a girlfriend for three years. After we split up, we discovered that we were both transgender and started transitioning separately. In retrospect, I realised we were both gay men and had fancied people who saw and treated us as near to our real (male) selves as possible, whilst presenting as butch lesbians.

I always assumed I would adopt in a couple and didn't realise that single men could adopt. My 40s were looming and I was single, so eventually I decided to do it anyway. I bought a house in a real little community in a cul-de-sac, which feels a very safe space for children, with a good support network.

Coming out

I was out from the start with the agency. They said I was their first trans adopter, but they were happy to proceed. I tell people I'm trans on a need-to-know basis. Most of my neighbours are just acquaintances and so I wouldn't tell them. It seemed obvious to go to my local authority first to see if they were happy to take me on, and I'm glad I did, as they were great.

Assessment

I was put onto an initial course with seven straight couples. I didn't out myself as trans to the rest of the group, but I might have outed myself as gay, I can't remember. I was told we were a very unusual group, as we all got on well with each other and have stayed in touch. We met up regularly for a long time. One couple who didn't go on to adopt have become kind of aunt and uncle to Joshua.

The social workers handled my gender identity really well. I felt well looked after by them. The only difficult person was the medical adviser who looked over my medical report and picked holes in what hadn't been written. She asked the social worker to get my full medical records released and I assumed it was common practice, so I gave my permission. But it wasn't protocol and it should have gone to another medical adviser or my consultant for a second opinion. She trawled the full records for evidence and picked out some things that she used to refuse to approve me, based on psychological integrity; there was no mention of all the material in there about my transitioning. She clearly had no experience of trans issues.

It was upsetting, but my social worker stood up for me and brought her line manager to see me. They concluded that they wanted to take me to panel and offered to pay £700 for an assessment from an independent psychiatrist. The psychiatrist chosen happened to be the lead consultant in the gender identity clinic and wrote a positive report. The social work team also did some trans awareness training with the panel before my panel date. They picked panel members who they felt would be most receptive to me as a trans adopter and used a different medical adviser on that day, and the adoption approval went through unanimously. I attended both approval and matching panels. They were very friendly and it was a lovely experience.

Since being approved I have made a video for agencies training others in how to assess a trans adopter – everyone needs to be aware of the Gender Recognition Act.

I was approved for a male child aged 0–3. I was open to nearly everything apart from mobility because of the stairs in my house – it's a 'rustic', small terraced house. I also expressed concern about some communication issues; my parents are my back-up carers, so I also had to consider what they could cope with too. They were interviewed during the assessment.

When the approval looked like it would never happen – because the medical adviser refused to approve me – I did very briefly begin to regret having had a hysterectomy. I know other trans men who stopped the hormones so they could get pregnant, but I don't think I could have coped with that, so it's a good thing that was taken out of my hands and it wasn't possible.

After the course I went through an old-style assessment, as the agency was only just introducing the new assessment format, but wrote up my PAR (Prospective Adopter's Report) in the new style, based on a set of parenting 'competencies' rather than the former list of 60-odd questions. One thing that did come up during assessment was a concern that I would not be able to convince children's social workers with my trans identity. Another question I was asked was: 'How will you deal with bullying? What if your child outs you as trans and gets bullied for it?' I just talked about building children's resilience. My parents were both great role models in being positive about difference, and I'm part of a supportive community and have a really strong support network.

While the medical adviser was blocking my assessment, I got involved in New Family Social and volunteered at their summer camp. I got lots of support, and that was a really important part of the process. I've found the group really supportive and I used a lot of online support through them as well.

Joshua

Joshua was nine months old when I saw his profile for the first time. I was going through my assessment and I was really drawn to him, but when the medical adviser put a block on my approval I put him out of my mind because I assumed he would be placed really quickly.

When the approval panel was finally going ahead, my social worker brought a few profiles for me to look at and Joshua was one of them! I was really surprised and decided to get more information and went to see his paediatrician. I can't understand why, but I was the only person interested in him.

So I was matched with Joshua two weeks after approval by the same local authority. Within two weeks of that matching panel I met Joshua. We had ten days of introductions and then he moved in! It was very fast.

I delayed going to go court for the adoption order until all his appointments and assessments with professionals were completed. At 18 months he wasn't walking, so I just wanted to know if anything had been missed. They only said after placement that they hadn't been sure he would ever walk, even though I had ticked 'no' to mobility issues because of the stairs in my house. Joshua has not been diagnosed as yet; he has some developmental delay and motor delay so there are expectations that he may have some difficulties in the future.

I took nine months' statutory adoption pay when Joshua was placed, and I'm now really very part-time. I am self-employed with a small IT business and I'm part of an allotment community enterprise. Since Joshua came to live with me I haven't had any new IT clients, but I'm used to living on a small income.

Joshua is only in nursery in the mornings and it's really important for me to be here for him; he still needs me and he can be on tenterhooks when I'm not there, even if I leave him with my parents. I wouldn't consider leaving him with other people yet. Even though he has been with me for two years, I still don't know what each day will bring – he can have a great day or a total anxiety meltdown.

I have to advocate strongly for Joshua and I'm probably seen as a bossy parent who doesn't let things lie, but the way I see it, all that stuff benefits not only the adopted child, but all the children in an area like this, where a lot of children have development and attachment issues.

Joshua was 18 months when he came to live with me. He's three-and-a-half now. I'm lucky that my parents are so supportive, and I also have a good support network with a child of a similar age and his parents living next door to me. I have ongoing contact with my preparation group and one couple in particular, who didn't go on to adopt but who are an important part of Joshua's life.

I think organisations like New Family Social and their summer camps will become more important to us as Joshua gets older.

Letterbox contact has been agreed with his birth parents and I've written them two letters. We've not had anything back, but the social worker visited his birth parents after the first informal letter. The offer is there for face-to-face contact with me, but they haven't taken it up. I'm in contact with the adoptive parents of an older half-sibling and have (anonymously) found other half-siblings on Facebook.

I think as an adopter, particularly as a single adopter, it's important to be proactive about training. I've done an 'Introduction to Theraplay', and I've also had Filial Therapy training. I am open to anything on offer and I'm hoping to get on a post-adoption course about therapeutic parent training.

The adoption support team did a presentation to a whole school staff meeting on attachment and developmental delay, which was much appreciated. I think the school is very enthusiastic about having a parent who 'gets it' about these things!

DILIP and JAMES (2015)

They've Got Two Dads!

Dilip and James are a gay couple who have adopted three brothers, although, at the time of our first interview with them, they had only adopted two and were not expecting a third. Dilip is mixed race, with white and South Asian parents. His father's family is Hindu. James is white and Christian, and they are both qualified social workers. Dilip and James were discouraged when they first approached an adoption agency, but a second approach to their local authority swiftly found them approved as adopters and parents. Here they are in conversation about their decision to adopt, their assessment and the reality of being parents to Anthony and Jake.

Dilip: We'd both decided we wanted to be parents before we got together eight years ago. We thought about different ways of parenting, considered other avenues, but once we had explored adoption, we decided it was definitely the way, the best option for us. It was more being a parent that was important to us, rather than having a child that was genetically ours. I think the fact that we both worked within social work meant we had a sense of reality about what adoption meant and how it could work.

James: I know quite a few people who have been adopted, or families who have adopted, and I've seen that working, despite all the challenges that those families have had to face. So we had a feeling that adoption could work for us.

Dilip: The first time we explored it, three or four years ago, we rang a voluntary adoption agency and it wasn't very positive. They didn't do anything particularly badly and we only had minor contact, but on the phone they asked me what my wife's name was and I remember thinking, 'Well maybe this isn't right', as they were an agency that marketed themselves as having expertise in lesbian and gay adopters!

The other thing that was discouraging was the implication from them that we wouldn't be considered seriously until we'd lived together for a certain length of time. Although we had been together for about five years, we hadn't lived together for very long. We were told, 'Oh well you need to leave it, you don't really know each other well enough. You don't really know what it's like until you've had to share a bathroom with somebody', or something like that. It rubbished our relationship and I felt they were seeing us as a less valid couple.

James: It just didn't feel right. Even though they hadn't met us, our relationship wasn't quite right in their eyes. They were using these arbitrary measures to judge us rather than being interested in finding out more about us. I did wonder if they were a bit heterosexist.

We decided a few months later to apply to the local authority. I filled in an online form and we had a phone call from them within a week. We had the sense that we were just exploring the possibility of adoption at the beginning, that at any point we could just call a halt to it or put it on pause, but this time it just felt like it was working and was going in the right direction. The social worker said that she really wanted to document the nature of our relationship rather than putting any emphasis on the length of time we had lived together.

Dilip: And that was nice, it cleared the way. We're not in a civil partnership or married and I don't think they asked about that – that's never been a stumbling block, and it wasn't an issue at panel.

Telling the family

James: As we were planning to adopt, we had to come out to extended members of our family. The majority of my uncles and aunts knew I was gay, but I'd never had a direct conversation with them about it. I think my parents had probably talked to them about it. As the adoption got closer, I realised we were just going to be outed all over the place once the kids were with us. We had to get on and tell people about the adoption and about being gay because the kids would just tell everybody.

One of the sticking points, the reason why I hadn't been more open about being gay, was that I'd never come out to one aunt who I am particularly close to but who doesn't live in the UK. I'd never had the conversation with other uncles and aunts because it felt like it would be a deception not telling her first. So I emailed her and we had various email exchanges and tearful phone conversations. I'd left it far too long and wished I'd done it a long time ago.

Adoption preparation

Dilip: We met our social worker in February and we went to the preparation groups in July. There was a two-day course one week and then a one-day course two weeks later. Once we had completed the preparation course, we were assessed, and within six months we went to panel for approval.

James: They 'fast-tracked' us, although we were never sure why. There were about 11 couples on the training course and we were the only gay couple and, although we have never had to talk openly about our sexuality to professionals, the only time it was raised was during the adoption training.

Dilip: It didn't feel uncomfortable, I don't think they necessarily did it because we were there, but they talked about gay couples. They handed around two examples of adopters' life story books, preparation books for adoptees, and one example was from a straight couple and one from two gay men. It was nice they'd done that – they might have done that for us, but I reckon they might have done it anyway, because they were just good examples.

The sessions were not about personal exploration really, more about introducing us to the system, talking about children in care, attachment theory, grief and loss. They showed some quite ropy video about attachment in infants, which felt very general and didn't really address specific issues that might come up for adopters, like attachment in older children or those children who have been separated from foster carers and birth parents.

James: But in lots of ways the training was quite good. A challenging aspect was the inclusion in some sessions of a student social worker who was not a good advert for our profession! It was clear she hadn't prepared anything and didn't know what she was talking about. It was really embarrassing for her and for the social workers. They brought in the assistant team manager who intervened on her behalf.

Dilip: They talked about situations you might find yourself in; how you might deal with these, what you would need to consider and how you might help children who might have issues of separation. That was really good.

James: I think a lot of those involved in the course relied heavily on their own practice and experience, different situations they had been in. There was also a little bit of assessment going on – every now and then I caught the deputy team manager just watching people. I got the sense she was sussing us out.

Dilip: At one point she said, 'You'll all be great', and I felt that I was no longer being judged. I don't remember gender being an issue. There was a discussion about homophobia in schools. One of the social workers said she had been telling her 15-year-old daughter that, when she was young, there was a stigma about being out as a lesbian and her daughter said, 'Well, that's not an issue these days.' Someone in the group disagreed with her and she said, 'Maybe it's different, easier for boys', which suggested that she thought young gay men don't face as much homophobia. Then there was some discussion about homophobic bullying in schools, but although it was good that it was discussed, it wasn't dealt with in a complex way, because it's important to recognise that some young people still face homophobia.

Then there was this exercise where you had to put yourself on one side of the room if you thought something was okay and on the other if you thought it was bad. One of the questions was, 'Is it ever okay to slap your child?' Then there was, 'Should you force your children to eat everything on their plate?' And loads of people said, in some circumstances you should (I don't know if 'force' was the right word). And the social worker said we shouldn't do that, 'We don't want fat kids, do we?' I was standing next to some quite chubby people and they just thought that was really funny. So there was some insensitivity and they were a little bit dogmatic. Bringing up children can be complicated; rules are not always clear-cut.

James: I don't remember race being discussed a lot. There was a Pakistani couple there: he spoke English, his wife didn't, and he only interpreted things for her occasionally, so she was just sitting there not participating in much of the discussion or the group sessions. That did bother me.

The assessment

James: The social worker came to our home maybe four times; it was shorter than I expected. She expected us to fill in the assessment form ourselves. I assumed that a lot of it would be about getting us to understand what we were doing and why we wanted to do it. I thought there would be more discussion, but it was mostly about us getting everything down on paper.

They didn't want our life histories – they were more interested in us exploring issues about how we'd be parents, how we would deal with certain situations. It was about us completing the form rather than the social worker helping us to understand situations. We emailed our answers to her and she would come back the next time with a few questions arising from our emails that she wanted to explore further. But even then, it was less about wanting to explore our answers; more about what would come up at panel and trying to anticipate their questions.

Dilip: She didn't really ask us about coming out. I remember she described your parents as 'evangelical Christians', but she never asked about their views on your being gay.

James: It felt as though generalisations were being made during the assessment. The social worker almost skated over questions of sexuality, in a funny way. It didn't sound like she had registered the implications in her mind and we didn't really talk about our sexuality. We talked about a support group where there are a lot of men and she said that, in her experience, there are a lot more gay men than lesbians wanting to adopt, and she wondered why. I said that it was possibly more complicated for gay men to create a family biologically, but she'd not thought that through, even though she had worked with both gay men and lesbians.

Dilip: But there was a lot of conversation about ethnicity and skin colour. I think the way people look is quite a feature of adoption. She wanted to know if we would take on a child with two black parents. She talked about these Zimbabwean kids who've got two black African parents, but we didn't feel we would be right for them. We were asked whether that was because of the way they looked and part of it was – not for our sake, but for their sake – these kids would have had two dads who they were clearly not biologically related to, as I am mixed race Asian and James is white British.

Skin colour is often one of the things that people actually talk about when they talk about likeness or belonging. I found it quite hard, as these Zimbabwean children were the first children they'd mentioned to us. We didn't know our social worker that well at that point and we were still treading water a little bit and she sort of discouraged us from 'narrowing our sights' to Asian mixed race children only. She said there were a lot of Asian parents wanting to adopt and only a few Asian children coming into the system. She did ask us how we would deal with racism and whether I'd experienced racism as a child and how I'd dealt with it.

James: She asked me sort of parallel questions, but not relating to race, more about religion. Things that might make me part of a minority group, I suppose.

Dilip: She reflected on how gay men had become more visible over the past five or ten years. Basically, she was saying that there are loads of gay adopters around, there's nothing 'weird' about it anymore and there hasn't been for a long time. It 'just isn't an issue', and she was 'cool' with that.

James: I think ten years ago this issue of whether you were out or not was an issue, sometimes the only issue.

Dilip: I think loads of straight people are offended by the idea that you need to be assessed to become an adoptive parent. My GP said, 'Oh, this is ridiculous, why should you have to answer these questions on the medical?' And I was thinking, 'Well, of course I should, because I don't want looked-after children being adopted by someone who's more likely to become really ill or die when they're still young.'

James: My GP was much the same. She said, 'As long as you appear fit and healthy, you'll be fine, you'll be able to cope fine with two little ones.' So she just ticked loads of boxes and that was that.

Dilip: During the assessment we were asked if we wanted to adopt boys or girls, and it came up at panel. I think you wanted boys and I said boys or girls. There was no talk about how we would cope with girls with puberty and periods etc. It was just presented as, what do you want, and ethnicity was talked about in a similar way. In adoption today, there's more of a 'what do you want?' than a 'let's match you', which was, I suppose, the situation ten years ago.

James: I was surprised that there wasn't much discussion during the assessment about our own experiences of parenting, which I expected. We worked hard on the workbook, crafted that, though I don't think it really said anything that we hadn't thought about before. It made me think about my own experiences and about our different styles.

Dilip: I remember talking to a friend who's a safeguarding officer and she was saying, 'Well, they won't be fooled by this stuff. You know, if you say you have your niece and nephew round every month they'll want to see evidence of it.' But they took everything at face value. From the start it was like, 'Well, we know you're good, we just need to get this through.'

At the beginning, they asked if we had plans to enter a civil partnership, but we said we didn't and the social worker just moved on. One social worker referred to us as a gay couple and the other as a same-sex couple but that doesn't feel problematic; they don't avoid the issue. We did feel during the assessment that they hadn't realised what would be different for gay adopters, but nothing said or done by our current social worker suggests to me that she hasn't thought things through.

We talked about a gay support group and she kind of just shrugged her shoulders, as if to say, 'Fine, if that's going to be useful.' It was a non-issue. We weren't asked, but we did point out early on that we had straight families and friends. We did feel we needed to make it clear that we had heterosexual and homosexual friends. If I was doing the assessment, I'd be concerned that a couple might not bother with straight people. I would also ask a straight couple if they knew any LGBT families, but I wonder if many social workers would do that.

James: We do know quite a few LGBT families who have adopted and we put some of them down as members of our support network. There is a definite shift from the days when social workers would steam in and ask, 'Are there any heterosexuals in your life?' That would never happen now.

We talked a bit about lifestyle. I think they were talking about the differences between foster carers and adopters and not to assume anything – some of that was clearly about class but I don't think it was labelled as such. The social worker was talking about a girl who liked fish fingers and then her adoptive parents cooked them and she didn't like them because they were grilled and from Bird's Eye and she was used to having Morrisons fish fingers fried. So class was talked about in those terms, like, 'Do you put your ketchup in the cupboard?', that sort of thing! When you start talking about culture, you soon realise that everybody assumes all sorts of things without realising it.

Dilip: During the assessment we were given a lot of feedback on what we said and the social worker explained how she was interpreting or analysing that. It felt like a gathering of information that our social worker then reflected on. I don't think we ever saw the full report.

James: She got us to sign the form by faxing the back page of it and getting us to fax it back. We never saw the full form, we just saw page 35, which is not cool, really, but it doesn't worry me.

We were approved for two children under six; gender wasn't specified. They did ask about whether we were prepared to take on a disabled kid. The social worker had us in mind for a group of three children, but we weren't sure we could manage that. But by the time we went to panel we already knew about the two children who are now with us – they were three and one-and-a-half at the time – and after we had heard about them for the first time, we just thought about those two children – our children.

Matching

Dilip: We said we were looking for children with a mixed race heritage, reflecting our heritage to some degree. They discussed a number of children with us with different profiles.

James: That came up at panel. We were asked how we would promote the children's racial heritage, which is Indian and White British, Hindu and Christian, different generations of different religions.

Dilip: When you talk to the children's social worker, the fact that one of us is Christian is a real positive.

James: Their mother was adamant she wanted her children to go to church regularly. She became Christian almost as a way of rejecting her family who were Hindu. It's interesting how racial and religious identity is perceived.

Dilip: But if they want to have a relationship with her when they're adults, and they've been brought up going to church, that is some commonality isn't it? I mean, that's the whole point of matching, isn't it? That's, for me, the most important bit: to create some connections with the family that you might have in the future.

James: That's true, although it's hard to know in 18 years' time, if they will still want to go to church and, given their mother's volatility and mental health issues, she could have become Muslim by then or something completely different. But I suppose the intention was to get as good a match as possible.

Dilip: Both panels were lovely – the approval panel and the matching panel – very positive. The woman who chaired the second panel started off by saying, 'This is a match with some complexities, but, on the whole, we're optimistic.' The complexities weren't about being gay – these brothers had a very difficult start to life. They asked a lot of questions – two couples ahead of us had both cancelled for different reasons, so they had been twiddling their thumbs waiting for us to arrive.

The only time they talked about us being same-sex was when they talked about schools and recommended a school that they felt was positive towards LGBT families. They probably just wanted to make it clear that they didn't have a problem with our sexuality. Their major concern was the approval of our families and whether the children would be embraced into the wider family unit.

James: They know that neither of our families are geographically close, so there wasn't an assumption that any of them would be jumping in to babysit.

Dilip: They didn't do the 'gender role model' thing or ask if the children would come into contact with people of the opposite sex.

James: We did talk about the kids we knew. We had three referees, all of whom have children. They didn't ask us if we knew any other gay or lesbian parents. They did ask us if we planned to join a support group and we said we would, but we haven't as yet.

The children

Dilip: They are mixed race brothers, Anthony and Jake, with an Indian mother. They don't have any additional needs. The introduction process was fairly quick. It happened over ten days in February. It was really cold; there was still snow on the ground. The idea was that we spend a day with them in the foster carers' house and then take them out, so that we gradually took on more responsibility for the boys before they came to our house. But there were only a limited number of indoor places we could actually go to with them. They wanted to run around and go to the playground. But we were trampling through snow to get to these swings and bringing them back with red hands. Anthony slipped and grazed himself. They were freezing and we were a bit knackered and terrified.

James: We met them on a Wednesday and the following Monday we brought them to our home for the day and that made things a lot easier because we could plan lots of things to do inside. Every day that week they came for longer and longer and then they stayed the night on the Friday and they never went back to their foster family.

Dilip: Driving them back to the foster parents during the week had been difficult, as Jake has quite severe eczema and, when he's anxious, he starts scratching himself, so the whole process was really quite traumatic for him. His skin was really bad. In the car on the way back we couldn't really stop Jake scratching and he was crying and we were stuck on the M60 in a traffic jam. It was just really awful.

James: It's funny – at the time you just think, 'Well, this is just parenthood.' We didn't fret about it and just thought it would get better. The foster carers were lovely. We'd put the boys to bed when we got back to their house and then have a cup of tea with them. They had really mixed feelings about Anthony and Jake leaving. They really wanted the kids to have a good placement, but were upset to see them go. It was very moving.

Dilip: They were really amazing and supportive towards us. They visited us here during the introduction process and brought their son, who was older than our two but had a good relationship with Jake. It helped him because the foster family's son was a big figure in his life – and still is. He was so excited about showing him his new bedroom.

James: I remember when we had the inter-agency meeting – the planning meeting for the introduction process – looking at this really detailed plan of what we'd do and what time we'd arrive at the foster parents and thinking, 'This is never going to work, it's never going to be that quick', but actually it was. They were bang on about the pace and how many days it would take. The social worker knew how excited Jake would be when the foster carer's son visited us. I thought Jake might become really withdrawn but he didn't. She got all these things right, and I think it's partly because she knows the children, but probably because she knows how these things work.

Dilip: We felt that the introduction, if anything, could have been slightly shorter because by day eight or nine, we were all getting tired going back and forth to pick them up. However, it was traumatic when the children finally arrived because Anthony was so distraught when he realised he was never going back to the foster family.

James: The introduction process is not really about building anything more than a superficial connection; the relationship comes after that. I know that Anthony really wanted it to work but I remember the journey bringing him back here to stay; he was so tense and on the verge of tears. You could tell he was just being really, really brave. I can't imagine how I would be, really, at his age. But it's good that he feels he can communicate his feelings.

Dilip: He can't help himself!

James: That's perhaps why they chose gay men to look after him, because it's a match, you know?!

Dilip: Well, we are good at sharing emotionally. Since they arrived we have had to have more dealings with schools, doctors and other services as a couple, so in that sense we have had to be 'out' as gay in lots more situations. Not long after they came to us, we went round to the nursery where Jake now goes and we went together so it was kind of pretty clear from the start that we were his dads.

James: Our relationship was just acknowledged and embraced without anything explicit being said. They were kind of nice about it and they say, 'Is it daddy or is it papa?' but they say it in a nice way. At playgroup I talk about Anthony's other daddy and sometimes they address me as Anthony's 'mum': 'Anthony's mum, can you sign here?' Actually, Jake calls me 'mummy'. I'm getting used to being called mummy!

We had a more difficult experience at the GP's.

Dilip: That wasn't great.

James: There was a whole lack of understanding about adoption.

Dilip: And some very officious behaviour from the reception staff.

James: The GP was lovely, but the reception staff made problems because the children had one surname on their health records and another that we use – this was before their adoption, so the children's health records still had their birth surnames. But there are particular reasons why we didn't want them to be known by the name on their health records, and reasons why the social worker didn't want them to be known by that name either.

Dilip: The social worker wrote a letter to that effect and we got a letter back from the GP saying they were happy to make appointments under our surnames so that the boys' birth name wasn't announced in the waiting room. Then, when we got there, the receptionist ticked us off because in her view that wasn't appropriate, even though they had a letter from the GP approving the plan.

And there was some stuff specifically about us being a gay couple. We took the boys to the surgery the day after they were placed with us to get registration forms to fill in. This was before we had the letter from the GP. We tried to explain, but they didn't get it, and they called someone else from their office who was really officious. When I rang up she effectively said, 'You come here with your new partner and these children from a previous relationship, and we can't treat your partner as their dad.' I told her that we were adopting the boys together. But she had filled in her own backstory from nowhere that these were my biological children from a straight relationship and I'd just moved to the area with my new gay partner! It was really odd.

And meanwhile, behind the reception desk is a big certificate with five stars from the Lesbian and Gay Foundation saying that this GP's surgery provided a wonderful service to lesbians and gay men!

James: Well we've got a gay doctor there, that's probably how they managed to get that, but it doesn't matter what the doctors are like, it matters what everyone is like. I suppose it just showed that a lot of people can't compute this actual relationship and so they invent something else. But that's the only trouble we've had actually, isn't it? Everyone else has been lovely – our neighbours, friends, everyone we come regularly into contact with.

Dilip: We told them all in advance that we were adopting these boys. We made a point of telling them so that they didn't suddenly make some strange comment in front of the kids, and they were all quite excited for us.

James: I'm getting less willing to talk about the adoption because a lot of people don't know what to say and so they talk about it as if it's just unproblematic.

Dilip: If they were our biological children, they might not ask so many questions, but because they're adopted, they feel they can, even in front of the children.

James: And it's all about what's happened to them before, which is why I'm getting more guarded. Well of course they'll have to tell people they're adopted because, clearly, they are not a product of our relationship, but there are other explanations, though adoption is the one that I'd like them to feel okay to use. But it's up to them. Sometimes there is a stigma attached to being adopted and we don't want to reproduce that at all. It's not a secret but it is private. I think that was a phrase used during the preparation groups.

Dilip: One thing that was interesting was when we were filling in the registration form for school. There was only a space for the name of a child's father and the name of the child's mother. So I signed as 'mum'! But that wasn't the case at the nursery. They asked for name of carer.

James: It's incredibly gender normative, that playgroup. You soon realise, though, that all the nursery rhymes that we sing go on about chattering women and snoring men.

Dilip: The foster carer pre-empted any problems the children might have about coming to a gay couple. Jake had a negative experience with his birth mum. The foster carer talked to him about the type of families he might go on to, and one of the options she suggested to him was a family where there were two dads. And he said he'd like two dads and he apparently then asked her to go and find him a family with two dads! And by that point she'd already met us. She told Jake she would have to speak to the social worker and see if she could find him a family like that, and then 'we'll check to see if they're alright and then if they're alright we'll see if you can meet them.' It was all quite cleverly done. But I don't think at this point he has any awareness of any negativity. It'll be interesting to see how he starts to process that once he encounters any sort of homophobic behaviour, as up until now he's not encountered anything.

James: So much depends on the school they go to. We've got a lot of choice about that, and we don't need to make any decisions for a while. It's nice that he feels that he's chosen us.

Dilip: Some women work associates feel they need to come and see them with the feeling that they do need more women in their lives, that kind of thing.

James: There was one really nice incident in Morrisons supermarket. We went there one evening and we were all tired and we hadn't had any tea, so we thought we'd just go to Morrisons' café and get a quick meal for the kids. I was in the queue and you went and did some shopping and Anthony and Jake stayed with me to get the food and the woman behind the till said: 'Oh you've got the easy job tonight, while mummy goes and does the shopping', or something like that, and the kids were calling me 'Papa'. And she said, 'What do they call mummy?' and I said, 'Oh no, it's daddy.' She said, 'Oh they've got two dads! That's lovely.' It was kind of completely unexpected, but it was kind of nice.

Dilip: She was really nice. When I joined you, she was chatting to the kids and very smiley. I think sometimes you can feel on the defensive in public situations like that, but actually there are lots of unexpected responses. You just get all this positive stuff from strangers when you are with children that you never, ever get as an adult man on his own. As soon as they reach eight or nine they'll be seen as potential troublemakers, but at this moment they're really cute and yeah, that's really interesting. Women talk to me in the park or in shops, you know, those sorts of things. They never would have done that before. All that's nice. It carries a lot of weight, I think. The fact that you're a parent means that you can be talked to in some way. And I think, as a dad, I behave differently as well.

James: Everyone around here knows the situation. We go to the park most afternoons around five together with the two kids, and, if anybody really stopped to think about it, it's pretty clear what the setup is. Walking along this street, I think people know that we live together with these two kids, even though it's quite a big street. So, it's alright really. What do you think?

Dilip: I think it's alright.

DILIP and JAMES (2018)
The Arrival of Stanley...

Anthony and Jake's younger brother Stanley was born a week after they were placed with us and went straight into a foster placement. At the time that the interview was done it wasn't confirmed that he would come to live with his brothers. At first we weren't sure whether it would be right for the two older boys, or whether we could cope with three children, and the legal proceedings also went on longer than first anticipated. However, when Stanley was eight months old, he was placed for adoption with us. The adoption orders for all three children were made at the same time, about ten months after Stanley was placed with us.

The three boys are very settled now (three years after Anthony and Jake arrived), although, looking back, it probably took two years for this to happen. The older two boys are in school and this has been really positive in lots of ways, such as helping with routines and developing friendships with other children. The school's demographic reflects the local area, so around half the children are white and half are Asian, mainly of Pakistani origin. There haven't been any problems with the school about us being gay or the children being adopted. Almost all the other parents seem very accepting. Occasionally we've had other parents who are confused that the boys don't live with their mother, but we've not had to deal with any offensive remarks so far. There is a child in Jake's class who has two mums.

We still see Anthony and Jake's foster family regularly. They're really supportive and the children are close to them. Stanley's foster carers do not want direct contact, but we exchange letters once a year.

The boys talk about their birth parents from time to time and look at photos. During the first year or so this was more upsetting for Anthony as he still had vivid memories of his parents, but this has become easier over time. Stanley has quite a vague understanding of who they are but talks about his birth daddy from time to time. We exchange letters with the boys' father and mother once a year, and are keeping these for the boys to read when they are older.

Our families are involved in the children's lives to varying degrees. James' parents are really loving grandparents to the boys, and we stay with them for a few days most school holidays.

BARBARA and SHAZIA (2014)
Getting Caught Up in the System

Barbara and Shazia are an African Caribbean and an Asian woman who have been fostering as a couple for seven years. Barbara has worked in education and is now a psychotherapist. Shazia is a doctor in general practice. When Barbara and Shazia decided to go into fostering, Barbara's childhood in care deterred one agency from taking them on, while convincing another that the couple would make ideal foster parents. Barbara tells of the rejection they faced when they first attempted to become foster parents, and of the joys and challenges they have faced since becoming foster parents.

We wanted to offer a home to children whose parents and homes were no longer available to them. I felt that this was a group of children that we could help through that trauma and make them feel okay. I've got two birth children – they're now 27 and 22 – so I knew what was involved. We thought about adoption, but for me it was always fostering, though Shazia wanted us to think about adoption as well as fostering.

We didn't hide the fact that we were lesbian. It was always very evident and we were clear about it, but we never actually talked to the agencies about it, which is a bit bizarre. I thought it might be an obstacle; even though I know in all the literature and media we'd seen that lesbians can adopt and foster, I still thought it might come up. But although they didn't bring it up with us, I think it's clear from the children who come to stay with us that the social worker has discussed it with them. You know that by the conversation.

It's almost one of the first questions for some of the older ones, and even for some of the little ones that have gone on for adoption. During the introductory period with adopters, the adopters will come to us and say, 'Oh, you sleep in the same bed', so again there's been this conversation with potential adopters about what it is that goes on in this house. It's never been an issue, but it's not an open conversation.

First application

We first applied to foster through the local authority after going to one of their information days. Afterwards a social worker came to talk to us about whether or not fostering was a viable option for us. That decided, we went on a two-day training course and were allocated a social worker to talk us through the process. They started the assessment straight away. The social worker said that they had to get references from the people we worked for and discussed the people she'd need to interview, like my children, and that seemed all right to me. Shazia's reference came back immediately; mine didn't.

This became an issue and I reminded my team leader and she would say, 'Oh yeah, I need to do it.' But she kept not doing it. The social worker actually wrote to me saying that unless she got my reference she was going to close the case. I was outraged. They didn't close it, but they did make it very difficult. So five months later, the reference did come. And the social worker said, 'Oh, we've got your reference and we were really surprised by it because it was a really good reference.' What were they expecting?

Our social worker had overlooked the fact that we both worked full time and said that one of us needed to work part time. We had always planned, if we were approved as foster carers, that I would reduce my working hours or give up my job. I had discussed and already agreed this with my employers, but our social worker wasn't terribly happy with that. She wanted me to give up my job, while at the same time telling me that being asked to give up my job wasn't an indication that we were going to be approved. So that was a bit of a stumbling block. Why would anyone give up their job for something that might not happen? We were at loggerheads; there was no doubt about that.

They had quite an outdated model of family life, that you have a full-time breadwinner and a full-time house person before you even know the ages or the capabilities of children who will be placed with you. I certainly think that at that point, during assessment, you've got no idea how fostering will influence your life, what impact it will have.

I had brought up two children while working full time. I wasn't completely ignorant of the demands children would place on our lives. But when my kids were young I picked them up at the end of the day from school or from daycare. There wasn't the demand to attend meetings on their behalf that there is with a child in care. The only meeting I had to go to was parent evenings at school. But with foster children there are a whole host of meetings, hospital appointments and medicals that must be attended – all sorts of things that really pinch at your day. If you are working full time those meetings can be hard to accommodate – someone has to be available.

The whole process with the local authority social workers was difficult. We had thought deeply about fostering children and about the different issues that might come up, like different cultures and different religions. But our experiences weren't valued, or even seen; it was like we were being tested but we didn't know what we were being tested on.

Things go wrong

Now I don't really understand why there was this clash with the social worker, but there was. From our point of view, you're in a strange situation where you want to be helpful so that you can get on with this process, and you don't want to upset that process. I don't want someone to see the worst side of me. You want your best clothes on, don't you? You're in this artificial situation. But there came a point when I began to think, 'Actually, you're being unfair.'

So of course she begins to see a bit of my personality when I say: 'Actually I don't want to give my job up, I don't think it's the right thing to give my job up at this point. I will give my job up, you've got my word – you can ring work to find out that I've said to them. I will give up my job – as soon as I'm approved, but at this stage?' Anyway, in the end I decided that I would go part time. So I work three days. She felt she could then proceed with the assessment. So you can see where it's become a bit of a battle, and not a good battle. I don't know why, but it just felt like we were in this fight.

She agreed to start the assessment and then, even before she actually started, she told us she was going to close the case. I asked why and she said, 'Well, I feel like you're really aggressive.' I said, 'I wonder why you'd use that word, because there are many words you could use for me but I don't think aggressive is one of them, I don't think it describes me anywhere near accurately.'

She said, 'You're really sarcastic.' I said, 'Oh, why do you think I'm sarcastic?' And she said, 'Well, when I asked you when I could interview your son in September, you said Christmas Eve.' I said, 'Oh, so why do you think I said that?' She said, 'Well, I think you were being rude.' I said, 'Well, you know he's in the army, that's the day he comes home, on Christmas Eve. Why didn't you just ask me if I was being funny?' She said, 'Well, okay, I take your point.' I said, 'But now you've written that down and it makes me look like an arse actually, like I was being sarcastic when in fact maybe you'd misunderstood that he's in the army, he doesn't come home all the time. I haven't said that you can't talk to him.' So that was another misunderstanding.

We had a series of unfortunate mishaps. I suspect with somebody else maybe those things wouldn't have happened. Anyway, she agreed to carry on with the assessment. But of course I began to wonder whether I wanted to. Anyway, we wanted to foster, we had to get through, so we decided that we'd get on with it. So they then interviewed each of us separately, talking about our lives from birth until we met. I don't know why they do that, but that's how they do it.

She spent three sessions with Shazia getting her story, and the idea was to spend three sessions with me. Maybe we did two sessions. Now, I think that they were fine actually, but obviously she felt very differently, and this was all against the backdrop of what had gone on in the last few months, which doesn't bode well, does it? Eventually she said, 'Actually, I don't think I can sponsor you.' She felt that my story wasn't coherent. She didn't think that I was ready to foster or that I'd thought about it. It was quite shocking actually.

It's ironic. I have worked in education for years and trained as a counsellor. But she didn't think I could work with professionals either. So I told her the schools I worked with and suggested she talked to the head teachers who could give her a picture of how I worked with professionals. But she never did talk to the schools.

She also felt there was a conflict of interest with my job. Looking back, I can see why she said what she did, and one of the reasons is my early life, growing up in care. When she wanted to talk about my early life, I couldn't tell her that much about it. I didn't know where I'd lived, and I always had this idea that I'd been fostered, but wasn't sure. The thing I did remember is living in this children's home in Halifax Road from the age of 9 to about 16; then I went to live in another children's home, and then I got a flat, and the rest is kind of history. But she felt that there were too many gaps. I did point out that, back then, when I was a child, social workers didn't take care of your history. There was no life story book; I haven't got any photos of my childhood. I bought a camera when I was about 11 and most of the photos I have are those. So my record of my childhood is as coherent as I think it can be.

And there was a point in the second interview where I was talking to her about living at Halifax Road and she was trying to work out my relationship with my mother and the people who looked after me – my schooling, attitudes, interests, things like that. My relationship with the principal at Halifax Road wasn't good, actually. I don't know why. That's another story. There were all sort of problems there I've since learned about. But as a young child then, you've only got what you can remember.

So there was a point in the interview where she said: 'Do you think anybody loved you when you were growing up?' And of course I'd not considered that question myself, and even if she was aware of it, the way she gave it to me was like a bomb. It was like, hmm, maybe she has a point actually. I remember going out to the toilet and thinking 'Oh my god, maybe they didn't love me.' Anyway, I answered that question, I said: 'No, maybe not.' But I don't think she realised the enormity of that question, and maybe that was part of her decision. She said that I had no self-awareness. Maybe she was right, but I don't think it would have stopped me from bringing my own children up and holding down a full-time job and making this huge decision about wanting to foster and whether or not I would be capable of fostering. These are questions that I've had to ask myself; that I'm doing it for the right reason and not the wrong reason. So it's not a subject that I've taken lightly.

So we come to a point where she decides that actually I can't go any further because she doesn't think it'll be a very positive F1 report that she has to write for the panel. We have a meeting together, all of us, and I remember Shaz saying to her, 'You know, you're really on at Barbara and you need to get off her back, and I'm not sure why you're doing that.' Now, I hadn't been aware of that, though I had been aware that there was some tension, but I think I thought I could rectify it by providing what it was that she needed, but it was obviously more than that. So Shaz said, 'I wonder if we need to have a different social worker because maybe things can't go right now.' So we then had a meeting with her and her manager.

It was interesting because her manager said: 'I always knew when she was coming to see you because she was really anxious in the office.' So I said, 'So you knew that she wasn't in a good place to be doing this and yet you let her come?' I really wanted to be a foster carer, I wanted to get through the process. I told her that I had to accept what she was saying, but I found myself wondering if it was true. So we kind of came to this stalemate. I think I'm a really fair person, I can see things from most angles, and that probably gets in my way sometimes.

So I suggested it might be better if two social workers carried out the interview assessment; that way, if one of them felt concerns they could talk to one another. I felt that if they knew she was struggling to assess us, it was not fair to her to let her come. And not fair to us. These were objective things, but actually they affected us. But they said they wouldn't reconsider and by then I was thinking, 'I'm not sure that I want you to reconsider. Even if you send another social worker, I'm not sure that I can manage that now.'

At that final meeting – it was such a damning meeting, like we were the worst people in the world – I said, 'Has there been anything positive in the last eight months?' So the social worker said: 'Well, you've both got very good jobs. I don't know how you do your jobs.' But that wasn't what I was asking. So, I asked again, 'Has there been anything positive? Even if it was just: "you've been welcoming, there's always a cup of tea, you've always made some cakes" – I don't know.' And she said: 'No, there hasn't. No, nothing.' So, for me that was it. I just said: 'Okay, I have to leave now, I can't continue. For me there's no point.' But Shaz did continue. I think she was very angry and felt like she needed to kind of say, you know, what are you saying about us?

It was absolutely awful. Damning. And they had let us continue through the process for eight months. So we went into this complaints procedure. But I think at that meeting I'd withdrawn, to be quite honest. It was Shaz who really wanted to complain. But there came a point in the complaints procedure where I had to say: 'Shaz, look, we went into this to foster, either we're going to fight this organisation, and give it all our energy, or we're going to think about trying to find a way to foster.'

I think by then I had begun to wonder if I wanted to foster. If my life, or my house, or me, wasn't good enough, then fine, we'd tried, we should just leave it. But Shaz really wanted to foster. So I decided to do something completely different and I did a diploma in photography. The time came time to apply for the degree course and I was thinking 'I'm not sure I really want to do this', at the same time thinking 'I'm not fostering.' That's when I decided to get some counselling. I felt I needed to talk to somebody neutral to make sure that I'd made the decision because it was the right decision for me and not because of the process that I'd been through. Anyway, it became apparent with the therapist over a number of weeks that actually I did want to foster, I really did, and so we said that we'd try again, and that was when we went through an independent fostering agency.

Starting the process again

That was an interesting process because they have to make their checks with social services. So they got the reports, read them, and came back to us and said, 'So why do you think the case was closed?' I said, 'Because there was a personality clash and a lot of misunderstanding. It was just an unfortunate set of circumstances.' They agreed to start the fostering assessment again to see how it went. I think they were expecting to hit a brick wall, to find out what went wrong, because from the paperwork they couldn't see what went wrong.

So we started the process again – and as part of that we were sent to a preparation training session with other potential fosterers. We were probably the only lesbians in the group – probably the only lesbian, gay and black people in the group, actually. That wasn't acknowledged in the preparation groups for social services or for the private company. They say anybody can foster and adopt, but you get the feeling that the other couples don't expect there to be gay and lesbian people amidst them. It's like something they read about but that doesn't exist.

The fact that we were a lesbian couple wasn't particularly addressed in the assessment. I think one of the social workers asked us what we would say to the kids about our relationship and about our sleeping arrangements. In our house there are three floors and we're on the top floor, and we don't have kids on the top floor anyway. That was just a rule, and a rule that's worked really well.

I wonder now whether the real concern was that we'd be kissing and having sex or something instead of looking after the kids. But well, that's not how it is really. We're quite busy doing other things. We picked up on this unspoken concern of theirs, but they're not children's concerns actually. They did talk about male role models. It was never a concern of mine. I mean, I've brought a son up and he's fine, he doesn't have any problems, and we do have male friends. I think they asked us if we had a civil partnership. They would refer to us as a 'same-sex' couple rather than a 'lesbian' couple. For some reason people find that easier to say.

Racism and diversity

Race issues are not handled, full stop. There have been issues that both of us have had to bring up. There was an incident during a course on equality and diversity training that I was on. This guy was telling us all about diversity and getting people to be interactive. Anyway, he wanted a lift down to the station. I gave him a lift and he said, 'What does your husband do?' So that's his take on diversity?

There was another support group meeting about culture. I was in this room with all the other foster carers and one of them said: 'I don't see what's wrong with using the word "Paki" or "nigger". We all use it. It's real.' And the trainer was black. I said: 'Well, I don't use that word.' And he said: 'I bet everyone in here uses the word Paki.' I said 'I find it offensive', and then had to explain to him why. But he found it very difficult to take on board. Anyway, I spoke to my social worker about it and said: 'There are some things you can let go, but I don't think you can let that go.' I hadn't heard that kind of language since I was in the playground at the age of ten. But they didn't deal with it and I didn't go back to those group meetings.

The trainer didn't address these issues. He made it clear at the beginning that he was there to hear what we had to say. And in one sense I thought actually he was quite good in how he handled it because he allowed people to say what they needed to say, and he said that he wouldn't be running back to the providers of the course to tell on us. So I think in one sense he dealt with it and in another sense he didn't challenge it, because he was there to hear them. If he'd have said in the beginning, 'Right, I'm going to challenge you', I don't think people would have spoken. So I think actually it was quite clever – because at least he heard the truth of the situation. So race isn't really dealt with.

We're both black, we want black children. We know that there's this disproportionate number of black children in care. But the agency advised us not to say that we would just take black children. And we'd hear other foster carers talking about the children they were looking after. One said, 'Oh we've got three Asian kids, we just get them a takeaway for food.' And I asked him what language they speak, and he said, 'Oh, Muslim.' And I said, 'That'll be their religion, not their language.' I mean, I can't imagine how it was for these children.

It's interesting that we are not used as a resource for black children. There was this email that came to me via my supervising social worker suggesting I book on this course about plaiting hair and creaming skin and looking after black children. I said: 'Do you really want me to book on this course? I'm black for god's sake, and you're going to tell me how to manage my own hair and skin?' I don't think it occurred to them that I'm black so they probably didn't need to send it to me.

One of the things that disturbed me on the culture course was that all the foster carers kept saying 'Oh, we'll look after any child, they're all the same.' But we're not all the same. Different children need different things. But if you say that people get offended – like, 'What, we're not good enough to look after black kids?' You can't even start that conversation.

One of the things that I remember from my childhood, when I lived at Halifax Road, was that nobody knew how to do our hair. I remember this woman, she'd obviously got fed up with our hair and she went to buy a steel comb that she proceeded to comb our hair with. It doesn't work, does it? I've got school photos from that time and you can see that nobody gives our hair any attention and our skin looks very dry and patchy.

Becoming foster parents

So, we are going through the fostering process with the new agency and it is a good process. We're anxious about it, but we sail through it. They did their F1 form – that is the standard form whether you are going through social services or a private agency. After you have been approved the form is added to; records are kept of all the children you have fostered and how successful those placements have been. It becomes an ongoing case file.

We got a copy of the report before we went to panel. It was shocking to read, because you're reading your life on paper. But our social worker told me not to be shocked. She'd used my history to inform the rest of the report. She felt that my difficult start in life would help me to foster. They looked at that part of my life in a very different way. It was really reassuring. The panel asked us a few questions – I don't think they asked us enough questions – and that was it. Almost straight away we got a referral for three kids, even though we were only approved to take two.

Diversity policy

I'm sure the agency has a policy on diversity, but my guess is it's a piece of paper – and unless an issue comes up, it's not dealt with. They don't really have to give it any attention. They told us that they don't get many referrals where children are black but they could have dealt with that in a different way, like maybe putting our profile out to agencies looking locally for foster carers and saying: 'We've got carers who are black, if you've got children, particularly long-term children, who might benefit from being placed with black foster parents.' The agency does advertise the fact that it takes sibling groups, but children are often split up, and here's a house that would welcome them. I feel very strongly about having sibling groups, particularly black sibling groups. I think that's where we've missed being with a local authority. We were invited to this foster carers event and I noticed how many white foster carers had black kids. It was depressing.

When they go to court, the judge will say, well, if you've got a placement today we'll give you the care order. So they then just accept anybody. There's not even an attempt to acknowledge that black children are better off in placements with black carers. What would be the saving to the state through the rest of those children's lives if those children were in a placement that affirms their identity, gets them on the right track at school, gets them achieving educationally, and gets them into employment? I don't think it's good enough.

One of the shortfalls of the system is that there is too little thinking ahead for the children. We've had a lot of little ones, under-fives, and we always say that we'll get them reading before they leave us. That is one of our aims; it's not difficult. We need to have more aspirations for children. There is a tendency to give up on them – even when they are only small. One little girl, who we were told would never read, was reading and learning and at the top of her class after she had been with us for a while.

The children in our care

At the moment we're fostering a disabled boy called Calum. We had said that the one group of children we wouldn't foster would be children with disabilities – unless they were deaf, as we both sign. But we were sent him by accident apparently. He has considerable disabilities and needs and has been with us now for 18 months. He's our ninth placement.

Before Calum we had three able children – a huge difference – and adjusting to those differences has not been acknowledged at all. I know that people expect you to go from placement to placement, but for me the placement with the three children was probably my perfect placement – I felt really engaged with the children and managing them kept me challenged. This placement with Calum does the same thing but in a totally different way. We have often done respite care, and usually care for groups of siblings. We have looked after about 28 kids – though we have not had anyone else since Calum arrived.

One of the reasons we hadn't wanted to take disabled children is because the house is on three floors – there aren't any downstairs bathrooms or bedrooms – just because of the practicalities really. We were approved to foster one child, or two children if they were siblings, of any age up to 16. And we did a mother and baby course so we could look after a mother and baby; we have to go back to panel every year, and it was suggested that we might train for that.

Looking after a disabled child is a challenge in terms of the range of healthcare professionals we have to deal with and be involved with. I felt at one point that I couldn't go on doing what they were asking us to do. So we have 'professional morning' now, once a fortnight, where people come between 9:00 and 11:30, and that's worked really well; so much so that the doctor we deal with is planning to roll it out to other parents.

There's an equivalent set of meetings with the local authority to review a case like Calum's. The same people are at the same meetings except for the people who lead the meetings – one by the social worker and one by the consultant. Now we are going to try joining these two meetings up. The social worker wants the information the consultant has and he has information the social worker needs, so it is a practical solution and cuts down how many meetings we actually go to.

In all the placements we have had, our sexuality has rarely come up as an issue. We had one boy who was 15 and I don't think it was appropriate for him to be here, mainly because of his history. But we were told 'It's for one night, possibly two nights.' He was here for five months, and it was clear that it wasn't the right place for him. We really had to manage that placement and just get through it. He was very, very abusive about our sexuality and he was always calling us 'Nigger' or 'Paki'…a whole range of things. It wasn't the right place for him to be. We could take that abuse, but I don't think you should be in a situation where that's what was happening. It wasn't healthy for him or for us. The problem was, there wasn't anywhere for him to go. Everybody agreed that he needed to be in a unit rather than a home, a family home. That was sad, but true. Eventually they did find a therapeutic unit in Northamptonshire that he went to, a beautiful place that I think he would have really benefited from. That is the only placement that we have had that I think was inappropriate.

Our sexuality hasn't been an issue with social workers or birth families when I've taken children in our care for contact. There was one set of kids we had, and the grandma complained because she said she couldn't understand what her grandson was saying anymore, he sounded too posh! That was really funny. They were from West Yorkshire, so I'm guessing they've got a much broader dialect or something.

We had a set of three under-fives, which was a nightmare of a placement in terms of management. We always try and take a placement that one of us can manage alone so that we don't always both have to be here. Obviously in the day time I'm going to be by myself. These children were all under four and two of them were autistic. It was hard. They were placed here because they had to be in three separate rooms because they weren't sure about the injury that had happened to the youngest child, just a baby. They arrived under police escort and throughout the placement were well protected. They had contact three or four times a week with their family and, in order to protect them and us, I would take them somewhere, somebody else would pick them up, and then they'd get to the contact. Part of that was to do with us being black, and part of it was to do with the kids being in care and the parents not accepting it.

Then, in the third week of the placement, there was an issue when they'd come home after a contact visit with their family. The social worker came to see us and said the parents had made an allegation that the kids had been abused by us. She was on the phone to her manager and said: 'I've got to strip them off and check them.' So she went through the kids and made a note, and one of them had some bruises. I didn't know he had bruises. She asked how he got them. I said: 'I don't know actually. He does throw himself around a lot; you can read my reports, I often make reference to that.' The manager was still on the phone and insisting she remove the children. Shazia was cooking their tea. But the social worker told me to pack their things and asked to take our car seats.

It had been difficult settling these kids down, but we had got to a point where we could communicate with them, and we were sorting out a school for the four-year-old. But they moved the kids.

It was a real shock. No negotiation. And they knew they've had problems with these parents all the way through.

Anyway, we were told that the kids were going to be examined at the hospital. And we were kind of in this limbo where we were waiting, and we were told the police would come to interview us. Poor Shazia was traumatised. But we know how we look after kids. We knew we hadn't done anything. As luck would have it, the children were examined by the same doctor who examined them three weeks earlier when they had come into care, and that doctor said: 'I'm amazed by the kids, they're very responsive, they're sitting down very quietly, they look very healthy, and they've put on weight'. That was really nice for us. The social worker apologised and said they didn't think there was anything but they had to go through the procedure. In one sense we needed protecting because it would have just gone on and on. The children then had to go to separate placements. It was really sad. And that incident goes on record actually. But there was also a letter from the consultant that will go on record saying that there was no case to answer.

One of the strangest things that happened in the middle of that was that the social worker came to discuss our taking on another child. It was really inconsiderate. We were in the middle of this turmoil and we just needed to take a breath and just think about what had happened.

Support

We're not in any support group actually. We did ask about other gay and lesbian couples or parents who were fostering, and we've not heard anything. But I think that's one of the difficulties with an agency, it's very hard to access that kind of support, and I think you miss out on a lot of support not being with the local authority. They don't know what other foster carers are in the area, not to mention who's black, who's gay, who's got any disabilities. There's no database that collates that information.

I don't really discuss anything with our social worker. He would probably faint anyway if you mentioned anything to do with being a lesbian. He writes these forms and says things like we are in 'good health', but how does he know? I remember when I had this lump on my breast, and it was a real worry, but I didn't discuss it with our social worker, and he was placing these children with us. We ring him if we need him and he rings every Friday to see if everything is all right. It would be really nice to have a black social worker or a gay social worker, actually. I think it would make a difference.

The agency did provide a support group, but it was becoming a bit of a complaint group about pay and numbers of children. There are a whole host of things that you could complain about. But if I've got any issues or difficulties, then I talk to my therapist.

And in terms of friends and family support, well, neither of us have access to family, so that's out. That's a whole half a body cut off actually. The friends we do have – well, you learn that some people will tolerate your unavailability and some people will come along with you and do whatever it is you need to do. Definitely people have dropped out of our circle while we have been looking after Calum, who is so severely disabled. That is really sad. It does tend to sift out who's up for you plus child.

The current placement with Calum is difficult as he is not expected to live. And to be fair, I don't think social services knew what was entailed in looking after a child like Calum. There's a whole host of things that surround this placement that haven't been taken on board. Now we've got Calum everybody thinks that he needs to stay here because he's doing well, and that is pleasing for all of us. You kind of get caught up in this system.

Three-and-a-half years later (2017)

Calum lived with us for just under five years and died suddenly and unexpectedly a few months ago in a special hospital for children with brain injuries. When he came to us at seven months old he had suffered a severe brain injury and was in constant danger of choking. He had to be suctioned often and had to be fed through a tube. No one knew if he could see or hear; he wasn't expected to communicate or ever be able to move or sit up, and he was expected to die within the year.

He hadn't been with us long when we he started responding to sounds and movements around him, and we realised he could see us. He just kept progressing. After a while he started to copy basic signs and he gave people his own signs for them and was interested in everything around him. He went to a special nursery school at three, which involved huge training for everyone to learn how to use his equipment; drivers, escorts, even the staff in the special school – all had to be trained to use the suction machine and on how to feed him. He went through nursery and reception and he was involved in integration initiatives between the special school and the mainstream primary it was attached to, and he had a really good friend in mainstream. He loved nursery. He went to a residential therapeutic unit for children with brain injuries at the other end of the country for six weeks in 2014 for intensive treatment. They tried to teach him to kneel up, but it was a struggle. Then we took him to Jamaica and he suddenly started kneeling there. Then he started to try to stand up. So we got a new scooter that he could scoot around the house in, and in 2015 he got a self-propelled wheelchair that gave him more control indoors and outside in the park. He could also move around on his own inside and climb on furniture and up the stairs.

After a long battle with social services about Calum staying in foster care with us, we went to court about a year before he died. We were going to go for permanent placement with responsibility to lead on his care, and were gearing up for a big fight, when social services suddenly turned round completely and conceded everything. We became named as his carers and he would remain as a permanent fostering placement with us until he was 18.

Just after his fifth birthday, we went back to the residential unit to help him learn to walk, as he was really trying to. He had a very detailed care plan at the unit about his communication, his needs – they have a beautiful holistic approach, it's like being admitted into hospital and they take over the care and they're teaching the parents.

He was very excitable, except at night, when he had a really good regime of calming down and going to sleep. The day he died he had an infection and was on antibiotics. It was really bad so the nurse said she would arrange for a doctor and a dietician the next day. He took out a special bike that day that his wheelchair fits on to and we went around the grounds, which he loved. He had a great time.

The next morning I got a call to come to the ward straight away and I was told that he had died. I was very shocked and some of the things I was told didn't make sense. Some of the information only came out recently in the final report from the hospital after seven months, and bits of it are still conflicting.

We had supported contact with Calum's birth parents over the years, so I spoke to the social services manager because I wanted to let the birth parents know. They said they would do this. His dad then rang me, and I talked to him about what had happened because I thought he had been told. He hadn't been told and was in shock. He got a taxi straight down to the hospital and started talking about his plans for the funeral, though I tried to suggest it was too soon. That evening he asked, 'Does the care order end when a child dies?' We had organised a funeral company to bring him home, but the social workers said Calum's dad wanted to use a funeral director of their choice. The social workers explained that they now have to go with everything the birth parents ask for, as parental responsibility reverts to the birth parents immediately on the child's death, regardless of the circumstances of the care order. We wanted a humanist funeral with a willow casket; his birth father wanted it in a church. In the end it was agreed by all parties that the funeral would be in the cathedral. The funeral director was very tactful and persuaded the parents to go for a willow casket.

When there is an interim care order or a full care order, the local authority and birth parents share parental responsibility. When a foster child dies, the birth parents regain full parental responsibility, which seems to be a flaw in the system. There were so many arguments between us, like where the body should leave from. Thankfully the social worker insisted Calum needed to leave from where he had lived for most of his five years. Still there is no headstone on the grave. I planted loads of flowers and his dad just digs them up. I've realised we have to treat it like any foster child who goes for adoption and we have to hand over that responsibility. It's not what we would want for a child we were so caring and meticulous about for so long.

I got a lot of support from someone else who had lost a child. I had to tell my clients because they had known I was taking Calum down to the Children's Trust for a spell of treatment. I did take a break from my work as a counsellor. Friends and neighbours have been really supportive; for example, someone from playgroup has been leaving little pots of flowers by our front door. Our own fostering agency was really good – they didn't pressure us to take more children. The agency gave us a choice and were led by us. They carried on paying us for a while, even though it wasn't clear we would be carrying on.

Calum's social work agency was shocking; they didn't support us at all. They could have managed it all very differently. It was really unfortunate that his social worker had just left so the new social worker didn't know us at all, but the manager knew us and was wholly supporting of the birth parents throughout, with no recognition that we'd been doing a job for them for five years, and even though the birth father had made things difficult for them too.

The whole church thing was very much about us being lesbians, the way the social workers kept talking about the 'family' needing to come first, meaning the heterosexual birth parents. However, it was very clear in church that we were his family, from the photos and memories of his life. We had so many people from his life with us, from our choir, his school, the children's hospital, the children's centre, neighbours, local shopkeepers, people who used to meet him walking their dog. The realisation unfolded in us slowly that his dad wanted control of everything and knew he had the law on his side. He said, 'You're just foster carers, you get paid for what you're doing.' He didn't understand what was entailed in looking after Calum. We gave a lot of time and support to the birth parents and I won't do that again.

We're fostering again now, a teenage mother and her new-born baby. We chose them because it's a very different kind of placement from Calum, and the connection is kind of at one remove because we're supporting her to bond with her baby. Even so, it was hard to bring her home from hospital, because that's what we did with Calum when he first arrived, and hard to prepare the house for someone different. Lots of Calum's stuff is still around and we had to move some of it. On the first day of the new placement I felt like I was leaving him behind. But she doesn't know the significance of the stuff in the house, like the specially adapted wet room; she just uses it, which is quite good. We do need to move on and it's good to be working again and to have a different focus. Christmas will be hard.

MIKE and ANDREW (2015)
Being an Advocate

Teacher Mike and his partner, Andrew, who works as an accounts manager, talk about the positive support they received through the assessment process and the joys and challenges they have experienced in the first 15 months of adopting their son, Jack.

Andrew: Mike and I feel very positive about society's current stance towards homosexuality. My parents and my sisters were looking forward to us having a kid, as was Mike's mother. We have a very supportive extended family environment and friends.

Mike: We've been together for eight years and there's a gap of nine years between our ages. I've been a respite carer before. When we decided to do this, we'd both reached a certain stability and income level; we'd got a dog, and we'd just bought our first house. I've worked with children most of my life, so I was aware that there are lots of young people out there needing placements. My work has been predominantly with children with special needs and challenging behaviour.

Andrew: I've helped Mike with respite care and I really enjoyed working with one family of four or five children who had been affected by foetal alcohol syndrome.

Making the first approach

Mike: We went to our local authority because we had heard through the New Family Social network for LGBT adopters and foster carers that they were already working with same-sex couples and were very positive and supportive. The social worker we spoke to was very keen on us as candidates. At the time I was transferring from being a student teacher to teacher, so she said to call her when we were ready. I was working in a primary school, but we were about to move house so we thought we'd do that first before starting the process. New Family Social (NFS) has been important to us; they have encouraged us and we have kept in touch with them. We soon realised that the issues people in the group faced were mostly to do with the needs of the children placed with them rather than homophobic attitudes and concerns.

Andrew: NFS is a fantastic organisation; we met some really supportive people who were kind enough to share their experiences. It gave me the chance to meet children other than the children I met when helping Mike with his respite care. That first-hand experience was so much more useful than any books. It was odd afterwards seeing straight couples at motorway service stations with their children!

The assessment

Mike: We told the social services department dealing with our assessment that because of my work experience we would be interested in taking on older children or children with special needs or challenging behaviour. A lot of my work has been with autism, but we weren't sure about going down such a challenging route. We thought it might be too much; maybe we needed to give ourselves an easier time. We were thinking of maybe one child, or a sibling group of two, as we were moving into a two-bedroomed property, and probably male children, although we were quite open about that. We thought about fostering as well.

Andrew has Polish heritage in his family and we would have been open to cultural difference; we would definitely have been committed to exploring the heritage of our child. We have lots of women in our lives and good networks in the area. When we were looking for a house, we looked for a house close to my mum and in a nice area.

Approval

Andrew: Regarding approval, we had a very easy time and found that we had a lot less to talk about than other adopters, who had to address the loss of not being able to conceive naturally. Adoption was our first choice and it made the whole process very exciting for us. We also had no past relationships, and a history of working with adopted children with behavioural problems meant we knew what to expect. This meant everything happened very quickly and we had no real delay or hurdles. We spent a lot of time talking about our dog and if he would be okay with a child in the house. We even had to make an indoor dog gate (which was huge because our dog is huge!). We never used it, but we did what we had to do to keep everyone happy, as in the social workers.

Placement (2018)

Andrew: It took about a year from us first enquiring about Jack to adopting him. It took about nine months before he moved in and then we fostered him with a view to adoption for about four months. The process was all very positive; we were unanimously approved at matching panel and had a very nice judge at the adoption hearing. Jack was just seven years old when he was placed with us. For the first nine months he settled really well. It was a kind of honeymoon period and he settled into school as well, joining Year 2 at the end of the first term.

Mike: Things started to fall apart at school at the end of the summer term of that year. It's hard to know if it was the transition at the end of year, or if that's how long it took for him to settle enough for the impact of his history to start to surface. It also coincided with starting attachment-focused therapy, so that might have had an effect. He has a lot of problems with school and that creates a lot of fallout at home. He can't control his rage at home or at school, and can go instantly from calm and affectionate to very angry. He's extremely anxious and hypersensitive all the time; he gets very upset and takes the smallest comment as a criticism. He's also hypervigilant and school constantly overwhelms him with stimuli.

Andrew: In Year 3 he moved into a split year class of Year 3 and Year 4 children with a newly qualified teacher. It was a very challenging class with a lot of children with additional needs, and the teacher wasn't really coping. She shouted a lot and shouting is a trigger for Jack and can take him instantly back to being a very young child in an environment with extreme domestic violence going on. In that year the head teacher was suspended and fired, and Jack's class teacher changed six times. We stuck with it, though there was no funding to support Jack in school, and not even a special educational needs coordinator (SENCO) when he started. The only way it worked for a while was that the school was employing Mike on a part-time basis to keep Jack in school. I work full time and Jack is out of school so often that Mike has had to give up working completely so he can be available in case the school phones.

Mike: I can't work anywhere else as I need to be on hand in the morning in case school call me in. If Jack has a meltdown, we are the only people who can deal with him. He has learnt to bait adults all the time because he is so hugely affected by witnessing extreme violence in his first six years. His life was chaotic and that's going to affect him for the rest of his life, which we feel very angry about.

There is now a SENCO for one day a week and they've just done an Educational Health Care Plan (what used to be called a Statement of Special Educational Needs) for him after 15 months of difficulties. He is also registered as disabled now, and we get Disability Living Allowance for him, because of his difficulties and frequent exclusions. We are committed to him going to his local school; he's settled and loves it there and they do mostly understand him, so we feel it's better to stick with it and hope the plan gets him more help. Success happens when he's working one-to-one with a teaching assistant in a room on his own. He goes to school for the playtimes and being with other kids, but that often ends in failure and rejection. He may get a place in a pupil referral unit and we know there may be a stage later, at high school, where he may need to be in a specialist unit. We're pushing for sensory therapy to help him manage his feelings and address his hypervigilance and anxiety. It's all fire-fighting. We make a lot of noise, but we're not unpleasant. We've had to be firm about advocating for our child and asking for what we need.

Andrew: We were provided with a lot of information before Jack was placed with us. Everyone was nervous about whether we would be able to deal with him. They gave us a timeline of all the social services involvement in his life from being a baby, so we knew what we were taking on. He was in that situation for six years, which was shocking. What wasn't made so clear to us was the level of support that would be available to us after adoption. We have to fight for things all the time that would be provided automatically if we were still fostering him. Just before the adoption we asked about continuing fostering. We still get foster payments because Mike had to give up his job – the payments are renewed annually and they're a lifeline for us financially. They do that because of the high level of his need and to maintain the placement.

Mike: He has direct contact every two months with his younger birth brother who has also been adopted and is going through very similar problems. The other adopters are positive about us, but we're all concerned about the brothers' traumatic bond – they love and hate each other. Jack's brother is being raised in a very traditional, disciplined and kind of militaristic regime, whereas we're very therapeutic, so that's difficult. The contact is also usually at emotionally heightened times, like Christmas and birthdays, which doesn't help and is not supposed to be a good idea. We may try to scale it down over time.

Andrew: On the positive side, we both love him to bits and are fully bonded with him. He does love us; he loves his home and his family. He really wants things to improve and tries so hard. He's affectionate and polite and caring. His loving, caring side is the polar opposite to his rages and meltdowns; he just swings from one to the other and that pushes us to be vigilant, so we can divert things before they happen. We're fortunate that he generally sleeps through the night. I work full time, so I try to give Mike time off in the evening and at weekends. We've been doing meditation and mindfulness every day with him, and sharing hobbies together to keep that connection with him. We have subtly persuaded him to adopt things we like, so he now watches the superhero films we like too! Unfortunately, he doesn't have that with his peers. He generally finds it easier with girls and he enjoys playing with two girl cousins around his own age in the family. My twin brother and his girlfriend are also very positive people in his life, and he loves spending time with them.

Mike: We can give each other time off, but it's very difficult to get time off together. My mum lives nearby and is our main support, but he had a difficult incident with her recently and we have had to rely on her a bit less. He's such a sponge with our emotions and when we're tired, or have had a bad day, it triggers him. The most unsafe times of his life have been when adults are in a bad mood.

Andrew: Our sexuality has not really been an issue and we haven't experienced direct discrimination since the start of our relationship. There's been very little negative impact on our family, and probably a huge lot of positives in not having the triggering of his past that he might have got with a heterosexual couple. There are no other distractions and stimuli here and he needs that space and attention just for him. There have been no issues about us being a same-sex couple outside the house. Occasionally we've had to pick up on homophobic language he's picked up at school, but generally he's quite protective of us. We have good relationships with the social workers, we're asked to attend adoption evenings and Mike now serves on the adoption panel as an expert adopter. We're still part of NFS and do volunteering for them. The annual NFS summer camp is our main family holiday. The environment can be over-stimulating for Jack at times, but we have a lot of fun, and he gets loads out of being with the other kids.

TERESA and CATH (2015)

They'd Been Left in Limbo

Teresa and Cath are a mixed race couple who adopted two children, a brother and sister, ten years ago. Teresa is a counsellor working with children and families and Cath is a social worker and therapist, also working with children and families. After a very traumatic early life, the children spent two difficult years in foster care before being adopted. Teresa and Cath talk about the challenges they have faced throughout the adoption process, highlighting the huge difference good support – from the school, social services, specialists, friends and the LGBT community – has made.

Teresa: I always wanted children. I used to want to be pregnant, very, very badly, painfully so, looking back. I tried getting pregnant but it just didn't happen, didn't work out. So eventually we decided to adopt. We were both in our 30s by then. My brother is adopted so it had always been there for me anyway. I mean, I can remember, as a teenager, thinking, you know, even if I married and had children, that I would always adopt. I can clearly remember that, because of him. He was such a great brother.

His is a classic story of the 1960s. His birth mother was a nurse and his father was here from Africa studying engineering. He went back to Africa and she felt she couldn't keep him so she handed him to neighbours, a nice couple, lovely people, but they had problems of their own, learning difficulties. It was completely informal, and subsequently a social worker got involved and somehow my mum got involved and said, 'I'm here.' He used to run away to our house and eventually he just stayed. So adoption was always there in my mind as an option.

Becoming adopters

Cath: The first people we approached to see if we could become adopters gave us really short shrift. They were really rude. Somebody sent us a really short nasty letter telling us where to go, which was a bit off-putting.

We were out to everyone from the start. We found ourselves being described as a 'same-sex' couple rather than as lesbians; the term 'lesbian' is rarely used these days. I think it's an attempt to lower negativity. Society is a long way off attributing anything positive to being lesbian. Homophobia is just too rife, too deep in people's souls.

Teresa: After a few false starts we found a voluntary agency that was positive. They were great, they were looking for black and minority ethnic families for hard-to-place sibling groups so as a mixed race couple wanting to adopt two children, we fitted the bill.

The voluntary agency first sent us to a preparation group. It was very mixed. There were some bods who were bright and on the ball and others less so. There was only one other mixed race couple and we became quite good friends with them, kept in touch after the adoption. I don't remember any hostility to us as a couple.

Cath: It was a very strange experience. You meet these people you don't know and you're put in this really vulnerable situation, talking about really emotional issues. Things would sometimes come up in those group discussions that people hadn't considered and they would break down. It wasn't easy, but we got through it.

Teresa: After the preparation group came the first home visit. I was very anxious about that. One of the first things we were asked by the senior social worker visiting that first time was: 'Who's going to be mum?' We looked at each other and one of us said, I think it was you, 'As opposed to what?' That did put me off, that lack of understanding.

I found the assessment process horrible. They scrutinise your relationship, and I found that really raw. I think when you talk about that and you are a lesbian it feels much more precarious; you feel more vulnerable. That was the worst bit for me because you worry about how they see the relationship. When you look back on your own life and you think about the development of your own sexuality and relationships, I think it's quite a painful experience. It's quite difficult talking to somebody you don't know about it.

It was also hard because you feel 'we've got to be really together on this', and worrying that they are looking for cracks to explore, and that's exactly what you don't want to show them. Obviously, they need to know that you're not going to fall apart and split up, but that part of the assessment didn't feel too great.

Cath: During the home visits we filled in the Form F, which is long – it has about 60 questions on it. We did it over about 12 sessions. We did our own write-up each time, answering the questions and then going through our answers with our social worker, the one assigned to us after that first home visit.

We also filled in this form where you tick boxes of what you will and won't find acceptable – and yet when we looked at that form about a year after we had adopted, we found we had ended up adopting children with almost all the problems we said we didn't want!

Teresa: We understand that assessment and scrutiny is important, but I wish at the group stage there'd been more discussion and information about disassociation and secondary trauma, stuff like that. Looking back, I don't think we were properly prepared for what was to come. I wish there had been certain things at the beginning of the home assessment, like an attachment therapist visiting you who can talk about attachment and trauma, that kind of stuff. I think it would have helped us understand a lot more a lot earlier on.

The reality is that a lot of professionals working in the system don't really understand the situation themselves. During the home assessment we were pointed in the direction of lots of books. The problem is not just understanding the context of the book, but understanding how it works in practice, something that can't really be explained.

One book that turned out to be a real life-saver later on was a book by Richard Delaney and Charley Joyce, *Behavior with a Purpose* (2009), which looks at problems faced in adoptive families. That saved my life; I used to come downstairs at night after the children had gone to bed and read it and go, 'ha, found it, that's the one.' He uses cartoons and humorous explanations for what is going on.

They did ask us during the assessment about male role models. I found that quite stressful because there aren't that many really, and all the ones that there are, or would be, are either dead or cracking on – my uncle, my dad, and one or two friends.

Once we were assessed we went to panel and they telephoned us later to say we had been approved as adopters. Our sexuality didn't come up at all. Initially one of us was actually going to be the adopter and one of us was going to get a residence order, but the rules changed while we were going through the process and so eventually both of us adopted the children, as a couple. We must have been one of the first lesbian couples that adopted as a couple.

Finding our family

Cath: We were approved for two children up to the age of seven. It was pushed up to seven, as we had originally given a younger top age limit. We wanted young children, though not necessarily a baby. I was nearly 40, so I felt that too much time had passed to do the baby thing.

Teresa: It got more complex because we got the *Be My Parent* magazines and we started seeing all these social workers. All these young children seem doomed and pull at your heart strings. It was hard once you were approved; there were so many children.

Cath: We wanted a boy and a girl.

Teresa: So there it was. We got what we wanted. A boy and a girl, Joseph and June, aged six and four-and-a-half when they came to us. They could have come earlier, but the process of getting them was absolutely hideous. It was the worst thing I've ever been through. We went down to their local authority to talk about them in September and they didn't come to us until the end of April the following year – seven months later. And in the meantime, they had a foster care placement breakdown.

Cath: The foster mother made up some story about her mother being ill, but her husband clearly couldn't stand Joseph. He hated him.

Teresa: How can you hate a child that small?

Cath: But he did hate him. I remember we were in a meeting and he beckoned to me and said pointedly: 'He's horrible.' Just like that.

Teresa: So the placement broke down and they went to another carer. We asked if we could have them earlier rather than moving them again. But as it turned out the new foster carer was good. She worked with them. That was a stroke of luck. But the week before we met them we went to the post-adoption centre and were told they weren't placing them together. And that is when we got angry.

Cath: I was beyond angry and upset. They were being idiots and telling us we knew nothing about attachment.

Teresa: So we went to see a trauma specialist, Dora Black. She was brilliant – she specialises in helping children. She'd seen them much earlier on, when June was two, and then again two years later, because of their attachment and trauma issues, which expressed themselves at various times in violent, sexualised and dissociated behaviours. She spent a long time with us and swung things in favour of our keeping the children together. Her opinion overrode everyone else's.

Cath: The good thing about her was that she talked about trauma and the impact of trauma and how that completely messes with your mind. She warned us to be prepared and to expect nothing. She told us to expect nothing back. She was down-to-earth. She spoke a language we understood and she knew what she was talking about. I just thought: my kind of woman.

Teresa: And she was really cross because the children had been in limbo for two years and they had done nothing, and she had seen a massive deterioration in June. She thought the children should go with us and so that's how we got them. We didn't officially adopt them for another three years. We took time cutting the ties because we didn't want to be left high and dry; we wanted the support that we knew would disappear once they were adopted. It sounds mean now, but it was the right thing at the time.

The children

Cath: When we had decided to take on Joseph and June – we had seen them on videos and everything – we told the social worker, 'Teresa is going to be "mum" and I'm going to be Cath.' Then we walk into the foster carers' home and she introduces me as mum and Teresa as Teresa! Joseph ran up the garden shouting to the neighbours, 'We've got a mummy and a Teresa!' You were heartbroken and I was horrified. They were calling us Teresa and Cath for a few months and then we said: 'Enough of that – it's Mummy Teresa to you.' It was important to put in those hierarchical distinctions: 'You're the child and we're the parents.'

There were some problems at first. I remember June sitting in the living room at midnight with a sheet over her head and a tiara on top, whinnying and neighing. She went on for hours. She couldn't stop herself and she would do that until she was completely worn out.

Teresa: We got some help and we were told to just ignore her.

Cath: We had a baby monitor and it sounded like she was having a party in the bedroom after she had gone to bed. There were all these different characters. It wasn't ordinary play. It was quite bizarre, well to us, anyway.

Early on, it was soon after Easter, I remember their social worker coming up from their local authority, and she wanted to see them on their own. So we had our swimming stuff packed and we had left sandwiches for them all and we were going off for an hour-and-a-half.

We got to the end of the road and realised you had forgotten your cozzie, so we came back and, in the space of those few minutes all the furniture had been tipped up, cushions everywhere, Easter eggs open all over the table. And the children were so pleased to see us because we had come back unexpectedly – and that was wonderful. And the social worker said, 'Please don't leave me on my own with them again.'

Teresa: We had some difficulty understanding each other when they first came. I remember Joseph asking: 'Can I have a car door?' and thinking what is he talking about? It was a cuddle! And because they spoke like that at school, that made it quite difficult for them to settle and make friends. They didn't have a 'posh' accent but kids around here didn't recognise the accent so thought that it was posh. They had us running up and downstairs with toast at 10 o'clock at night for the first couple of weeks.

Cath: Toast and milk.

Teresa: 'I'm starving.' And we'd think, 'Ah, poor kids, deprived'! I went outside once, shortly after they came here, and saw them standing on the window ledge in the middle of the night chatting to the neighbour's cat – trying to stick a broom handle up its bottom!

They had had a really deprived start to life. Their parents, whatever their background, had got involved in drink and drugs and their lives were every way a total mess and enmeshed in the benefits system. I have a sense of them still being conscious of that.

There is a huge difference between the birth family and the adoptive family for most children. There was a huge difference between what we'd experienced and what they have experienced in their early years. But I knew the kind of place they came from – it was round and about in my environment. I don't think it is material differences that matter; it's education and aspiration. And that continues to cause conflict. I don't know why but it does – that lack of motivation and aspiration. That sense instead of entitlement. I don't get it. I expect them to be able to do this, that and the other, and I don't get why they would want to spend a Sunday just watching telly. Why would they want to do that? I get terribly frustrated by it.

I feel upset that they don't want to learn. I know they're learning all the time in a lot of ways – life experience is learning and, in many respects, more rewarding – but it doesn't pay the bills. So I do get very frustrated by the lack of ambition educationally. I have to keep reminding myself that just being who they are is very difficult; that their day-to-day existence is hard. It's a struggle. And I have to remind myself of that all the time.

I found it took me longer to understand the effects of neglect on Joseph than to understand the trauma June had been through from sexual abuse. I understand the sexual abuse stuff, I got it really quickly, much quicker than I understood the effects of neglect. I understand now, but early on I couldn't understand Joseph's behaviour. It tears you apart. You feel incompetent as a parent and that's really soul-destroying.

Cath: Joseph is able to think philosophically to some degree. He always could. But June, his sister, although she's better, gets embarrassed. So the differences between us and their family have been an issue. And I think it should have been addressed more at the start.

The gender issue

Cath: When Joseph was quite small, one of the things he asked was, 'Well, how am I going to know how to be a dad?' And I told him, 'I actually think I learnt how to be a mum off my dad more than my mum, so what has gender got to do with it?' But we had never had these conversations with the social worker. And I think June as much as Joseph will have missed that male role model.

Teresa: One of the first things I remember Joseph saying, was, 'When will I be a man?'

Cath: I remember being in the supermarket once and he said to the cashier, 'Two mums, but no dad yet.'

Teresa: You do have to think out of the box when you get on to gender issues. What qualities are people referring to that they randomly call male or female qualities? Sons will not grow up to be women. You can only give your child your perspective. And yes, they do have to find different things, other things from other places. I don't think not having a male around has been a particular hardship for Joseph. I think he is more conscious now that he hasn't got a dad around; for instance, if he sees his mate Sam going to a football match with his dad he might wish that was him. But he has been going to the match with Cath for years now.

I think it's a bodily thing. We're not male. We have tried to find people who can embody that male role for Joseph. We have had to try to push that because he is very rejecting of adult men. But both children go to mixed gender schools, so they are, every day, with an assortment of male and female role models.

Cath: There are assumptions made at Joseph's school. All the furniture in this house has been put together by me and June. Joseph came home with his options for GCSE and he had put down 'woodwork' and we all fell about laughing because he can't hold a screwdriver or hammer a nail in – that's just not him. And we told him to play to his strengths like drama, which he is really good at. The attitude that 'boys do this' and 'girls do that' still exists in many schools.

He's also the more emotional of the two of them. And we tell him it's alright for him to cry, but it's absolutely not alright for him to be sexist. We have that conversation with him a lot. We have that '…and don't think that just because you're a boy that means you can get away with washing the dishes like this, go and do it again' kind of conversation. I do feel it's hard for him; he knows these sexist attitudes are nonsense, but they are out there and that can be difficult for him.

And then there is this thing about boys and pornography. We had to work through that. He accessed some site on his laptop once. I knew he'd been on a site and I said, 'Paul's coming to look at all the computers, so if there's anything you want to tell me now, there's an amnesty.' And then he told me. So I said, 'That's it, everybody can get away with that once, don't do it again.' End of conversation. Then the bill comes in for this iPhone, for nine minutes at £4 a minute! He'd accessed a site with his friend Sam. That boy got both barrels from us for about a month. I don't think that'll be happening again.

Teresa: Conversations we've had about this sort of thing have been very, very intense conversations about self-respect, and being a human being really. He does understand. The children are now 17 and 15.

There have been no massive turning points but there have been key things that have helped. One key thing was choosing the right primary school. We talked to several schools and they were just either unwelcoming or flat, but the head of this school was much more relaxed and welcoming and invited us along to the school.

Cath: He was brilliant, absolutely brilliant. We seemed to spend half our lives at that school when they were young.

Teresa: He made us feel that we and the children had given something to the school just as much as they had given something to the children, which is fantastic really, because they were an absolute bag of work. But he was prepared to take them on – he felt helping them would be an experience they could all learn from and he was open to learning. He was absolutely fantastic. Later on he sat on the adoption panel for the area.

Cath: He didn't want the children to be scapegoated. He said the children would not be excluded. And he never did exclude them, no matter what they did.

Teresa: And they did some bad stuff.

Cath: Sometimes he'd call and say, 'Can you come up?' I remember one patch when I must have been in his office three times a week. I never felt told off. It was always, 'How are we going to get through this?' And we'd negotiate a strategy and then implement it together. It was sometimes 'he'll have to go home', or, 'she'll have to go home'. But always 'come back tomorrow and we'll start again'.

Teresa: We've had kissing under the table, oral sex in the toilets.

Cath: Joseph once threw a grate at a child that just missed the child's head.

Teresa: Tantrums at lunchtime. All the toilets bunged up and overflowing.

Cath: And they made up all these stories. The way they said things was so convincing – my mum's a burglar, we keep a dog in a cage under the stairs, grandma had an operation and she never came round from the anaesthetic! That was his news one morning. I went in and the teacher said, 'I'm ever so sorry to hear about your mum.' What? 'It was your mother who died wasn't it?' No.

Teresa: He was six or seven at the time. Hard to believe. The school made a big difference. If we hadn't had that school, I don't think we'd have made it.

Cath: No. It was a lifeline as well. It was a few hours' break. The secondary school has been good too, very supportive and flexible. They are not the only adopted kids at the school and they know that – so it's a school where it feels like it's okay to be adopted. It sounds really weird but it's a bit like being gay in a way. It's okay to be out about being adopted there – but I think there are schools where being adopted may not be a thing that you talk about. It's not such a big school. They went up as a class from the primary school. I don't think they talk about their home circumstances to many people; they don't talk about us.

Teresa: But they do know their circumstances. And we do talk to them about how tough their childhood was when they were very little, how that has impacted on their lives. June and Joseph are a bit of a package.

Cath: They have their own confusion about identity because they are mixed race. I mean, they've been racist. June was very muddled up. I remember her coming home and thinking she was a white girl for ages.

I can remember Joseph saying to me, 'I'm so glad I'm not black.' And it was very, very painful. He's got better. He has got a struggle anyway because of his appearance. Appearance-wise people think he's white a lot of the time. I don't think he really knows what to do about that. He did say he'd rather be black or white but not this, neither one nor the other. You can see that, because he's so much lighter than June is.

Teresa: He's the lightest person in the house.

Cath: 'Little lilywhite.' They did get picked on sometimes and this one girl would throw bottles at him – plastic bottles. The kids who attacked them when they started secondary school were excluded and their parents were called in. The school dealt with it really well. It's not a racist school.

Outside support

Cath: We've had good support all the way through the adoption. The LGBT adoption group, my mum's been great, especially as a place for June to go to. We also had support from Sue Golding, an attachment therapist and psychologist, who has been a real treasure and still works with the kids when things crop up. They go and see her on their own.

Teresa: They look forward to talking to her. She feels like one of the family now.

Cath: And we see a therapist, Margaret Wilkinson. We saw her once a month for a few years.

Teresa: And there has been other post-adoption support, and organisations like the London Centre for Child Mental Health. One thing that has been critical for us has been the stables. June has a real interest in horses. It's a soul connection for her. June isn't frightened of anything, which in itself is a bit frightening. When we were introduced to June and Joseph, we spent a week on a farm and they had two Doberman Pinschers – terrifying.

Cath: And at one point we saw June being dragged down the lane. She had her arms round the Doberman, hanging onto it, and it was running down the lane. It was terrifying, but she was fearless.

Teresa: Another great help was Cool Springs, the play scheme – mostly for disabled children. They were very good with Joseph and June; they were nice to us and they were nice to the kids.

Joseph had a lot of kind of twitchy behaviour. When he was little he used to wave his arms and stamp his feet when he got excited, and his eyes would quiver. It was alright until other kids at school began to notice it. I remember watching him on the football pitch one day, waving his arms instead of playing football because he was excited.

We went to see this woman in the Midlands, Camilla de Jay, who was a primary movement therapist. She assessed him and then gave us a programme of exercises. I was quite sceptical but it actually led onto lots of things, like showing us how difficult it was for him to follow a finger or point at something. Most children can do that by the time they are two, but Joseph still has trouble with that. He also couldn't balance. He couldn't walk on a straight line. But with the exercises, within probably the space of three months, all his twitching had gone.

We've had financial support from the council for therapy the children have needed. We pay for our own therapy.

We would have quite intense meetings here with someone from the placing authority, our social worker and the headmaster of their school. Everyone sitting on the floor, eating their lunch. Outwardly attractive as they are, they were kids with pretty disturbing features.

Cath: We do get problems even now and the school has been fantastic. June has had some problems at college. Just a couple of weeks ago she fell out with some girls and she wouldn't get out of the back of the car. And the college was really helpful.

Teresa: I can see a future where we are more involved professionally in adoption, sit on a panel or something. But I want to get the kids a bit older first. A bit more moved on. I think working in this area or paying some attention to it is on my mind. I work as a family therapist and I already do some ordinary family therapy and consultancy work with agencies, fostering agencies and others.

Adoption has changed me in terms of my understanding. I worked with a children's mental health team before and we did a good job, a good attachment-based, system-based job, but now I think I get it from everybody's point of view to some degree. It's made me more patient and, I suppose, given me some self-assurance. I have a more holistic approach today. I know this can be done if you get the right input at least most of the time, and particularly in terms of adoptive parents and foster carers.

Cath: We've had the children for 12 years now and I had hoped the systems would have changed a lot more than they have by now. I saw this teacher last night and I just thought, why are we still having these same conversations?

Teresa: And sometimes I think we assume people understand a lot more than they do. I think I take short cuts in what I say – because I have said it so many times before. And whoever I'm talking to says 'yes' and I move on, and then they ask a question and I realise they haven't really understood. I overestimate other people.

Our knowing so much can get on June and Joseph's nerves. There have been times in the past when they will say: 'Well you are a therapist – you will bloody know, won't you?' That kind of thing.

Cath: They don't get away with much.

Teresa: We've ended up being much stricter parents than I ever expected we would be, which has been a bit of a downside in some ways. I end up being somebody I almost don't know, as a parent of adopted children. You don't recognise yourself. If somebody had told me this was the kind of parent I'd be I'd have said: 'Don't be so ridiculous. I'm not going to be like that, I'm going to be my liberal, fun self.'

But that had to change. I think all parents probably have that fantasy. I remember my dad saying he couldn't believe how I was with the children – my sister called me Attila the Hun! But after a while my dad said I had been right to be tough. But it didn't come easily to either of us.

ROB (2013)

The Issue is Being in Care, Not Being Cared for by a Gay Man

Rob always knew he wanted children. At first he attempted parenthood with a lesbian couple, but when that plan fell apart he decided to become a foster parent as a single man and to use his skills as an educational psychologist, hoping to make a significant difference to children in his care. Today he is a strong advocate for gay, single foster parents.

I've always wanted kids. When I was a teenager I thought I was going to grow up and have kids and a family really early. I used to go down the local primary school and teach groups of kids when I was in the sixth form. I loved working with kids. And I always loved friends' kids when they'd come round – I'd always muck about with them in the garden and stuff. So, having a family and kids was always there for me.

I didn't come out until I was 27. I hadn't actually kissed a guy until I was 27! I had an army childhood, and being gay just wasn't an option so it took me a long time to come to terms with myself. There weren't any gay role models out there, or not for me; there was Julian Clary and Elton John, they were the only two people I knew were gay, and I didn't associate myself with either of them. So coming out was hard, and by far the hardest thing for me and for my family was that the family of my own that I'd always wanted just didn't look like it was going to happen. And I almost put it aside like it wasn't a possibility, and for a long while I just went out on the scene and kind of did all the stuff I wished I'd done when I was a teenager.

And then several things happened that led me down the path towards fostering. I work as an educational psychologist in schools, and I had often worked with foster carers, support workers and other people who carry out interventions and stuff to improve kids' lives. I realised that what was really needed was for these interventions to be followed through, and that this was somewhere I could help.

There were a couple of cases that affected me. The first was one of the kids I saw in a school where I was working. When I see kids I ask them to do drawings and I ask them to start by drawing an ideal world. I start for them, by drawing a very simplistic little picture – there's a little sun in the corner and a house and a tree, and I ask the kids to put themselves in the picture and whoever else they like, wherever they like. And this kid put various bits of the family in the picture and he put himself in the sun with the learning support assistant, just the two of them.

That learning support assistant had become such a key person for that kid. She was the only constant, the only person he felt was there for him. We were talking through the picture and he wanted to be with her because she felt safe so they were in the sun together and everyone else was down in the house. I realised how important she had become to him. This kid had been adopted and the placement had broken down and he'd gone back into care. It was horribly complicated and this kid really had done amazingly well, considering. And every time I went to the school, he'd come to me and he'd try to give me things, just to engage me, and I realised how these kids latch on to people, how important that one-to-one relationship is.

The second case was a kid in foster care who was in a special unit; he had been excluded from school. He was a lovely kid and I quickly realised he should not have been in that unit; it was ridiculous. And I was like, why the hell is he here? He's not fitting a profile of this unit. He was about to change schools and was destined for another special unit, but both his carers and I wanted to get him into a normal secondary school. We fought for that. The school we wanted him to go to had a holiday club and we wanted him to go along to give it a go in the hope the school would then take him. But he needed to be taken to the club and for someone to stay with him – that was the agreement. His carers weren't able to take him, so I went along as an educational psychologist and I just sat next to him and wrote reports whilst he engaged with the course. Of course, he did amazingly well because he was a lovely kid and they then let him in to the school. His foster family was so grateful that this kid was getting a positive start in a normal secondary school. But without the commitment of those foster carers, that wouldn't have happened.

That fed into my mind and I thought maybe I could try something like that, but I didn't think I could afford it; I hadn't realised that foster carers are paid. I ended up doing supportive lodgings for The Albert Kennedy Trust, supporting young LGBT people in a crisis. Through that I met a couple of people who had been foster carers who told me carers were paid, and I realised that if I worked part time, I could afford to do this, and so I started looking into it. I actually sold my old flat and moved so that I could foster.

The thing that I had struggled with, working in education, was not being able to influence a kid's social care. That is so important, and often foster carers don't feel sufficiently educated or empowered to challenge and change systems. Knowing the education system has made a massive difference to my ability to support these kids. I wanted to try to make a difference by being a constant for a child and being able to follow things through, though you never really know how much difference you make.

I cross the boundary between professional and carer and I see where the gaps are. There is so much diversity of practice. There's often a real lack of collaboration between social care and education around children in care. I think that's the big divide. School staff know a lot of stuff about kids and they're very good with some kids, but they get overlooked. Schools should be integral in care planning, in assessments. Why aren't schools – or indeed doctors – included in assessments of foster carers?

The big trigger that made me just pull my finger out and go for fostering was a lesbian couple, friends of mine, who asked me to be a donor for them. We went through a long process of legal stuff. They were lovely; they'd been together for 12 years. We went for it, but after three months of trying artificial insemination and it not working, they split up. It was totally unexpected, and they were devastated by the whole experience. It was a sad time, but it made me realise how excited I had become at the prospect of being a dad. And it made me realise that I couldn't just sit back and wait for it to happen. That's when I decided to do this, and within a couple of months I'd applied properly to be a foster parent.

The application

I didn't have an issue with applying to become a foster carer as a single gay man. I went to a few different authorities, but I applied to this particular agency because they were so instantly welcoming. One of the first questions they asked me was if I was gay, and when I said, 'Yes', they said, 'No problem at all, that's great.' And it just went on like that; it wasn't an issue, they were very supportive. From my perspective I was very glad that they had mentioned it and made their support so clear.

I went to an assessment group, for something like two days. There definitely wasn't any issue about my being gay. I certainly wasn't introduced as a gay carer. All the social workers knew, and if anything it was the other foster carers who were surprised, but actually it was quite interesting how much curiosity and support there was from several of them. I did make an effort on that first course, and on the week-long training course we went on, to make sure everyone knew by the end of the course, but I didn't want to push it in their faces at the beginning. I didn't want people to have preconceived ideas, but I also wanted them to leave knowing. I think that if I had announced it at the beginning, some of the other carers wouldn't have engaged with me as well as they did. I was single, so I was there by myself, and it wasn't so obvious.

I do remember on the week-long course there were several occasions when people were talking about how unsafe it was to leave your husband or your male partner with a child, or let them bathe the children or be with them by themselves. I'm like: 'Hang on, first, I am a man and I'm single and second, if I do have a partner, they're going to be a man as well. It's like, what are you saying?' I challenged that and it made them stop and think, but there were a couple of people who still spoke a little bit to that agenda, saying that the statistics were very damning – but that's not what you want to hear as a single male carer who is a little bit freaked out about possible allegations. Other than that, I think the course was quite supportive and most of the other carers were quite sensitive.

The home assessment

The social worker who carried out my assessment was independent [of the local authority] and told me I was the first gay person she'd assessed. She asked me to let her know if she asked me anything that I found offensive. She was actually very good. She was interested in how I was going to cope as a single gay man. A lot of people get a bit funny about those kinds of questions, but they are important, and she asked in a supportive way.

She asked about my sexuality but not in a threatening or nasty way. It was just part of a list of questions about my age, my gender, my address – and that is the way it should be. It wasn't seen as a major obstacle. I wasn't offended; my sexuality is relevant, it's part of me, part of my identity and my motivation. If anyone asks me why I foster, one of the first things I say is that I'm gay and my options are limited. That's the starting point, and then it makes sense to people. I think it'd be really out of order to start the process and not be honest about your sexuality.

She was very supportive about my being single. The local authority wasn't quite so keen about my working, but I have no choice; I don't have someone else to support me financially. As a foster carer I had to give up some of my job, but when there are no children in placement you don't receive any financial support – so I have to keep working. It was a bit of a catch-22; either I did this and kept working at some level, or I didn't do it. I currently work two days a week within school hours – but that time is spread over three or four days to give me the necessary flexibility I need as a foster carer.

The assessment was competency-based. There are a lot of questions, but they were ones I was expecting to be asked about my experiences. And they ask about how you have coped with difficulties in your life and with bereavements and loss.

We also talked about racial identity, but it is not such a big issue with fostering. I'm white British, I'd probably be defined as middle class, but I'm not a great one for definitions of that kind. A social worker's priority is to look after a child's best interests and, in an emergency, social workers rarely have a lot of choice.

The kids certainly don't care about your background or who you are. They adapt surprisingly quickly. It's kind of interesting but it isn't relevant to them – they are more interested in your looking after them, spending time with them. And you need to be resilient and ready to defuse stupid comments; that's important. I think one of the advantages of being gay is that you are used to having to be assertive and to challenging the system if you need to.

One of the other things we talked about was relationships and how I might introduce people to children in my care. She also asked about gender role models. It's an important question and it was important for me to think that through. I remember thinking at first that the children might have more men than women in their life with me, but it hasn't worked out like that at all. Most of the foster carers I know are female, and I ended up linking with them as well as with friends amongst the staff at the school where I work, who are also mostly female.

I remember thinking that I had a massive network of people I could turn to, because I knew so many people through work, the charity I was involved in, my family, university friends; I had so many different groups. What's interesting is that if I look back at people I saw as part of my network originally, very few of them are the people I really use in my network today. These things evolve and change. It's the kind of person, their availability, that makes them part of my network, and that wasn't so clear to me during my assessment. Once children are placed, everything changes. People I wasn't expecting to be involved took more of a role. A couple of my really good friends were and are brilliant; others not so.

I did speak to the fostering panel when my case application was put forward. They were lovely, very supportive and actually, interestingly enough, that's the one thing I've consistently heard other people say – that the panel was lovely. They'd obviously been through the stuff I had been asked in the assessment. They didn't ask any intrusive questions; they asked for some clarification on some things, but generally they were really supportive, really positive. There was no push then or at any other time to take any particular group of children. I'm approved for both genders and for children aged 5 to 12. I'd like to take younger children, but I have to be in school to work. I didn't want to take children any older.

I think my biggest fear about taking older children was their response to my sexuality. I felt that kids going into adolescence and going into care had enough to deal with – they could find it difficult being put with a gay carer when they were going through all that. It really worried me. I wasn't secure enough in my understanding of fostering to want to deal with that too. I was being encouraged to take older children, but I just didn't feel comfortable. That might change though.

Within a week of panel, I had a kid move in – and he's still here, two years and four months later – yeah, short term! Then another kid came who had been in several placements that had broken down. He was here for a few weeks and then they found him another placement, but that broke down after a few months and he came back here for another three months, right through his first term in secondary.

Eventually they found him a long-term placement. But the social worker nearly messed up the ending of his placement with me.

He was meant to leave on a Saturday and then suddenly his social worker said he would be picked up from school and taken straight to his new carer on the Friday and they'd send someone to pick up his stuff. I was like, 'Hang on, I've got endings and stuff planned, with a special dinner and things tonight.' I had to really fight to get that plan back. She was cutting the ending because she was fearful of it all messing up, which I understood, but it was also important that he ended his time here in a good way. I didn't want him to feel like he had been rejected again. It needed to be a positive move for him.

Then another boy moved in – he's a little bit older, about to turn 13 – and he's been with me just over a year. So for most of the time I've had two kids. The boys now with me are both from families where they lived alone with a single parent, so they find sharing quite difficult.

Relationships

Although I am a single carer, I am currently in a relationship, but at this point my partner hasn't moved in and he doesn't take any role with the kids at all, except as a friend when he's around. He didn't meet the kids for about eight months; he'd come round after they were in bed. Then I got him police-checked so he could stay over, but he only comes over once or twice a week. Asking him to get police-checked really freaked me out, but he was brilliant about it. His relationship with the kids is still quite distant; they know him but it's very much me that's the foster carer.

He'd have to be fully assessed if he moved in, and that's a huge step – it's a big commitment for somebody to make. He doesn't want to be a foster carer and even if he did move in, he wouldn't take a much more active role. You can't lean on someone in a new relationship; you can't start a relationship like that, because you'll scare them away. So I didn't, and haven't, used my relationship for that. My partner didn't sign up for this.

Changing social workers

My assessment social worker was brilliant but once I had been approved I was allocated a different supporting social worker from the local authority. She had assessed another gay couple and she put me in touch with them, but it wasn't the most productive relationship – just because we were all gay doesn't mean we are going to automatically get on; we were on very different pages.

This social worker was very practical, good at processing receipts, that kind of stuff. But she rarely asked me about my sexuality, my life, my emotions or my feelings. The one thing that haunted me as a single gay carer was my fear of having allegations made about me and stuff. She rarely visited, and after a while there was some issue that I complained about and she replied, copying in everyone, rather than phoning me up. I found that email offensive – she was just justifying why she hadn't done this or that, and that was the last thing I needed. I needed help!

I sent an email back saying that I may have reacted emotionally – it's difficult stuff that we're dealing with day-to-day – and told her that what I needed was her to pick up the phone and say, 'Are you okay?' And there was just no response to that, and so finally I sent another email suggesting I just change social worker. And she sent quite a rude email back. I never, ever heard from her again.

She does support the other gay couple she introduced me to and they are very positive about her. So they would say it's nothing to do with sexuality. But you know, if you're a good social worker, you ask about difficult stuff, you bring it up, and this couple is older, they don't want anyone prying into their emotions, and they have each other to talk things through with. As a single carer you don't have the support of a partner to lean on. And if you struggle with something, you need to talk to someone about it. That first year was quite tough, getting my head around it all.

So now I have a different social worker who is better at supporting me emotionally. There's always going to be a good match or not with a social worker – different people click with different people.

The children

As an educational psychologist, it did worry me that they would give me all the hard-to-place kids, and to be honest, they have! And whilst I was very reluctant to take on these challenging kids at the beginning, at the end of the day, they're the kind of kids I can make the biggest difference to.

The thing with fostering is that local authorities have limited resources and they have to think who can cope with certain types of children. It's the kids who have emotional behavioural difficulties who have been thrown towards me. Those are the kind of kids who need the most understanding. You need to be quite resilient, understanding about attachment and trauma and transitions and stuff. So I suppose I had some of that understanding and I could help these kids. We all want these kids to have the best chance. There have been times when it gets extra stressful and I inevitably cross the boundary between profession and carer. Whilst, because of my profession, I think I can make a hell of a difference, some social workers find that knowledge a bit of a threat.

Interestingly, the other gay couple I mentioned had one of the kids I have looked after before me. His placement with them broke down and he was then placed with me. It wasn't that they did anything massively wrong; it's just he was a tough kid, that these kids challenge. In some ways it can be easier being single – kids in these situations can try to split couples up, to get in the middle of a relationship and be destructive, but they don't have that opportunity with me. My boundaries are very clear; it's my way or the highway. It's simple. I think that makes it easier in some respects. That's why I needed my supervising social worker to really be there and to support me emotionally.

I'm currently looking after two boys, a 6-year-old and a 12-year-old. The 6-year-old has needed a lot of help. He has a complex history and was sexually abused by his mother. I have an understanding of these issues because of my training. He's needed a lot of help and should have had more earlier on. Another child I looked after had a history of bereavement and suicide and death and stuff. These kids have got lots to deal with. The 12-year-old has received help for the past six months through the NHS child and adolescent mental health services (CAMHS), but it took a long time to get that organised. Two-and-a-half years is too long to wait; earlier help would have made such a difference to him. It is frustrating the way barriers are put up and it has only been organised now because he will be moving – and they want to start it while he is in a stable situation.

It sometimes feels that as long as things are stable and you are managing, nothing is done. Only when a move is imminent or something dramatic happens will the help you've been asking for happen. We had a couple of major incidents – one was a kind of sexual incident involving another foster child that freaked everyone out, and the other incident was when he rubbed shit all over my car. These were big enough incidents to worry the authorities, but the little stuff has always been there. We all knew the history. Other people sometimes need to experience the extreme nature, the trauma stuff, to actually acknowledge a child needs help.

Role models are really important for kids, and I was worried about how the kids would respond to me. And one kid, who understood more about my being gay, was challenging and I just said to him that I found what he was saying offensive. He just stopped and sort of shut down and then he kind of disappeared and was on the phone texting his mum and I thought, 'Oh shit, here we go, what's going to happen now?' But half an hour later he was back, bouncing around and it was never mentioned again. That's kids.

I had a lot of contact at the beginning with one of my foster children's families – sometimes two or three times a week. It's not about who you are; it's about mutual respect. I really try. I really make an effort to engage with parents and families, and they appreciate that. I think as a single gay man I am seen as less threatening. A lot of kids are taken away from their mothers and the mothers can see I'm not going to steal their maternal role.

It is better to take a low profile about being a foster carer. My older kid hates the idea that he's fostered and would hate other people to know he is in care. The issue for him is that he is in care, not that he is cared for by a gay man. He's been with me for a year now and he's about to turn 13. He's got a mate from his school who lives just around the corner. He's gone back to their house a few times, and I've told him that once the other boy I'm looking after has gone, he can have his friend for sleepovers and stuff. He's told the friend's mum that I'm his uncle. He's not told them he's in foster care. That's the difference between fostering and adoption. I know quite a lot of LGBT adoptive families are very proud of their family identity and they promote it – this is who they are. It's not like that with fostering – you are there to support the kids and, ultimately, it's about the children. You can't put them in a difficult position because you don't know what their futures hold. And you can't commit, because they are not going to be with you forever. That can make it difficult and hard as a carer because no matter how much you want to tell people, you've got to put that second to the needs of the child. That's really important.

Fostering and The Albert Kennedy Trust

Before applying to be a foster carer, I worked with The Albert Kennedy Trust (AKT), which finds safe homes for young LGBT people in crisis because of their sexual identity. When I started fostering there was an AKT placement living here. He was 17 when he moved in and 19 when he moved out – and he was here when the foster child still living with me moved in, and so had to be police-checked. That worked really well, the three of us – it was a nice time.

I would have been happy to have another AKT placement, but social services came down heavy on me, because then I was moving someone into the child's space, not the child into their space. It doesn't really make sense, because they'll happily move another foster child in without assessing the impact it could have on the child already here. I thought it'd be incredibly positive, both for the kids and for the young gay people, to see a positive family. That was certainly true for the AKT placement who was here when I started fostering. He could see that having kids was a real possibility. It's nice to feed that in, it's an important part of life. It was also great for me because he could babysit while I popped to the shop, and it was positive for the younger kids who love having a much older sibling role model. It worked really well.

I'm considering, when my current foster kids leave, taking in an AKT young person and going through the process that way again, but it'll be a bit frustrating if that's what I have to do every single time.

Being a gay carer

I don't hide my sexuality, but neither do I go around wearing a badge saying, 'I'm gay'. A lot of people think I'm straight. I'll mention it if I feel it's relevant, but I don't make a big issue about it. People make assumptions. I've got a very close friend, Helen, who's a single carer who lives near me and people often think we're together or have something going on. It doesn't bother me, it's not about me, and the kids are under no illusions. They don't really understand what it means, but it's not relevant to them at their age. I would never lie to someone about it, but I'm not going to go shouting about it.

I can imagine some gay people getting quite offended that the children don't want to bring their friends home, and wonder why they are embarrassed by their identity. But I think as a parent it's about the children and what makes them feel comfortable. You can help them through that. Young people, teenagers particularly, can be embarrassed by their parents whoever they are and whatever their sexuality. I've heard a lot of stories around gay carers getting very offended by certain things that are said to them – but when you sit back and think about it, you wonder 'Was that really about sexuality, or was that just about being a teenager?'

School, particularly secondary school, can be a challenge. You can be persecuted for having the wrong bag or the wrong shoes. You've got to build up a child's resilience before you force another 'difference' on them and get them to own it. But in some ways, that's a good thing about fostering – you can compartmentalise things. It can be 'this is who we are here' and outside you can make up a story about who you are there – they don't have to take being fostered or my being gay personally.

Fostering versus adoption

I decided on fostering rather than adoption because I wanted support – not just social work support, but also a whole network of support. A lot of people say, 'I just want to be left alone'; well, I don't want to be left alone. I know damn well that actually, for a kid to really survive, you need a really good network around them. It was the head of fostering who introduced me to Helen, who's the foster carer round the corner, and we get on really well and we're really good friends now. She's brilliant.

All parents have to develop a network, but instead of it slowly evolving around a baby, you're thrown this half grown-up kid and you're expected to have a network ready. Many foster carers, and some adopters, go into fostering having already been parents, already having children in their life, and they've already got a lot of systems set up around them.

I have struggled with going in with a kind of ready-made kid into a school where I just don't fit. In the entire time I've had my six-year-old foster child, very few parents have ever made any effort to talk to me. A couple of them have been friendly, but generally I'm seen as the person looking after the naughty kid. And if they talk to me, it's usually to moan about my child, or to say something nasty. It's tough.

You kind of hope that you're going to be a part of this community, but actually what you become is the victimised parent of the victimised child. It's horrible, and I've found that hard and quite draining. I remember a few weeks after this little boy arrived, one parent attacked me, saying she was getting a petition to get him excluded because he'd pushed her daughter down the stairs. She was yelling at me in the playground. It was really upsetting. This woman wasn't going to give this kid a chance. He was six years old and already people had just given up on him and blamed him. That's horrible.

That same parent chased him round the playground last term, trying to hit him with a stick, yelling abuse at him. She got reprimanded for it, but then demanded a meeting to get my six-year-old excluded and started a petition. As a result, one of the other parents came rushing up to me and said how sorry she was at what this woman was doing. I almost felt like crying – she was the first person in the playground in two-and-a-half years who had really talked to me and shown some support. She's been lovely. Her daughter's in the same class as my child, though I'm not sure she massively likes him. He's very likeable, but he doesn't know when to stop – with other children he can be too in their faces, in their spaces. He never gets invited to anyone else's house. He's just got an ADHD diagnosis. But that mum has been lovely, and every time she sees me she's really friendly and gives my foster child a hug. When we were talking the other day, it turned out she had been in care.

I do wonder how much difference I can make with these kids if I can't give them positive role models in other children and families. As a foster carer you're a bit stuck, because you do end up socialising with other foster carers who have kids with issues too.

This little boy is now going into long-term fostering with a family in Kent. It could be really good for him, a fresh start. This is the first family that has come forward, the only family. The social worker's a bit worried and I think she's secretly hoping I'll just cave in and say, 'Oh just let him stay.' He's the kind of kid that needs a lot of commitment. If I had a partner who was really keen, then we could do that. But that's not the situation.

Gay family camps

One thing I have found really helpful are the New Family Social picnics and camps. There are 300 odd people at these events, adults and kids – a field full of LGBT families. For me and my kids it was not so much about my being gay, but more about my kids knowing there were other children in care like them. That is so important for them. It's a link. They had a lot of freedom, because they had a field full of police-checked people. Everyone was safe. And you could share your stories and your support.

I felt normal; I didn't feel like I had to hide who I was. I didn't have to worry about being with someone and people judging me – all that gay paranoia. It was so not an issue that it helped me to realise that this fostering is just about parenting. There was no difference between this group of people and any other campsite full of people and their families. It helped me. My partner came too, and he loved it. He's younger than me and for him having kids is really important. He's not that involved in the fostering, but he does want kids in his life, so to meet all these other families was lovely.

Role model

I am comfortable in my life and where I live. I've got a real mix of friends, especially amongst other foster carers; they're a real mixed bunch of people from different walks of life. I think it's nice for kids to see you have a range of friends from different places. I think all of it is just about being non-judgemental and letting the kids know that you're accepting and tolerant of difference, really. It's not usually how they've been brought up.

I am a role model for Diversity Role Models, a group that goes into schools and holds workshops talking about sexuality. We go into a lot of schools, including primary schools, because in primary you talk about your family and how families can be different. The children are sometimes a bit curious that I've got a same-sex partner and I'm a gay parent and they ask a few questions, but they seem to be cool with it. It feeds into their minds that being gay and being a parent is a possibility, an option. It's the adults who struggle with the concept.

DARRELL and DAVID (2015)

Becoming a Family

The first step towards becoming an adoptive or foster parent is to find a local authority prepared to assess you. In 2014, teacher, Darrell, talked about the process he and his partner, David, who works as a gardener, went through, and the positive support they received. Three years later he talked to us again about their journey to adopting their son, Ieuan.

David and I decided to look into adoption because we felt we had reached a very settled stage in our lives; we've been together for 13 years and had a civil partnership in 2008. Our friends were settling down and having kids and we were looking after the kids and really enjoying that, having fun doing that, and friends would tell us 'You're really good at this.' That was encouraging. Also, attitudes to same-sex couples who have children have come a long way in recent years, helped by well-known couples with children such as Neil Patrick Harris and Elton John. Gay marriage, high-profile same-sex people in all walks of life and the work of groups such as New Family Social (NFS) and Stonewall have all helped make adoption easier for same-sex couples.

Making the first approach

David and I were a bit worried when we first approached our local authority. Although we used to live in the city, we now live out in the sticks, and living in a village we wondered what our neighbours would think, but they have been very supportive. We were also worried about how we would be perceived by the local authority as a gay couple, but actually they told us, 'You're not the first.' They had approved several same-sex couples already and their policy was to support diversity. And they are not alone in actively recruiting same-sex couples; their attitude was that we come to the adoption process 100 per cent invested in it having only considered this route, whereas heterosexual couples may have suffered many setbacks and heartaches before deciding to adopt.

Preparation

We went on a preparation course first. We were in two minds at that time about whether we really wanted to go ahead, so we used the course as a kind of fact-finding resource. The people on the course were really positive. There was no 'mummy and daddy' kind of language at all, whereas friends in the neighbouring authority had experienced real old school attitudes to gender on their course. After the course we still weren't totally convinced, but we decided we wanted to go to the next stage of assessment. Our concern was that we felt we didn't have enough experience with children or know enough LGBT families who had adopted. We contacted local nurseries to get some more experience with children and the local authority put us in touch with the LGBT support group, New Family Social (NFS), and even paid our subscription.

We signed up for the NFS summer camp and that was great. There were lots of different families with different make-ups on the camp, and there was a real feeling of community. This face-to-face contact with other LGBT families was fantastic. We made a lot of new friends at different stages in the process, some with children, some just matched and some still waiting. It helped us to feel really positive about the assessment and our decision to adopt.

The assessment

The assessment was basically five interviews. We were worried about how the social worker would be with us, but she was lovely, very open. She drove huge distances to come and see us. Talking through things with her was like being in therapy! With some questions we weren't really sure what she was getting at, but we really trusted her to represent us honestly. We got the report about two weeks before panel and she had managed to capture exactly what we meant in each answer – it was as if we had written the report ourselves.

She had been reluctant to give us a tick list of disabilities or circumstances that we thought we might or might not be able to cope with, as she said this wasn't always relevant in the end when a couple was matched with a child. We did make it clear that we would both continue to work so we would find it hard to cope with a child with serious disabilities. However, we could cope with a child with learning difficulties; these are very common, and as a teacher I felt confident in being able to deal with this. We would also consider a deaf child as my mother has a cochlear implant, so again, it's something I was familiar with.

Our social worker suggested that we should go for one child initially as we would find looking after one easier to start with. We told her that we wanted to adopt two children and would like a sibling group, and she went with that. We also told her that we would want to adopt boys. We did talk about identity and how we would support a child's identity, but our social worker seemed confident that we would obviously be able to cope with a range of identities. I think she made these assumptions because we were very confident, but she did seem to have a very good handle on who we were.

The panel

The adoption panel was all women. One member had been present on the preparation course and she grilled us harder than the rest because she knew us from the course. We were in with the panel for

40 minutes. The questions we were asked were really encouraging us to provide evidence in our favour. It was only five or six minutes after coming out from the meeting with the panel that we got a positive decision. We were approved for two children aged two to six years. We weren't sure at this stage how much time we would need off work when we had children placed with us.

It took six months from us first contacting the local authority at Easter to being taken to panel for approval in October. For the first few months, we didn't mind too much about the wait, but we felt that we would be disappointed if it went on much longer as we were worried that we would forget some aspects of the training we had been through.

Support networks

Throughout the process we had lots of support from friends and family, the social work team and the people at our work who knew we were being assessed for adoption; both of our employers are completely open to diversity and now we're approved, they all know.

NFS was the support group we decided to join. They were fantastic. Some of the online message boards can be quite negative, but this is often just people venting. Face-to-face support was by far the most useful. We were able to go to a picnic organised by our local group and then we volunteered at summer camp which, as we said previously, was a great experience and really paid dividends in our panel. It's also made us lots of new friends at different stages in the process, some with children, some just matched and some still waiting like us.

DARRELL and DAVID (2018)

That was all three years ago. Our son, Ieuan, has been with us for two years now. After we were approved in autumn 2014, we had to wait a whole year to be matched with a child. Social workers are very surprised when they hear this – it's the longest they've heard of – but there was a change just at that time in the regulations around how decisions are made on putting children forward for adoption. As a result, there was a sudden drop in the numbers of children being put forward and a corresponding surplus of adopters waiting for placements. Now, there are about 40 children waiting for placement in the county, but at that time the average was only two or three.

In that time we did look at a profile of a sibling group, but one of the children had a lot of needs and would have needed one person to be at home all the time, and we decided we weren't ready for that. In the end our social worker came to us with a child from our local authority. His social worker knew our social worker and thought of us for Ieuan. After such a long wait, with various other profiles not coming off and other enquiries being turned down, we were quite cautious. But when we met his social worker and saw how enthusiastic she was about us as a potential match, we got very excited.

We had been approved for a sibling group of children aged two to six, with at least one boy. Ieuan was a single child and was 22 months old, so we had to adjust our ideas, but we were prepared to be more flexible. He had no particular identified needs and was actually one of the simplest children whose profiles we saw. His medical assessment was pessimistic and predicted global developmental delay because of poor parenting, but it was unnecessarily negative. He had been fostered at about 12 months and was behind then in speech and movement. At 22 months he had only just started walking.

The long wait we had was difficult in places, but meant we were really ready for Ieuan when he arrived. He was placed quickly, with the only delay being because of me, as I had to take a school trip to the US in the half-term holiday, so we met him after that. Both our jobs have been very supportive, and because of the delay we had time to give them notice of our parental leave. David works for the National Trust, which is very forward-thinking in its adoption leave policy. I work in a secondary school and didn't have the leave written into my contract initially, but it's an academy, so they let me write their adoption leave policy for them to mirror the maternity leave terms. I worked full time and David worked part time. I took parental leave first and David took two weeks of paternity leave. Then we split the parental leave between us and I went back to work before the summer holiday in order to get paid over the summer while David took over with his parental leave.

We had a week of introductions before Ieuan moved in, but it was cut short by a day because he bonded with us so quickly. The foster carers were brilliant. When we first heard they were a retired couple who were fostering out of a religious commitment, I thought they would be really difficult about us – that was my own prejudice – but they were totally supportive. They had never placed a child with a gay couple, but they didn't even blink. Their first question was, 'What do you want to be called?' They prepared Ieuan really well.

Family life

Ieuan settled really quickly. In our first meeting he came straight across the room and hugged us. He's done really well. He had a speech and language appointment in his first few weeks and was assessed as being six months behind. He was tested again a couple of months later and had already caught up with his age group. We think his comprehension was always better than people thought, and once he started talking, he was off. It was a combination of us knowing his needs really well, great pre-school input, and him really wanting to learn, plus getting tips from my sister who works in a nursery on how to help him. It's also about being aware of what's out there and being willing to take up anything he needs without worrying about it. My sister says he's on target for his age now and slightly ahead in speech and vocab. While David was still on parental leave he started taking Ieuan to pre-school. Then he got 15 hours' free childcare a week from when he was two because he was adopted. When David went back to work part time he was able to arrange his part-time hours to almost match the 15 hours of pre-school. David's parents live near us and help us with picking him up from pre-school. Pre-school has really benefited Ieuan and helped his development. It means he's really positive about moving on to school, now he's nearly four. My brother, sister and mum all live within an hour away and they're all brilliant. We're also still in contact with several adopters from our preparation course, so that's a great network – we really bonded as a group on the course and they're local, whereas other friends are all over the country.

Ieuan was never to have any direct contact with his birth mother. We were very up for meeting her, but it never happened. Initially there was also an idea about him having direct contact with his older brother, who is in long-term foster care. But the brother may now have direct contact with their mother and that would preclude any direct contact with him for Ieuan. We did have another request for a meeting with his birth mum more recently, but again it wasn't followed up. We also volunteered letterbox contact and the local authority has all the paperwork for us to do it, but nothing was set up on the other side, so it hasn't happened.

We live in a small rural village and had wondered about people's attitudes towards our family. When we were on adoption leave together, we took Ieuan to a church playgroup and we were virtually the only men. There was one other man, who was a shift worker and brought his child along because he was available then. He said he'd not known any gay men before, but he was very open and said we'd taught him something. There was no problem with anything at pre-school either, it was just, 'Of course he can do everything, we'll do cards for his grandmothers on Mother's Day and two cards on Father's Day.' We've not encountered any problems from the other parents at pre-school or playgroup, and we've been invited to all the parties and so on as a family. The primary school seems pretty clued up too. It's a church school, but they were celebrating a Jewish festival when we visited. I would be very surprised if there are any problems. Attitudes have changed and family make-ups have changed, with so many children living with divorce and with one parent, or in second families. The other day we were out at a restaurant as three families, all with two fathers, and everyone just accepted us.

Within the next year or so we will probably have that conversation about whether we adopt again, but not while Ieuan's going through starting primary school. We're quite positive about adopting again, but we can also quite easily see it just being him and us, and we know we've had a relatively easy time with him and it might not be so straightforward a second time. If we do adopt again, it has to be right for him. You can have an idea of what you will do when you start out and then you have to adapt your ideas as you go on. Adopting Ieuan has obviously meant a complete reordering of our lives, changing our mindset and adjusting to not thinking like a couple but a trio, learning to be patient, tolerant and understanding of each other (especially when we're tired!) as new fathers with a child younger than our initial training, reading and experience had prepared us for. It's challenged our self-confidence and rapidly built our understanding of our own respective roles parenting a child who's still bonding to us, and us to him, whilst getting to know him not from birth but from when he was a toddler. Ultimately, it's been about being open-minded, affirming and reassuring of each other, and we obviously wouldn't change a thing now!

Some Resources

Books

Clay, R. (2011) *Is it True You Have Two Mums? A Story of a Lesbian Couple who Adopted Three Girls.* London: British Association for Adoption and Fostering (BAAF).

Fernandez, P. (2011) *Becoming Dads: A Gay Couple's Road to Adoption.* London: British Association for Adoption and Fostering (BAAF).

Hicks, S. and McDermott, J. (eds) (1999) *Lesbian and Gay Fostering and Adoption: Extraordinary Yet Ordinary.* London: Jessica Kingsley Publishers.

Hill, N. (2012) *The Pink Guide to Adoption for Lesbians and Gay Men.* 2nd edn. London: British Association for Adoption and Fostering (BAAF).

Hill, N. (2013) *Proud Parents: Lesbian and Gay Fostering and Adoption Experiences.* London: British Association for Adoption and Fostering (BAAF).

Nelson, M. (2016) *The Argonauts.* London: Melville House UK.

Rivers, D. W. (2013) *Radical Relations: Lesbian Mothers, Gay Fathers, and their Children in the United States since World War II.* Chapel Hill, NC: University of North Carolina Press.

Film

Symons, J. (2002) (Producer & Director) *Daddy & Papa: A Story about Gay Fathers in America* [Motion picture].

Support/agencies

After Adoption: www.afteradoption.org.uk

The Albert Kennedy Trust: www.akt.org.uk

CoramBAAF Adoption & Fostering Academy: corambaaf.org.uk

The Fostering Network: www.thefosteringnetwork.org.uk

New Family Social: www.newfamilysocial.org.uk

Proud 2 b Parents: www.proud2bparents.co.uk

References

Almond, B. (2006) *The Fragmenting Family*. Oxford: Clarendon Press.

Averett, P., Nalavany, B. and Ryan, S. (2009) 'An evaluation of gay/lesbian and heterosexual adoption.' *Adoption Quarterly 12*, 3–4, 129–151.

Barrett, D. (2012) 'Presentation, politics, and editing: The Marks/Regnerus articles.' *Social Science Research 41*, 6, 1354–1356.

Benson, A. L., Silverstein, L. B. and Auerbach, C. F. (2005) 'From the margins to the center: Gay fathers reconstruct the fathering role.' *Journal of GLBT Family Studies 1*, 3, 1–29.

Berkowitz, D. (2011) '"It was the Cadillac of adoption agencies": Intersections of social class, race, and sexuality in gay men's adoption narratives.' *Journal of GLBT Family Studies 7*, 1–2, 109–131.

Berkowitz, D. and Ryan, M. (2011) 'Bathrooms, baseball, and bra shopping: Lesbian and gay parents talk about engendering their children.' *Sociological Perspectives 54*, 3, 329–350.

Biblarz, T. J. and Stacey, J. (2010) 'How does the gender of parents matter?' *Journal of Marriage and Family 72*, 1, 3–22.

Brodzinsky, D. M. (2011) *Expanding Resources for Children III: Research-Based Best Practices in Adoption by Gays and Lesbians*. New York: Donaldson Adoption Institute.

Brodzinsky, D. M. (2012) 'Adoption by Lesbians and Gay Men: A National Survey of Adoption Agency Policies and Practices.' In D. M. Brodzinsky and A. Pertman (eds) *Adoption by Lesbians and Gay Men: A New Dimension in Family Diversity* (pp.62–84). Oxford: Oxford University Press.

Brodzinsky, D. M. and Goldberg, A. (2016) *Practice Guidelines Supporting Open Adoption in Families Headed by Lesbian and Gay Male Parents: Lessons from the Modern Adoptive Families Study*. New York: Donaldson Adoption Institute.

Brodzinsky, D. M. and Pertman, A. (eds) (2012) *Adoption by Lesbians and Gay Men: A New Dimension in Family Diversity*. Oxford: Oxford University Press.

Brodzinsky, D. M., Green, R-J. and Katuzny, K. (2012) 'Adoption by Lesbians and Gay Men: What We Know, Need to Know, and Ought to Do.' In D. M. Brodzinsky and A. Pertman (eds) *Adoption by Lesbians and Gay Men: A New Dimension in Family Diversity* (pp.233–253). Oxford: Oxford University Press.

Brodzinsky, D. M., Patterson, C. J. and Vaziri, M. (2002) 'Adoption agency perspectives on lesbian and gay prospective parents.' *Adoption Quarterly 5*, 3, 5–23.

Brodzinsky, D. M. and Staff of the Evan B. Donaldson Adoption Institute (2003) *Adoption by Lesbians and Gays: A National Survey of Adoption Agency Policies, Practices, and Attitudes*. New York: Evan B. Donaldson Adoption Institute.

Brooks, D. and Goldberg, S. (2001) 'Gay and lesbian adoptive and foster care placements: Can they meet the needs of waiting children?' *Social Work 46*, 2, 147–57.

Brooks, D., Kim, H. and Wind, L. H. (2012) 'Supporting Gay and Lesbian Adoptive Families Before and After Adoption.' In D. M. Brodzinsky and A. Pertman (eds) *Adoption by Lesbians and Gay Men: A New Dimension in Family Diversity* (pp.150–183). Oxford: Oxford University Press.

Brown, H. C. (2011) 'The Assessment of Lesbian and Gay Prospective Foster Carers: Twenty Years of Practice and What Has Changed?' in P. Dunk-West and T. Hafford-Letchfield (eds) *Sexual Identities and Sexuality in Social Work: Research and Reflections from Women in the Field* (pp.105–120). Farnham: Ashgate.

Brown, H. C. and Cocker, C. (2011) *Social Work with Lesbians and Gay Men*. London: Sage.

Brown, H. C., Sebba, J. and Luke, N. (2015) *The Recruitment, Assessment, Support and Supervision of Lesbian, Gay, Bisexual and Transgender Foster Carers: An International Literature Review*. Oxford: Rees Centre, University of Oxford, Department of Education and University of Bedfordshire.

Cheng, S. and Powell, B. (2015) 'Measurement, methods, and divergent patterns: Reassessing the effects of same-sex parents.' *Social Science Research 52*, 615–626.

Clarke, V., Kitzinger, C. and Potter, J. (2004) '"Kids are just cruel anyway": Lesbian and gay parents' talk about homophobic bullying.' *British Journal of Social Psychology 43*, 4, 531–550.

Cocker, C. (2011) 'Sexuality Before Ability? The Assessment of Lesbians as Adopters.' In P. Dunk-West (ed.) *Sexual Identities and Sexuality in Social Work: Research and Reflections from Women in the Field* (pp.141–162). Farnham: Ashgate.

Cocker, C. and Brown, H. C. (2010) 'Sex, sexuality and relationships: Developing confidence and discernment when assessing lesbian and gay prospective adopters.' *Adoption & Fostering 34*, 1, 20–32.

Dalton, S. E. and Bielby, D. D. (2000) '"That's our kind of constellation": Lesbian mothers negotiate institutionalized understandings of gender within the family.' *Gender & Society 14*, 1, 36–61.

Delaney, R. and Joyce, C. *Behavior with a Purpose: Thoughtful Solutions to Common Problems of Adoptive, Foster, and Kinship Youth*. Brooklyn Park: Better Endings, New Beginnings Publishers.

Delvoye, M. and Tasker, F. (2016) 'Narrating self-identity in bisexual motherhood.' *Journal of GLBT Family Studies 12*, 1, 5–23.

DfE (Department for Education) (2013) *Statutory Guidance on Adoption: For Local Authorities, Voluntary Adoption Agencies and Adoption Support Agencies*. London: DfE.

DH (Department of Health) (1990) *Foster Placement (Guidance and Regulations) Consultation Paper No. 16*. London: Her Majesty's Stationery Office.

Doucet, A. (2006) *Do Men Mother? Fathering, Care, and Domestic Responsibility*. Toronto, ON: University of Toronto Press.

Downing, J. B. (2013) 'Transgender-Parent Families.' In A. E. Goldberg and K. R. Allen (eds) *LGBT-Parent Families: Innovations in Research and Implications for Practice* (pp.105–115). New York: Springer New York.

Dugmore, P. and Cocker, C. (2008) 'Legal, social and attitudinal changes: An exploration of lesbian and gay issues in a training programme for social workers in fostering and adoption.' *Social Work Education 27*, 2, 159–168.

Dunne, G. A. (2000) 'Opting into motherhood: Lesbians blurring the boundaries and transforming the meaning of parenthood and kinship.' *Gender & Society 14*, 1, 11–35.

Eady, A., Ross, L. E., Epstein, R. and Anderson, S. (2009) 'To Bi Or Not To Bi: Bisexuality and Disclosure in the Adoption System.' In R. Epstein (ed.) *Who's Your Daddy? And Other Writings on Queer Parenting* (pp.124–132). Toronto, ON: Sumach Press.

Epstein, R. (2002) 'Butches with babies: Reconfiguring gender and motherhood.' *Journal of Lesbian Studies 6*, 2, 41–57.

Fulcher, M., Sutfin, E. L. and Patterson, C. J. (2008) 'Individual differences in gender development: Associations with parental sexual orientation, attitudes, and division of labor.' *Sex Roles 58*, 5–6, 330–341.

Gabb, J. (2008) *Researching Intimacy in Families*. Basingstoke: Palgrave Macmillan.

Gates, G. J. *et al.* (2012) 'Letter to the editors and advisory editors of Social Science Research.' *Social Science Research 41*, 6, 1350–1351.

Gianino, M. (2008) 'Adaptation and transformation: The transition to adoptive parenthood for gay male couples.' *Journal of GLBT Family Studies 4*, 2, 205–243.

Goldberg, A. E. (2010) *Lesbian and Gay Parents and Their Children: Research on the Family Life Cycle*. Washington, DC: American Psychological Association.

Goldberg, A. E. (2012) *Gay Dads: Transitions to Adoptive Fatherhood*. New York: New York University Press.

Goldberg, A. E. and Allen, K. R. (eds) (2013) *LGBT-Parent Families: Innovations in Research and Implications for Practice*. New York: Springer.

Goldberg, A. E. and Gianino, M. (2012) 'Lesbian and Gay Adoptive Parent Families: Assessment, Clinical Issues, and Intervention.' In D. M. Brodzinsky and A. Pertman (eds) *Adoption by Lesbians and Gay Men: A New Dimension in Family Diversity* (pp.204–232). Oxford: Oxford University Press.

Golombok, S. and Tasker, F. (1994) 'Children in Lesbian and Gay Families: Theories and Evidence.' In J. Bancroft (ed.) *Annual Review of Sex Research* (pp.73–100).

Golombok, S. and Tasker, F. (1996) 'Do parents influence the sexual orientation of their children? Findings from a longitudinal study of lesbian families.' *Developmental Psychology 32*, 1, 3–11.

Golombok, S., Spencer, A. and Rutter, M. (1983) 'Children in lesbian and single-parent households: Psychosexual and psychiatric appraisal.' *Journal of Child Psychology and Psychiatry 24*, 4, 551–572.

Golombok, S., Mellish, L., Jennings, S., Casey, P., Tasker, F. and Lamb, M. E. (2014) 'Adoptive gay father families: Parent-child relationships and children's psychological adjustment.' *Child Development 85*, 2, 456–468.

Green, E. R. and Peterson, E. (2003) *Gender and Sexuality Terminology*. Berkeley, CA: LGBT Resource Center, University of California, Riverside.

Green, R. (1978) 'Sexual identity of 37 children raised by homosexual or transsexual parents.' *American Journal of Psychiatry 135*, 6, 692–697.

Hequembourg, A. (2007) *Lesbian Motherhood: Stories of Becoming*. New York: Harrington Park Press.

Hicks, S. (2000) '"Good lesbian, bad lesbian…": Regulating heterosexuality in fostering and adoption assessments.' *Child & Family Social Work 5*, 157–168.

Hicks, S. (2006) 'Maternal men–perverts and deviants? Making sense of gay men as foster carers and adopters.' *Journal of GLBT Family Studies 2*, 1, 93–114.

Hicks, S. (2008) 'Gender role models…who needs 'em?!' *Qualitative Social Work 7*, 1, 43–59.

Hicks, S. (2011) *Lesbian, Gay and Queer Parenting: Families, Intimacies, Genealogies.* Basingstoke: Palgrave Macmillan.

Hicks, S. (2013) 'Lesbian, Gay, Bisexual, and Transgender Parents and the Question of Gender.' In A. E. Goldberg and K. R. Allen (eds) *LGBT-Parent Families: Innovations in Research and Implications for Practice* (pp.149–162). New York: Springer.

Hicks, S. and Greaves, D. (2007) *Practice Guidance on Assessing Gay and Lesbian Foster Care and Adoption Applicants.* 2nd edn. Manchester: Manchester City Council Children's Services.

Hicks, S. and McDermott, J. (eds) (1999) *Lesbian and Gay Fostering and Adoption: Extraordinary Yet Ordinary.* London: Jessica Kingsley Publishers.

Hines, S. (2007) *TransForming Gender: Transgender Practices of Identity, Intimacy and Care.* Bristol: Policy Press.

Hitchens, D. and Price, B. (1978) 'Trial strategy in lesbian mother custody cases: The use of expert testimony.' *Golden Gate University Law Review 9*, 451, 451–479.

Hoeffer, B. (1981) 'Children's acquisition of sex-role behavior in lesbian-mother families.' *American Journal of Orthopsychiatry 51*, 3, 536–544.

Holloway, J. (2002) *Homosexual Parenting: Does it Make a Difference? A Re-evaluation of the Research with Adoption and Fostering in Mind.* Newcastle-upon-Tyne: The Christian Institute.

Hunter, N. D. and Polikoff, N. D. (1976) 'Custody rights of lesbian mothers: Legal theory and litigation strategy.' *Buffalo Law Review 25*, 691–733.

Jennings, S., Mellish, L., Tasker, F., Lamb, M. and Golombok, S. (2014) 'Why adoption? Gay, lesbian, and heterosexual adoptive parents' reproductive experiences and reasons for adoption.' *Adoption Quarterly 17*, 3, 205–226.

de Jong, A. and Donnelly, S. (2015) *Recruiting, Assessing and Supporting Lesbian and Gay Adopters.* London: British Association for Adoption and Fostering (BAAF).

Kirkpatrick, M., Smith, C. and Roy, R. (1981) 'Lesbian mothers and their children: A comparative survey.' *American Journal of Orthopsychiatry 51*, 3, 545–551.

Lewin, E. (2009) *Gay Fatherhood: Narratives of Family and Citizenship in America.* Chicago, IL: University of Chicago Press.

Logan, J. and Sellick, C. (2007) 'Lesbian and gay fostering and adoption in the United Kingdom: Prejudice, progress and the challenges of the present.' *Social Work and Social Sciences Review 13*, 2, 35–47.

Lott-Whitehead, L. and Tully, C. T. (1999) 'The Family Lives of Lesbian Mothers.' In J. Laird (ed.) *Lesbians and Lesbian Families: Reflections on Theory and Practice* (pp.243–259). New York: Columbia University Press.

MacCallum, F. and Golombok, S. (2004) 'Children raised in fatherless families from infancy: A follow-up of children of lesbian and single heterosexual mothers at early adolescence.' *Journal of Child Psychology and Psychiatry 45*, 8, 1407–1419.

Mallon, G. P. (2004) *Gay Men Choosing Parenthood.* New York: Columbia University Press.

Mallon, G. P. (2006) *Lesbian and Gay Foster and Adoptive Parents: Recruiting, Assessing, and Supporting an Untapped Resource for Children and Youth.* Washington, DC: Child Welfare League of America Press.

Mallon, G. P. (2007) 'Assessing lesbian and gay prospective foster and adoptive families: A focus on the home study process.' *Child Welfare 86*, 67–86.

Mallon, G. P. (2008) 'Social Work Practice with LGBT Parents.' In G. P. Mallon (ed.) *Social Work Practice with Lesbian, Gay, Bisexual, and Transgender People* (pp.269–312). New York: Routledge.

Mallon, G. P. (2011) 'The home study assessment process for gay, lesbian, bisexual, and transgender prospective foster and adoptive families.' *Journal of GLBT Family Studies 7*, 1–2, 9–29.

Mallon, G. P. (2012) 'Lesbian and Gay Prospective Foster and Adoptive Families: The Homestudy Assessment Process.' In D. M. Brodzinsky and A. Pertman (eds) *Adoption by Lesbians and Gay Men: A New Dimension in Family Diversity* (pp.130–149). Oxford: Oxford University Press.

Mallon, G. P. (2018) 'Practice with LGBT Parents.' In G. P. Mallon (ed.) *Social Work Practice with Lesbian, Gay, Bisexual, and Transgender People* (pp.165–197). 3rd edn. London: Routledge.

Mallon, G. P. and Betts, B. (2005) *Recruiting, Assessing and Supporting Lesbian and Gay Carers and Adopters*. London: British Association for Adoption and Fostering (BAAF).

Mamo, L. (2007) *Queering Reproduction: Achieving Pregnancy in the Age of Technoscience*. Durham, NC: Duke University Press.

Mellish, L., Jennings, S., Tasker, F., Lamb, M. and Golombok, S. (2013) *Gay, Lesbian and Heterosexual Adoptive Families: Family Relationships, Child Adjustment and Adopters' Experiences*. London: British Association for Adoption and Fostering (BAAF).

Moore, M. R. and Brainer, A. (2013) 'Race and Ethnicity in the Lives of Sexual Minority Parents and Their Children.' In A. E. Goldberg and K. R. Allen (eds) *LGBT-Parent Families: Innovations in Research and Implications for Practice* (pp.133–148). New York: Springer New York.

Morgan, P. (2002) *Children as Trophies? Examining the Evidence on Same-sex Parenting*. Newcastle-upon-Tyne: The Christian Institute.

National Resource Center for Permanency and Family Connections (2012a) *LGBT Prospective Foster and Adoptive Families: The Homestudy Assessment Process*. New York: National Resource Center for Permanency and Family Connections.

National Resource Center for Permanency and Family Connections (2012b) *Supporting and Retaining LGBT Foster and Adoptive Parents*. New York: National Resource Center for Permanency and Family Connections.

New Family Social (2015) *Statistics: How Many LGBT People Are Parents?* Accessed on 25/09/2017 at www.newfamilysocial.org.uk/resources/research/statistics.

Osborne, C. (2012) 'Further comments on the papers by Marks and Regnerus.' *Social Science Research 41*, 4, 779–783.

Parmar, P. (dir.) (1989) *Fostering and Adoption by Lesbians and Gay Men*. Short film for Channel 4 television (UK) *Out on Tuesday* series.

Patterson, C. J. (1992) 'Children of lesbian and gay parents.' *Child Development 63*, 1025–1042.

Perrin, A. J., Cohen, P. N. and Caren, N. (2013) 'Are children of parents who had same-sex relationships disadvantaged? A scientific evaluation of the no-differences hypothesis.' *Journal of Gay & Lesbian Mental Health 17*, 3, 327–336.

Pertman, A. and Howard, J. (2012) 'Emerging Diversity in Family Life: Adoption by Gay and Lesbian Parents.' In D. M. Brodzinsky and A. Pertman (eds) *Adoption by Lesbians and Gay Men: A New Dimension in Family Diversity* (pp.20–35). Oxford: Oxford University Press.

Phillips, M. (1999) *The Sex-Change Society: Feminised Britain and the Neutered Male*. London: Social Market Foundation.

Pidduck, J. (2009) 'Queer kinship and ambivalence: Video autoethnographies by Jean Carlomusto and Richard Fung.' *GLQ: A Journal of Lesbian and Gay Studies 15*, 3, 441–468.

Pyne, J. (2012) *Transforming Family: Trans Parents and their Struggles, Strategies, and Strengths.* Toronto, ON: LGBTQ Parenting Network.

Regnerus, M. (2012a) 'How different are the adult children of parents who have same-sex relationships? Findings from the New Family Structures Study.' *Social Science Research 41*, 4, 752–770.

Regnerus, M. (2012b) 'Parental same-sex relationships, family instability, and subsequent life outcomes for adult children: Answering critics of the New Family Structures Study with additional analyses.' *Social Science Research 41*, 6, 1367–1377.

Riggs, D. W. (2007) *Becoming Parent: Lesbians, Gay Men, and Family.* Teneriffe, QLD: Post Pressed.

Riggs, D. W. (2010) *What About the Children! Masculinities, Sexualities and Hegemony.* Newcastle-upon-Tyne: Cambridge Scholars Publishing.

Riggs, D. W. (2011) 'Australian lesbian and gay foster carers negotiating the child protection system: Strengths and challenges.' *Sexuality Research and Social Policy 8*, 3, 215–226.

Riggs, D. W., Power, J. and von Doussa, H. (2016) 'Parenting and Australian trans and gender diverse people: An exploratory survey.' *International Journal of Transgenderism 17*, 2, 59–65.

Rivers, D. W. (2013) *Radical Relations: Lesbian Mothers, Gay Fathers, and their Children in the United States since World War II.* Chapel Hill, NC: University of North Carolina Press.

Ross, L. E. and Dobinson, C. (2013) 'Where Is the "B" in LGBT Parenting? A Call for Research on Bisexual Parenting.' In A. E. Goldberg and K. R. Allen (eds) *LGBT-Parent Families: Innovations in Research and Implications for Practice* (pp.87–103). New York: Springer.

Ross, L. E., Epstein, R., Anderson, S. and Eady, A. (2009) 'Policy, practice, and personal narratives: Experiences of LGBTQ people with adoption in Ontario, Canada.' *Adoption Quarterly 12*, 3–4, 272–293.

Ryan, S. and Whitlock, C. (2008) 'Becoming parents: Lesbian mothers' adoption experience.' *Journal of Gay & Lesbian Social Services 19*, 2, 1–23.

Ryan, S. and Whitlock, C. (2009) 'Becoming Parents: Lesbian Mothers' Adoption Experience.' In L. R. Mercier and R. D. Harold (eds) *Social Work with Lesbian Parent Families: Ecological Perspectives* (pp.1–23). London: Routledge.

Shelley-Sireci, L. M. and Ciano-Boyce, C. (2002) 'Becoming lesbian adoptive parents: An exploratory study of lesbian adoptive, lesbian birth, and heterosexual adoptive parents.' *Adoption Quarterly 6*, 1, 33–43.

Short, E., Riggs, D. W., Perlesz, A., Brown, R. and Kane, G. (2007) *Lesbian, Gay, Bisexual and Transgender (LGBT) Parented Families: A Literature Review Prepared for the Australian Psychological Society.* Melbourne, VIC: The Australian Psychological Society Ltd.

Skeates, J. and Jabri, D. (eds) (1988) *Fostering and Adoption by Lesbians and Gay Men.* London: London Strategic Policy Unit.

Stacey, J. (2011) *Unhitched: Love, Sex, and Family Values from West Hollywood to Western China.* New York: New York University Press.

Stacey, J. and Biblarz, T. J. (2001) '(How) does the sexual orientation of parents matter?' *American Sociological Review 66*, 2, 159–183.

Stotzer, R. L., Herman, J. L. and Hasenbush, A. (2014) *Transgender Parenting: A Review of Existing Research*. Los Angeles, CA: The Williams Institute, UCLA School of Law.

Sudol, T. (2010) *LGBT Adoptive and Foster Parenting*. New York: National Resource Center for Permanency and Family Connections.

Sullins, D. P. (2015) 'Emotional problems among children with same-sex parents: Difference by definition.' *British Journal of Education, Society & Behavioural Science 7*, 2, 99–120.

Sullins, D. P. (2016) 'Invisible victims: Delayed onset depression among adults with same-sex parents.' *Depression Research and Treatment*, online advance access, doi:10.1155/2016/2410392.

Sullivan, M. (2004) *The Family of Woman: Lesbian Mothers, their Children, and the Undoing of Gender*. Berkeley, CA: University of California Press.

Tasker, F. L. and Delvoye, M. (2015) 'Moving out of the shadows: Accomplishing bisexual motherhood.' *Sex Roles 73*, 3–4, 125–140.

Tasker, F. L. and Golombok, S. (1995) 'Adults raised as children in lesbian families.' *American Journal of Orthopsychiatry 65*, 2, 203–215.

Tasker, F. L. and Golombok, S. (1997) *Growing Up in a Lesbian Family: Effects on Child Development*. New York: The Guilford Press.

Taylor, Y. (2009) *Lesbian and Gay Parenting: Securing Social and Educational Capital*. Basingstoke: Palgrave Macmillan.

Weeks, J., Heaphy, B. and Donovan, C. (2001) *Same Sex Intimacies: Families of Choice and Other Life Experiments*. London: Routledge.

Wood, K. (2016) '"It's all a bit pantomime": An exploratory study of gay and lesbian adopters and foster-carers in England and Wales.' *British Journal of Social Work 46*, 6, 1708–1723.

Wood, K. (2017) 'Families beyond boundaries: Conceptualising kinship in gay and lesbian adoption and fostering.' *Child & Family Social Work*, online advance access, doi:10.1111/cfs.12394.

Subject Index

Author Index